Sanctuary Almanac
State of Nature, State of Mind

Jim Stapleton

Cover photo credit: John Roden

First published by Dog Ear Publishing
4010 W. 86th Street, Ste H
Indianapolis, IN 46268
www.dogearpublishing.net

ISBN: 978-159858-595-7

This book is printed on acid-free paper.

Printed in the United States of America

For Diana

Adam, at Eve's grave: "Wheresoever she was, there was Eden."

- Mark Twain, Extracts from Adam's Diary

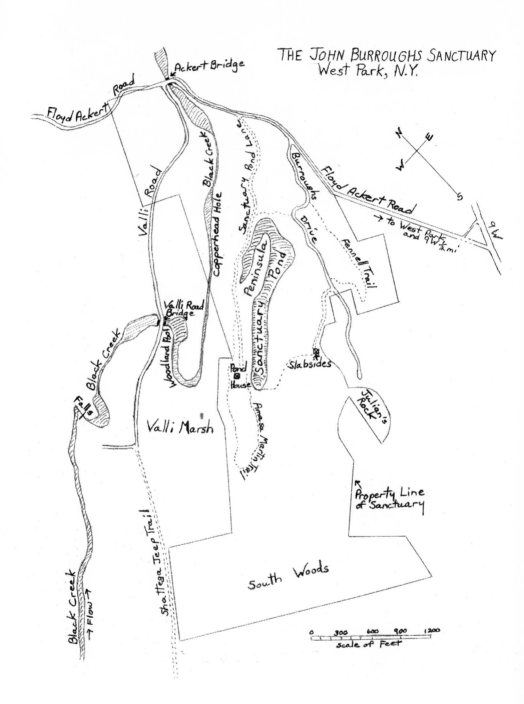

THE JOHN BURROUGHS SANCTUARY
West Park, N.Y.

PREFACE

I began this *Almanac* in 1987 during my last year as naturalist at the John Burroughs Sanctuary in West Park, New York. I lived there at Pond House with my wife, Diana, and her two school-age children, Jennifer and Eric.

The Sanctuary is named for the writer-naturalist, John Burroughs, who lived at Riverby in West Park and built his rustic writing retreat, Slabsides, in the woods nearby. The one hundred and eighty acre property, owned and maintained by the John Burroughs Association, straddles gently rolling wooded hills less than a mile from the west bank of the Hudson River, a two-hour drive north of New York City.

For the ten years of my time as Sanctuary naturalist, I developed the habit of noting passages: the stages of the pond, the development of plants, and the comings and goings of animals, including the dominant organism, *Homo sapiens*. I picked up a lot of lore about the Sanctuary, the natural world, and life, which I've shaped into the stories and meditations of this *Almanac*.

SPRING

March 21, 1987 - The first red-shouldered hawk of spring; Pond ice begins to melt along edges

Return of the Sun God

Hearing a faint scream in the blue Hudson Valley sky, I glance up from my work in the wood yard. The ax drops from my hands. I run to the front of the house and scan the heavens. I turn and call into the house.

In a moment Diana appears at the front door carrying binoculars. I point to a pair of dark shields slowly circling far above the wooded hill beyond the pond.

Our red-shouldered hawks are back!

Every year in mid-March we set up a watch for the return of this pair of sleek, graceful Buteo hawks that nest along Black Creek a half mile west of us. We expect them, we wait for them. And every year we are surprised by their mercurial arrival, bringing with them enough energy to melt the pond ice.

"I keep forgetting," Diana asks, "is it wide bands in the tail or narrow?"

"Narrow," I remind her.

"And windows in the wings," she adds, more or less as a guess.

"Windows, it is," I confirm indulgently. And indulgence comes easily as we stand in patches of snow above the frozen pond, gazing up at this sure-fire sign of spring, a flame-breasted messenger from the returning Sun God.

March 24 - Spring peepers singing at north end of pond; Ruffed grouse drumming in woods by Black Creek; Wood frogs singing in pond near lane

Quickening

The sun came out for fifteen seconds this morning. That's all we've seen of it this past week. Those fifteen seconds of light had an extraordinary effect on me.

I woke up this morning feeling glum, empty, physically ill at ease. The inpouring of yellow sunlight at 8:30 a.m. suddenly brightened the rooms with east windows and had the same quickening effect on me. I realized with that flash how long I've been without sunlight and how nourishing it is to my body, quite apart from vitamin D or photosynthesis or whatever else can be chemically documented. The fifteen seconds were a revelation, not only of my previous state of melancholy, but of my organism's dependence on periodic "hits" of sunshine, no matter how brief.

Occasionally I reflect on the course of this almanac. Perhaps I am simply "celebrating the sun" in these pages. The morning light makes this cliché fresh for me today.

March 25 - Ice retreats 20 feet along north and west shore; Canada goose fooling with her nest on island in pond

Loosening the Ice Pack

We suffered a cold winter this year. Until today the ice on the ten-acre pond in our front yard was almost shore-to-shore, and here it is the fourth week of March. Over the past ten years the event we call "ice out," the sudden thawing of the pond, has occurred at various times between the last of February and the beginning of April, but on the average it occurs in the third week of March.

I know these dates because for the past ten years I have kept records of the natural events along spring's passage through the Sanctuary. I record the first open pool at the marshy north end of the pond right through to "100% ice out." On the same calendar I log the earliest mourning cloak butterfly, the red-shoulders, the maiden blossom in a secret patch of trailing arbutus. Each region has its own set of spring harbingers - these are some of the signs in the Mid-Hudson region of New York.

Ecologists call these records of nature's timing "phenological" and have studied them with interest for many years. Despite this attention, no unified theory has been developed to explain why animals and plants do things *when* they do. But you can learn a lot on your own. By keeping a phenological diary you get to know and stay attuned to your own surroundings, whether it happens to be one hundred and eighty acres of mature woods, like the Burroughs Sanctuary, a suburban backyard, or even a patch of weeds between your apartment and the freeway. No patch is too lean a habitat to start making notes.

Nor should one pass over the familiar for the exotic. The daily hike from the house to the garage is packed with as much life as the average person can handle. Thoreau said the most novel and unexpected paths are the ones we walk every day. All of my own experience bears this out. If nothing appears on your walk to the garage, you aren't looking.

Recording phenological information is a venerable practice among naturalists. Aristotle is said to have kept a close-grained diary of natural events in the Peloponnesus, and Gilbert White inspired many modern nature watchers by doing the same in Selborne, England. Thoreau spent a good portion of his life noting down the minutiae of Concord in his attempt to divine the rhythms of the universe. John Burroughs himself writes about his practice of keeping a nature diary in his essay "Spring Jottings":

> For ten or more years, I have been in the habit of jotting down, among other things in my notebook, observations on the seasons as they passed - the complexion of the day, the aspects of nature, the arrival of the birds, the opening of the flowers, or any characteristic feature of the passing moment or hour which the great open-air panorama presented. . . . [A journal] is a sort of deposit account wherein one saves up bits and fragments of his life that would be otherwise lost to him. . . . There is hardly anything that does not become much more in the telling than in the thinking or feeling.

I picked up my own habit of recording the timing of natural events from a friend of mine, Dan Smiley, with whom I worked for a number of years at the Mohonk Preserve, an organization devoted to land preservation and ecological research in the Shawangunk Mountains near New Paltz, New York. For over sixty years, before his death in

1989, Dan recorded the daily happenings in the woods and lakes at Mohonk. He did most of this on his regular rounds from home to office and back. Dan's skills as an observer were largely self-taught and his discipline in keeping a sharp lookout was legendary, but not beyond the capacity of the rest of us, if we are willing to expend the energy.

I once calculated the simple correlations among Dan's records of natural events: comparing the arrival of the first song sparrow with the average temperature of February and March, the emergence of the black fly with the blossoming of the spice bush, and so on. One of the more intriguing relationships I found was between the dates for ice out of Mohonk Lake and the arrival of the phoebes and robins in mid-March. This makes sense if you accept the premise that early migrants move northward in response to general weather conditions and that the status of the ice on the lake is some sort of comprehensive summary of the local temperature, sunlight, and wind conditions over the previous months.

"Correlation" is the mathematician's word for connectedness. Like everything else in our lives, the natural environment is remarkably well connected. Phoebes and lake ice, snowfall and rhododendron bloom, hatching gypsy moths and emerging red oak leaves are some of the linkages I found in the Shawangunks. I find a few of the same and many new ones everywhere I go. In fact every locale has its own set of associations. I like to think of these connections as musical themes. One hears them best with a listening ear and well-tempered mind.

When I moved to the John Burroughs Sanctuary in 1977, I naturally paid particular attention to the development of the ice cover on Sanctuary Pond. I have no fifty-year record of observations to correlate, but I do have a pond in my front yard and a phoebe who nests over my front door. I've discovered I really don't need the time series or the statistical methods; the Pond House phoebe shows up every year within a week of ice out. This year's ice is only beginning to give way along the margin. My phoebe has not yet returned.

Many blessings flow from nature watching and diary keeping. For one, the practice keeps me in the moment. In my early years I spent a good deal of time lost in thought: solving physics problems in my head, inventing people on new planets, rescripting conversations from childhood. At my hermitage in the Pennsylvania woods I came back from three-hour hikes without recalling a single scene. Now that I have a nature diary, I am more attentive to each new fragrance, every snatch of birdsong, all the scurrying insects. My mind is quiet and present. I come home every afternoon with the tranquil satisfaction that I have been somewhere.

While watching for our phoebes to show up, we're wondering if the other spring events - the migration of the salamanders, the arrival of the song sparrows, the emergence of tent caterpillars - will follow the pattern and come correspondingly late this season. The evidence of previous years and the well-known caprice of nature advises us: don't guess, just keep watching.

March 26 - One quarter of pond is ice-free; Painted turtles on rocks in pond; Two spotted salamanders in the lowest pool on Burroughs Drive

Dear Old Friends

Diana and I are fond of walking. We rarely drive off to some other place to do a strenuous day's hike, but we find time every day, sometimes two or three times a day, to ramble through our surroundings and note what's going on. Frequently our objective is simply to reach the end of the one-half mile lane that leads from our cottage to the town road, and often enough we don't make that, getting caught up in the doings of a muskrat on the pond or sampling wintergreen berries off in the woods. Sometimes after dinner, we go out to look at the sky.

This afternoon is sunny and crisp, a day well made for revealing spring secrets of the warming earth. We stroll out to discover these new cast-ups and don't have to go far to find them. The Peninsula is a forested sandstone outcrop which projects into the pond and stands, at the highest, fifty feet above it. Walking to the far end we spy the first painted turtles of the season. They are lined up in a row on a half-drowned oak log in the shallow, ice-free, north end of the pond. We greet them as dear old friends who were away for the winter, but are now back again to while away the summer with us, as they have for the last ten years.

"Why do they always show up there?" Diana asks.

I describe their search for the warmest part of the spring pond, how the low winter sun catches the north end of every body of water best, while the other sides are often shaded by trees or hills. Also this end happens to be shallow, and the dark debris on the pond bottom absorbs heat from the sun.

I toss this off easily, all of it seems self-evident to me. In fact, I am often surprised by people who do not have an intuitive grasp of the physics of everyday situations. I would be hard put to prove that my own sense is intuitive, but it seems so, it's been with me a long time. This is different from my understanding of biology, which I gained later in life from books, from teachers and friends, and by watching.

For instance, I know that turtles sun themselves to get their interior temperature up to seventy degrees or so, in order to digest their food. I have a vivid image of when and where I learned this fact from Roland Bahret, a herpetologist friend of mine, while we were canoeing in a pond at the foot of the Shawangunk Mountains eight years ago.

───────────

My relationship with the science of the material world began early. As a young boy one of the things I admired about my father was his knowledge of mechanical things, how they were put together, what made them work. His information on these subjects seemed inexhaustible, matching my curiosity. Later at a Jesuit residential high school in Wisconsin, a physics teacher, Father John Scott, inspired me to look at the world as a system behaving according to laws we can discover by paying attention.

I started my freshman year of college in Detroit as a mechanical engineer, and passed in and out of the departments of chemical engineering, chemistry, and mathematics, all within the first week! At the end of that week I walked into the physics department as if coming home. I loved, lived, and breathed theoretical physics for the next seven years of my life, right through my graduate training in Göttingen, West Germany. I was on a lifetime track. Throughout these years physics was for me more than the science of matter, it was the ultimate explanation of the universe.

One October afternoon in 1962, a few weeks away from my Diplom degree at the University of Göttingen, I was packing up a few things from my house on Wilhelm Weber Strasse. The house was in the process of being demolished. I looked out the window and experienced a great revelation. I saw that physics was no more than a complicated set of assumptions about the world, like astrology or Buddhism, and had no greater claim to absolute truth. By the next morning I also knew that other parts of my life - my academic career, the Roman Catholic religion that I had professed since childhood, my social life - no longer met my needs. I had been moving through life propelled by other people's dreams. And worse, I didn't know what my own were.

In one day's time I decided not to be a physicist, not to be a Catholic, not to pursue an academic career, and to remove myself from the social environment. I left Göttingen and bummed around Europe and Africa for a year and finally sailed for America with a round-trip ticket. But I didn't go back. I became a hermit.

I found a patch of uninhabited woods in north-central Pennsylvania and built a twelve-by- twelve foot cabin. Supporting myself with a small inheritance and periodic work for neighboring farmers, I lived there for the next ten years, right through the noise and excitement of the sixties. I found out about it later.

I spent this time peeling off layers, finding out what I wanted, what I believed. My chief tool was writing. I wrote little stories that never got off the legal pads they were scribbled on, parables from the lives of the wild animals I observed on my walks: a grouse agonizing over each decision to freeze or flee; a school of salamanders studying how to avoid being stepped on. The animals bore a striking resemblance to me.

Every day at my cabin was a full page. I explored realities I had no time for in my previous, scientific life. By day I biked the Allegheny Mountains and hiked the forest trails; by night I invented melodies on my cello to capture the beauty of the day. I loved to walk at midnight along the abandoned railroad bed that lay behind my cabin. I learned the path by touch and could see my way in any light.

I bought my cello the day I left Göttingen. I had never played a musical instrument before, one of the little luxuries that didn't fit into our family life. At my cabin I played folk ditties, a few of the simplest pieces from Bach's unaccompanied cello suites, but mostly I improvised my own melodies. From the point of view of a professional cellist, my playing was an abomination; I loved it.

My chief contact with people was my monthly twelve-mile bike trip into Galeton for groceries. The grocer would say, "Nice day" or "Not too nice a day," depending. And I would reply "Yep" or "Nope," depending, until next month. That was it. I had more to do with the other lives around me: the beaver, oaks, goldenrod, and chickadees. I learned the plants and animals first hand. I look back in astonishment now at the time when "insects" and "mammals" were little more than conceptual constructs to me, like black holes and red dwarfs. The bird world was divided into robins, sparrows, and others; and I couldn't have cared less. At my Pennsylvania hermitage, I learned to care more, I bought bird books and tree guides, I spent whole mornings following deer over the mountain, whole evenings tracking the beaver as they worked their pond. I sat attentively among the trees, along the streams, around pools.

Around this pool in the northeast end of the Sanctuary, Diana and I continue our stroll, conducting the annual check of migrant salamanders. The geometry of vernal pools in this part of the Hudson Valley is largely a result of the north-south trending hills and glacial scouring, so that the mid-March waters are ice-free only at their narrow north end. This circumstance has many implications for life in these temporary ponds. When we do finally spot a few salamanders, the first of the new season, Diana observes:

"They always crawl toward these pools from the *north* side."

I correct her: "That's where we *see* them coming from, when we're on the road."

"No, even when we spot them in the woods, heading toward their pools, they're almost always heading north, right?"

"Yeah, I guess so . . . ." She is right about the migrating salamanders here in the Sanctuary, I check my memory of other migrants.

She is on to something. "Does that have anything to do with the ice going out at the north end," she asks.

My prejudice suggests a quick "no," but what do I really understand about any of this? Another domain ripe for rank speculation or, even more suspect, documented study. I have done my share of both in the past fifteen years.

At my cabin in the woods my writing grew from one page parables to short stories and finally a novel. When I considered offering the novel for publication, I knew the idyll was over; the present subject was for the moment exhausted. If I were to write more, I needed to learn something of the world outside. I left the woods to discover that world. I began on a local beef farm, moved to a dairy in western New York, and ended my farming career on an apple orchard near New Paltz in New York's Hudson Valley. After two years of struggle, the message was clear: I was not made for farming.

In the meantime I met Dan Smiley through a local nature club. We hit it off and I spent the next four years working as his assistant at the Mohonk Preserve. During this time I picked up a master's degree in biology at the State University at New Paltz. I think I learned more from Dan than all the professors at New Paltz combined. A humbling apprenticeship for a future professor!

In 1977 Bob Arbib, an editor at Audubon and president of the John Burroughs Association, asked me to live in the Pond House at the Sanctuary. He was concerned that the empty cottage was a target for vandalism. We made a loose agreement - I'd look after the place in return for living there rent-free. Despite numerous attempts to formalize the relationship, that essentially remains the deal. I live in the Sanctuary, but I make my living doing environmental research at Hudsonia, a non-profit institute I helped found, and by teaching at colleges in the area - Bard, the New School, Vassar, and SUNY New Paltz.

These latter activities would be a fall from grace if I were truly "professing" more than I am learning. Happily this is not the case. My checkerboard background in the hard and soft sciences, my unwillingness to be pinned down or be very sure about anything has kept me off balance, has made any question more interesting than all the answers.

"I wonder - is there a connection between those two 'north-end' things?" Diana is still puzzling over the ponds.

May be, I think to myself.

March 28 - Ice-out more than 3/4; Male phoebe for first (just in time for ice-out!); Robin singing in back-yard

Love Dance

Official ice out today, the pond is three-fourths open. The opening happened rather quickly in the last three days, a typically rapid development once the melting begins. What's more, the ice almost never returns when it goes the first time. Contrast this with early December: the pond grows a frozen skin a dozen times before it finally closes for the winter.

Why this lack of symmetry? Why shouldn't the pond surface freeze and unfreeze in exactly the same pattern? Questions like this brighten my winter nights. I suppose five or ten causes contribute to this fascinating phenomenon, factors ranging from the physics of crystallization to the rotation of the earth. Nothing happens in isolation in nature and the more complete explanations often reflect this complexity. In this case the dominant agent seems to be the wind. Wind frustrates the formation of ice crystals on the surface of a pool, while it furthers it on a solid substrate. Only rarely do the spring and fall winds in these hills stop for more than 6 or 8 hours at a time, so ice-out is favored over ice-in. A good test of this theory would be to watch the progress of the ice cycle in a calmer part of the country.

This year's ice-out date, March 28, is significant for another reason. It *probably* is a good date for the spotted salamander mass migration into the vernal pools. I can't prove this, I wasn't out watching last night (we miss the big move about half the years), but the weather profile for this event fits to a tee: "the first warm night-rain in the last week of March." Furthermore, I found spermatophores (sperm-carriers) on the bottom of the pool by the Sanctuary entrance this morning where none were yesterday. However, there is a hitch in this strong argument: we saw two spotted salamanders in a pool on Burroughs Drive two days ago, that is, before the "migration." So a couple of them came early. Possible. I still stick by my theory that if I had been out in the rain on Floyd Ackert Road at 3 a.m. last night, I would have seen dozens of tubular bodies urgently sliding over the soggy forest floor from their damp caverns to the mating pools. Everyone who has watched this spectacle has an enhanced mental image of the "force of nature."

After they have been in the water for a few days the ambystomids in our vernal pools engage the business of reproduction in earnest. Female spotteds position themselves near clusters of spermatophores. Males then begin the slow, languid dance around the stationary females, sliding in, under, and around them, undulating their long sensuous tails along the females' bodies, wafting the incense (so it is thought) of their own sperm to the females' odor-sensitive skin. This, to inflame her to pick up *his* spermatophores in her cloaca. His sperm then will fertilize the eggs she will lay along a twig or leaf at the bottom of the pool. In this way he insures his genetic representation in the next generation of spotted salamanders.

After the spotted salamanders lay their eggs in early April, they leave the pools and resume their solitary, mostly nocturnal activity in wet woodlands. The eggs in the gelatinous masses develop quickly and hatch in a few weeks. The emerging larvae breathe through gills and spend another couple of months in the pool before metamorphosing to land animals with lungs. This timing is critical, since the vernal pools by definition dry up in midsummer and no active, gill breathing animal could survive there. That of course is the point of using these pools as nurseries in the first place: the guaranteed absence of those great egg fanciers, the fish.

Watching this love-dance in full frenzy is one of the rewards of dedication in the naturalist's trade. I have seen low-key dress rehearsals perhaps a dozen times, but I was witness to the full performance only once, on a mountaintop at Mohonk. The dance is not easy to observe, several drizzly nights of all-night waiting at some forlorn woodland outpost are required. Not easy, but worth it: this image becomes part of your vision of life.

March 29 - Snow geese in 2 large flocks at 9 a.m.; Ice-out 100%; Pickerel frog calling in pond

Sanctuary Meditation

Lately I have adopted Diana's practice of meditating for a few minutes every morning. We sit relaxed on pillows in a room of the house we've set aside for this purpose. The exercise has been worthwhile for me. I have never succeeded in entirely clearing my mind, which is one of the goals of this practice, but I have had many satisfying insights in that brief space of quiet time. During this morning's meditation I came to understand *sanctuary* in a new way.

As I sat, I saw that to meditate is to enter a protected place, a kind of sanctuary in time, set aside from the confetti parade of the rest of the day. Being here is the temporal equivalent of a spatial sanctuary, where I may sit and rest my hand on the ground.

The practice of meditation serves the same purpose as preserving a serene, green place in the midst of chaotic bustle and maddening change, a space set aside to rest in. Both are *sancta*, places said to be holy, sources of peace and clarity. The long moment I linger over the mysterious pond creates enough calm to sense the bottom, even if I can't touch it.

March 30 - Spotted salamanders doing a half-hearted mating dance at end of lane; Arbutus in full bloom at station; Hepatica, 1 blossom at Ackert Bridge

Between Frost and Shadow

The spring woods has started its parade of botanical events. The trailing arbutus is always the first in early April, followed soon after by bloodroot, hepatica, and Dutchman's breeches, not necessarily in that order. Just about this time the red maple buds begin to bulge and the blossoms spatter red through the air all along the shore of the pond. The spice bush performs the same service in green for the vernal pools. These are the first flickering shimmers of the great illumination that follows in April and May.

When I say our Sanctuary spring starts with the bloodroot, arbutus, and hepatica, I am not forgetting plants like skunk cabbage, which pokes its nose through the snow bordering the forest pools in late February; or the pussy willows in our front patio in mid-March; or coltsfoot, which appears for the first time about a week later at Ackert Bridge. But I don't sense these as *spring* flowers; they seem more like experiments in late winter hardiness conducted by some botanical spirit; however, when the tiny white arbutus blossoms poke out from beneath their own unpretentious leaves, we take this as a definite commitment to spring.

To save them from the transplanters, I keep secret the Sanctuary stations of a few plants: the showy orchis, the yellow and pink lady-slippers, and the trailing arbutus. As the name suggests, the arbutus hugs the ground and spreads out in small patches from central plants. We find them often on slightly disturbed soil, such as the margins of forest paths. Even if a person happens to spot a cluster of the small tubular blossoms hiding beneath the blotchy, matted leaves, he probably wouldn't be much inclined to do the bending and twisting required to test the scent of the flower . . . not much inclined unless he knows already that the arbutus fragrance is one of the most rewarding in the eastern woods, delicately sweet and energizing. I always walk away from an arbutus patch feeling I can momentarily achieve some marvelous task quite beyond my everyday skills. The buoyancy lasts only as long as the incense fills my lungs, but I tend to go back again and again in the week that the blossoms are potent.

The sudden rush of April ground flowers - arbutus, hepatica, bloodroot, trillium, jack in the pulpit - makes botanical sense. They are engaged in one of the plant kingdom's ongoing resource wars. Most people think of animals when they visualize the struggle for survival, but to me nothing compares in biting and scratching to a young grove of saplings in a newly opened patch of forest. You have to imagine the howls of pain, the spilling of blood.

One of the resources most fiercely fought over is sunlight; all green plants need it, some more than others. The mosses and lichens that inhabit the shady forest floor through the year can survive on dribs and drabs of sunlight, but most plants require more. Opportunistic trees, like birches and poplars, maximize their sunlight by quickly outstretching the others skyward. Another strategy is to increase the photosynthetic surface, as the hemlocks do with their abundance of tiny green leaves and the moosewood does with its green twigs and trunk. A ploy of some soil-hugging plants is to sneak in their entire annual life cycle between the end of winter and the leafing out of the higher vegetation. This is the trick of the April ground flowers.

After the climbing April sun begins to warm the woodland soil but before the canopy and secondary layers spring to leaf, these forest-floor plants squeeze in everything that they are going to do this year: leaf out, bud, blossom, get pollinated, fruit, make seed, and build their root reserves for next spring's effort. It's a timed gamble between frost and shadow, just like the rest of life.

April 11 - Green frog in pool at end of lane; Bloodroot in bloom for first; Mourning cloak butterfly for first; Fox on Plutarch Rd. for first

Through a Hole in the Clouds

The day is still, the light comes from the north this afternoon through a hole in the sodden rain clouds that hang across the rest of the sky. Walking along the lane my gaze wanders over the familiar surface of a jumbled rock mass at the base of the Peninsula, made strange right now by the unusual lighting. I fix my attention on one especially striking boulder and slowly become unaware of the rest. A few moments later my eyes relax and I notice, to my surprise, the same scene below the waterline as above, the rock face mirrored perfectly in the quiet waters of the pond. I smile inwardly, amused at myself, at humans, for missing whole other worlds so plainly in our field of view. My eyes now scan quietly this other, softer rock face. I find another point of interest here. In a moment, I have forgotten the harder world above.

April 12 - Male cowbird for first; 12+ painted turtles on log at end of pond

Foxes and Developers

Yesterday I went for my first long bike ride of the season, an opportunity to monitor the progress of spring outside the boundaries of the Sanctuary. I didn't plan to make it a long ride. I started out to pick up a Sunday *Times* three miles north in the village of Esopus, but to get my copy, I ended biking ten miles in the opposite direction, to the Grand Union in Highland.

I'm glad I did the extra miles on my bike because the trip afforded me my first good look at a red fox this spring. He (or she) was scrambling up a sandstone cliff in a wooded section of Plutarch Road. He looked to be a fine specimen. Red foxes are common in our neighborhood (a fellow Trustee of the Town Historical Museum told me he trapped fifteen last winter in a single hay field a few miles north of the Sanctuary), but I only catch sight of two or three a year, so wary are they and clever at hiding themselves. This one was no exception. I held him in view as long as I did (thirty seconds), only because I surprised him in the middle of a fairly steep cliff abutting the road. He quickly found a small upturned tree stump of his own color to dodge behind, and if I hadn't seen him make the jump, I would never have guessed he was there.

Woodland lore has it that foxes, more so than most animals, know when they are hidden. I believe it, having watched foxes for twenty-five years in just such brief snatches as this. It is impossible to imagine a fox making the mistake of spotted salamanders, for instance, who carefully bury their heads under pond-bottom leaves with their brightly spotted tails sticking out the side.

I "pished" to let him know he was *not* a secret and he promptly bounded out of hiding and up the rest of the cliff, stopping momentarily at each switchback to estimate the size and imminence of the danger. He slipped over the top of the cliff with one last glance, making sure I was the right sort. Red foxes are a great pleasure to watch.

I would like to know: How have our foxes fared while the local human population has increased? Burroughs, in his essay on foxes, claims they thrive on the changes wrought by civilization. I am ready to believe that, if you think of civilization in fox terms: chickens, unwary cats and lap dogs, Norway rats, house mice, and so on; clearly a different perspective on civilization from that of the Great Books Series.

How the fox population correlates with the human population is theoretically interesting for an ecologist, but not my point here. What I really want to know is how do humans feel about foxes *vs* people as near neighbors. Let me confess my prejudice: I would rather see foxes than Joneses from my bathroom window in the morning while brushing my teeth. This is one of the thousand ways I can express to myself the elusive notion of Quality of Life.

This thought was much on my mind yesterday as I rode the back mountain roads - Old Post, Swartekill, Plutarch, Hawley's Corners - where a great deal of new construction has been undertaken since the last time I bicycled through these woods.

These backwoods have changed in my brief time here and by my lights they have changed for the worse. Whether more foxes or fewer foxes have survived this influx of people is not as important to me as my perception that the quality of this wild place has been degraded. An insidious consolation in this development is that the Burroughs Sanctuary is elevated in value as less and less of its environs look like it. This is an illusory benefit, however. A real benefit lies in the enhanced value of "sanctuary," the protection of our increasingly rare resources.

Nature sanctuaries were originally fashioned as preserves for animals and plants, set-asides where our beleaguered fellow creatures could co-exist with minimum harassment. More and more they are becoming asylums for humans, or rather for certain often-neglected demands of the human spirit. We should probably acknowledge what we are doing and start designing sanctuaries in this light. In some places this is happening. In fast growing suburbs, for instance, as the people-per-other-animal ratio moves toward a certain point, one hears louder calls for open space as a feature of the good life, even as a measure of progress. Neighborhood organizations around the nation, in a kind of reverse NIMBYism, are demanding better green planning for their backyard, as long as it doesn't happen everywhere else. Imagine if all these malcontents voted in a block, the way sportsmen are supposed to do! They will. I believe it's coming, but these things move at a glacial pace. The American idea of progress is now evolving rapidly and the friction between the old and new species is producing a lot of heat.

The notions of "environmental quality of life" and the "impact of human activities" are closely bound together. Unfortunately for the practitioners of environmental impact analysis (and for the rest who have to live with their shortcomings) the science and law of this discipline were developed by engineers rather than hairdressers. Engineers live in bondage to numbers; only the quantifiable is real. They can barely discuss the matter beyond that. Hairdressers may think in terms of an ounce of this or a half an inch there, but their bottom line is an intuition: the result is either "right" or not. Their inability to place that judgment in Cartesian coordinates doesn't get in the way of reworking the product until it is "right." This is closer to our sense of "quality of life" than is a list of numbers denoting cubic feet of soil eroded, parts per million in drinking water, or angle subtended in a visual field. The rural developer has, alas, only to present such a list to the Town Planning Board to gain approval for whatever. Asking whether the project seems "right" from the point of view of the Board, the developer himself, the neighbors, or the rest of the townspeople would be grounds for civil suit.

The individuality of a piece of woods has to do with its foxes, along with the other animals, plants, geologic features, climate, and history in a web with the memories and associations we bring to that landscape, fused into a sense of wholeness. Erosion rates and parts per million may be useful indices to suggest pieces of this whole; or armor, perhaps, to forfend the worst abominations against it. But they are not the whole. The whole resides in the imagination of each of us - communicable, if only we have the courage to speak over the head of the frightened little engineer within.

Swartekill Road is on the way down. I would say it's going fast. How will these changes affect the number of foxes here? I don't know; I doubt anyone does. What do the changes mean for the web of forest life that has given this area so much of its character? This is a weightier question. I still don't know what to say and I am even less sure that anyone does. What impacts do these changes have on the quality of this place in my imagination? Absolutely devastating. No blank space appears on the New York State Environmental Assessment Form for recording this kind of damage. The developers are safe, for the moment, from my radical views.

April 14 - Louisiana waterthrush at house for first; Watched injured muskrat resting by pond

Reptile Interiors

For the last few days I have been checking the snake den in our front yard three or four times a day. The emergence of the big black rat and black racer snakes is one of the highlights of our spring calendar. The third week in April is a good target date for first spotting the two kinds of "black" snakes that hibernate in the broken foundation of the hotel that burned down here in 1939. If we are attentive, we spot the first one poking his head through one of the cracks in the sidewalk that formed the promenade of the hotel - just checking out the state of the sun, I suppose. A day or so later, someone in our family will catch sight of a black snake stretched out on the broken rubble below the sidewalk, and in a short time three to five of them will be spread out over the terrace.

When Diana's children were younger, the emergence of the black snakes meant a fun day, because the kids loved to play with the snakes in their vernal torpor. I have dozens of slides of sinewy black rat snakes twined through Jennifer's long, blond hair or slithering over Eric's arms.

Eastern hognose snakes and milk snakes also share our front yard, but they have none of the dependability of the two black snakes. The milk snakes live in the basement and come out to the front porch to sun or find their way to the yard in the late evening. I believe I have run into them in every month of the year, save January and February.

I remember one year during Christmas week, I was in the cellar with Eric fixing the water pump (a ritual almost as regular around here as the rat snakes), when I disturbed a young milk snake that had curled up under a discarded water heater. Young milk snakes are even feistier than their elders, and this one was true to his genes, lunging at me with mouth gaping and fangs bared again and again in a good show of reptile savagery. The problem was that the temperature was a only few degrees above freezing and he could barely move due to the cold, so his fierce display played itself out in comic slow motion. His angry lunges became languorous waves along his slender body; coiling for the next strike seemed to take him forever. I found myself getting impatient for the next stab at my foot. I put him back under the water tank without warming him too much, to prevent his getting into any more trouble. I've often wondered if he made it through the winter in our basement, which drops well below freezing in January.

Our hognose snakes probably overwinter in the same cement foundation as the black snakes, at least I've see them around there in the spring. Someone or other in the household spots a hognose in the front yard on the average three or four times a year. A herpetologist friend of mine was surprised by this frequency, he goes out looking for them and never finds that many. They are wary and secretive and have a habit of not getting into trouble. I suspect that many more are here than we happen upon.

One reason hognose snakes are fond of our place is the abundance of toads hereabouts. The Sanctuary and our mini-environment in particular are rather wet; wetland forms abound - ferns, mosses, and amphibians. Among the latter are the American and Fowler's toads. On damp evenings in early summer the toads in the corners of the front lawn are so abundant we have to be careful where we're walking. Hognose snakes are known to be particularly fond of toads, some say they are *obligate* toad fanciers, that is, they eat only toads. I have my doubts about all such assertions.

Doubtlessly the most remarkable feature of the secretive hognose snakes is their behavior when surprised by a predator or a pseudopredator such as a human. (Humans aren't true predators of snakes because they rarely eat them or take any other benefit from killing them, but people certainly do wreak havoc in the lives of snakes.) A hognose is a wonderful performer, he is the old-time Thespian of the animal world. When first encountered, he will draw in air and hiss it out violently, no poisonous snakes have such a hiss as this. Simultaneously he blows up his body and especially his head to twice its normal size, looking for all the world like a cobra. If you haven't by this time run away in fright, he will lunge for you with distended jaws, his pallid gums flashing, a cottonmouth for sure! If you are still standing there, and if in fact you make a move for him, he strikes his final pose, which is to writhe horribly, roll over on his back and dangle his tongue out the side of his gaping mouth. Dead! Until you turn him on his stomach, at which he promptly rolls over again on his back. One part of the act that needs a little work.

Black rat snakes are much more straightforward as players on the world's stage. Their only ploy is to rattle their tails against some dry leaves at your approach, which many snakes will do. But they will protect themselves with a lunging bite if you attempt to grab them, as almost all snakes will do. What is different about black rat snakes is their readiness to be seduced.

I believe snakes are the animal world's greatest hedonists next to pussycats; they love to be fondled, stroked, and palpated, they spend half the year snuggling. You can bet that any animal that rubs its belly over wet grass for a living will develop a taste for the sensuous. Such as they are, many snakes can be sedated by plying them with caresses, once you have them in your hands. This may be one factor in the heart-stopping rattlesnake dances performed by the Hopi.

The black rat snake represents an extreme case: if you can get one soothing hand on him without his biting you and if you are otherwise gentle, you can easily pick him up without further defense on his part. One trick is to let the snake start to get away in a terrain of rocks or among woody stems. In this way he can not turn and bite as you run your hand firmly down his back or let his body slip through your funneled hands.

Some people may object that by telling this I am encouraging interference and disruption in the lives of wild animals. I disagree. I am strongly opposed to *harming* wild animals on trivial pretexts, even or especially those animals we may fear, like snakes. But I am in favor of *interacting* with them for just that reason. We have a lot to learn from snakes, not only about tolerance for other life forms, but about the geography of the wild mind. One of the great costs of civilization is our loss of daily contact with wildness. Some people may count this as a benefit, but I see it as a denial of reality, a frightened unwillingness to look at our own wild interior. Black rat snakes and chickadees and foxes help reopen that door ever so little.

April 17 - Female cowbird rattling nearby; Screech owl(?) warbling north of house

"I Tink Izza Coppahead"

None of the snakes I've encountered in the Sanctuary are poisonous, at least in a way that poses a threat to humans. Some "non-poisonous" snakes, like the hognose, are believed to have a weak venom in their saliva, but this affects only their small prey. The only poisonous snake that *might* be here is a copperhead. I have seen them in West Park and along the bluffs of the Hudson, but never within the Sanctuary boundaries for all my wandering up and down here. Nevertheless, about five times a season, someone reports spotting "the biggest copperhead I ever laid eyes on" in the Pond, shooting across my front lawn, waiting for them in a tree, etc., etc. Two or three questions invariably reveal that the eyewitness has no idea what a copperhead really looks like, probably has never seen one in his life, and has misidentified a water snake, milk snake, or something else, it almost doesn't matter. And this is the curious part: they *want* to see a copperhead so badly that any more or less elongate reptile without legs fits the description.

One of the few real copperheads I've seen around here merits a note. Diana and I were walking through the hamlet of West Park to the post office late one afternoon about two years ago. Slowly winding across the road ahead of us was a large snake. Naturally we ran up to see who it was. It was a copperhead, a handsome, healthy looking specimen. Before the snake made it to the other side, a dilapidated pick-up truck piled high with garbage clattered up to us and lurched to a stop in the middle of the road. A huge, squat fellow tumbled out wearing a soiled undershirt that didn't quite cover his beer belly. We call them "Woodchucks" here on the New York edge of Appalachia.

"I tink izza coppahead," he announced to us, dramatically pointing.

"You're right, that's right, you're right!" I encouraged him, ever the schoolmarm.

He looked dumfounded at this. "Walll, whaddya gonna *do?*"

"Do . . well. . . she's really a handsome looking snake, hunh? I'll bet she's three feet long. . . or more maybe? What do you think?"

Beginning to suspect the worst, the Woodchuck turned his appeal to my sense of civic duty. "Hey, they's people what has *kids* live here," jerking his thumb at the row of houses behind us on Ackert Road.

"Well. . . yes. . . well. . . .." I was not doing a great job of holding up my side of the argument. I wanted only to hold his attention for a few moments more, but I couldn't for the life of me think what would interest him right now more than that poor snake.

Meanwhile he went back to his truck, hauled out a two-by-four from the rubbish in the bed, and tried to shove it in my hands. "Here," he said, "dis here oughtta do it." He wanted *me* to bash it! This mountain of social conscience.

"I don't believe in killing animals that aren't harming anyone." I tried to make it clear and yet with the right measure of moral force to impress him. He just looked at me in amazement.

The man had a point: here is a poisonous snake; kids do live on this street; he lives around here too; maybe he has kids.

Then the encounter took an ominous turn. The door of the house in front of us opened and the owner walked out, a state policeman who works out of the barracks on Route 9W. He was naturally curious what was going on right here in his front yard.

I've talked with the man casually on a number of occasions, at the post office or the Grand Union grocery store; he waves cheerfully when I walk by. He always seemed to me a gentle, good-natured person; BUT . . . here he was with a poisonous snake that had just slithered out of his front lawn, he *did* have kids, and, well, he *was* a state cop . . . . I looked over to the copperhead, she was taking a damn long time to cross the road. I had a horrible mental image of the cop whipping out his .357 Magnum and blowing the little sucker away. `Make my day, make my day', kept running through my head.

The Woodchuck didn't waste any time. "Here!" he ran up to the policeman and handed him the club, "dis here oughtta do it. Izza coppahead."

The homeowner-father-policeman looked over to the copperhead, which was still in a position to be killed in ten or so different ways, all known to him. He handed back the board and said to him, quite simply, "I don't hurt snakes."

The tubby, would-be deliverer of natural justice was absolutely flabbergasted. Muttering to himself and shaking his head, he shuffled back to his truck, threw in the two-by-four, stuffed himself behind the wheel, and drove off to the dump.

It made my week.

April 19 - Easter; Blue-gray gnatcatcher singing for first at Slabsides; Shad-bush leaf-out; Flying squirrel lodged in dying elm

Sunrise Service
"Formation, Transformation, Eternal Mind's Eternal Recreation"
For the last couple of weeks my bedtime reading has been Carl Jung's autobiography, *Memories, Dreams, Reflections.* Jung often cites Goethe's *Faust* as an influence on his early thinking. I share that view. I am reminded of it this early morning as I sit on the rocks overlooking the pond and hear the bells calling to mass from Holy Cross, the Episcopal monastery on the Hudson in West Park. These bells are one of the few man-made sounds that we hear in the Sanctuary, along with the rumbling of the trains along the river. The bells have a new meaning for me at this moment. Everywhere I look are the tiny green avowals of renewal, of the commitment to life.

Life thrives here under the sun's blessing: the pushing buds of the beech, waterthrush songs in the woods, curly pondweed rising through the water, the maianthemum leaves, shadflowers, the hemlock pollen filling the air. From every pore of the soil spring natural acts of grace: moss, leaf, lichen, liverwort, bud.

I count the messages. Birds sing: chickadees, cardinals, flickers, redwings, cowbirds, robins, Louisiana waterthrushes, tufted titmice, phoebes, goldfinches, and a drumming grouse; butterflies - blues, skippers, and mourning cloaks - flicker through the dawn air; painted turtles push each other off sunning logs where muskrats have left their territorial markers; the monastery bells; the frogs - peepers, green and pickerel frogs - work at out-signaling the birds; and the fibers - the red notes from the shadbush, the yellow memos from the eastern hemlock, the purple signals from the fruiting grasses and mosses, and from every other nook of the earth, tiny signs of green started from the secret winter place.

Renew.

Continuing my walk out to the road to pick up the morning paper, I notice the arbutus is now brown and drooping, the blossoms are dry and without scent.

April 20 - Hermit thrush singing near pond; Chipping sparrow singing at house for first; Black rat snake at ruins for first

I Can't Help Asking

I took a short walk out on the Peninsula trail yesterday evening. I know now, after many years of confusion on this point, that most of my goings and comings in the Sanctuary are not so much to garner specific information on new blossoms or on the state of the goose nest as to deepen my rapport with this well known place. In my old goal-directed days I used to run back and forth filling out sheets of data describing the distribution of vegetation in the undisturbed valleys of the Sanctuary or the micro-climatic differences at the edges of the swamps. I still keep a lot of records, but my relationship to the columns of data has changed.

Yesterday, after my thirty-mile bicycle ride, I took a long shower, relaxed for an hour with the Sunday *Times*, and strolled out to the Peninsula. It was a warm, quiet, April evening and I was in a quiet mood, walking in the dusk. The Peninsula is just right for such visits. Sitting on one of the bare rock crests, I have a sweeping view of the greater part of the pond below, a stimulating and, at the same time, intimate and quieting prospect, the theme of the Sanctuary.

On my way out I took the "shore route," which means scrambling through the light woods on the east side of the Peninsula. Stepping over a large fantail of bedrock, I caught sight of a dead black-capped chickadee lodged between the rock and the base of a five-inch diameter elm snag. It was a lucky sighting because the bird had been cold only a few hours. The carrion beetles were already at it and the carcass would not have lasted, one way or another, two more days.

Dead black-capped chickadees are not casual business around here. To keep tabs on their population shifts, I have banded most of the winter flock that gathers at my feeder. Because chickadees do not migrate between seasons, this includes many of the breeding birds for an unknown radius around. Sure enough, he had a small aluminum U.S. Fish and Wildlife band on his right leg, which I pried off before recycling the carcass in the woods.

I have been banding birds on my own for the past ten years, ever since I moved in here. I use banding mainly to educate people about birds and the environment we share with them. A visitor with an interest in the life of any other animal will be mesmerized by looking directly into its wild eye. He will listen intently to whatever I say as I hold the living bird in front of him. I make use of the spell.

I wondered how this chickadee died. I saw no obvious signs of damage; it was not the work of a predator; and (apart from being stone dead) he appeared to be in good shape. I found out it was a male; my records show I banded him in May of 1986 and at that time he had a "cloacal protuberance," a bulge around the external sexual organ which males develop during the breeding season. He had this same bulge now which suggested he was healthy enough to get involved in the strenuous breeding cycle.

I looked around for a clue to his undoing. Next to him was the dead American elm. So -

Possibility #1: Fatal collision. However, chickadees don't usually bash into trees as they do windows; they are remarkably adept flyers, especially in short range situations. (I once saw a chickadee accidentally drop a sunflower seed after shelling it on a branch about four feet off the ground. The bird swooped down, caught the seed mid-air in its mouth, and recovered the branch without ruffling a feather. Deftness.)

Looking up at the elm snag, I noticed a two inch diameter hole in the tree, about ten feet high. Aha!

Possibility #2: The chickadee family was using this hole for breeding purposes. The opening was a little large, but within the range of other chickadee nest sites I have seen. Perhaps he was killed defending his nest. To test Possibility #2, I tapped lightly on the trunk at my level, hoping either to see the female chickadee stick her head out, or even hear the famous "Hissing Snake" defense. The hole was several feet away from my head, and the threat probably not great enough to elicit that extreme reaction. Surprise! Out pops not a chickadee head, but a whole flying squirrel.

Possibility #3: The male chickadee, in the course of investigating every single hole in the woods, as is their custom, poked his head in *that* hole and got a defensive response, a fatal one, from the tenant flying squirrel.

The real answer is any and/or none of these. I can't help asking.

April 21 - Goldfinch singing for first

Timely Connections

Our pair of Canada geese have returned this year and are nesting on the pond at the end of the Peninsula, upon the same island as they have every spring for the past eight years. I was mousing around the front yard this morning and happened to notice the gander feeding on the other side of the pond. He was doing what he always does this time of year: he spies some particularly tasty morsel of curly pondweed growing up from the bottom and tips up to rip it out with his beak, his rump pointing toward the zenith. He uses the full length of his neck and body to get the best tidbits.

I mused: How timely and convenient that the geese arrive as the first shoots of pondweed are reachable around the edges of the pond in March . . . the birds feed more and more toward the center of the pond as this plant slowly grows to the surface through April . . . and then . . . this idea never occurred to me before . . . and then the pondweed reaches the surface in the first week of May, just in time to accommodate the much shorter reach of the little ones who come off the nest to feed during that week.

I have thought a good deal about the timing of events in nature and here in the Sanctuary in particular. I think I have a relatively sophisticated grasp of these connections. In this light I examined the new idea - that the pondweed growth somehow influences the dates of egg-laying and hatching for the goose. The answer came back quickly, "No, that's not plausible."

Why not? In retrospect I'm not sure why I made that judgment, possibly a prejudice about the contingency of *this* pondweed growth versus the fixedness of nesting phenology for *all* those geese. Perhaps I assumed that the geese are locked into a pattern graven in their genes by their evolutionary history, while the pondweed growth depends on this spring's weather.

The question has returned to bother me, not whether that particular connection is a good one, but how I could put it aside so nonchalantly, so unreflectingly. Now I'm wondering: How many other provocative connections have I dismissed, unconsciously even, because they didn't pass this short-sighted test?

April 22 - Osprey on pond for first; Oak leaves in baby wrinkle, no gypsy moth caterpillars in sight

The Graceful and the Graceless

Yesterday evening I spotted my first osprey on the pond. I have been waiting and watching for a week; they seem late this year. Correction: yesterday evening my first osprey spotted me; it was her sharp, bright, querulous warning "Chee-Chee-Chee-Chee," as she left her perch on a gray birch overlooking the pond, that first alerted me to her presence. This is almost always the case, I can't remember ever spotting the year's first osprey before she spotted me.

Twice a year, April and September, Ospreys renew my faith in animal grace. They are fish hawks, and many people know them only by that name. They make their living around large bodies of water, hovering at a height above the surface and suddenly diving, feet first, to catch a surface feeding fish in their sharp talons. They are comely in all of their movements, especially in the act of hovering. Their wings are long in relation to their bodies, and supple. Most birds that hover do so by buzzing their wings (hummingbirds) or flapping frantically (phoebes and kingfishers). Ospreys send slow, graceful undulations from their breasts to their wingtips. The wings wave lithely under these impulses, maintaining their steady position for scouting fish. They allow me to believe this is effortless.

People who know ospreys want them around. When I first came to the Sanctuary and found that ospreys spend a few weeks here between winters in Florida and St. Lawrence summers, I was excited. When I discovered them performing pre-mating rites in spiraling flight above the pond, clasping talons and passing fish from feet to feet, I vowed to get them to stay.

To a biogeography student this makes less sense than it seems. Plants and animals are where they are for a variety of reasons. Biogeographers find assignable causes like climate, soil, paths of dispersal, predators, or prey. Chance also plays a strong part. In any case, if an animal does not reside in an area, no magic wands exist to make it do so. Never mind, I wanted ospreys in my back yard. I wanted them badly enough to pull the following stunt: In the dead of winter, 1980, I called up my friend, Al Brayton, a good birder and active member of the John Burroughs Natural History Society and asked him if would he be interested in an avian biogeography experiment. Sure, why not?

So a week later the three of us, Al, Diana, and I trudged out over the ice of the pond carrying a variety of tools and supplies necessary for the experiment. We picked out a chestnut oak on the east side of the pond that had the potential for being an osprey nesting tree. We started to work.

Ospreys make large crude stick nests near the water, either on solitary snags or in trees that rise above the surrounding canopy. They are fond of tall utility poles, much to the consternation of power and telephone companies. They seem to need clear avenues of approach to the nest. No trees around Sanctuary Pond would fill this bill. The canopy is fairly uniform in height because the whole forest around here is about the same age; it was released from agriculture sometime in the early part of this century. The chestnut oak that we chose was a compromise. It was a fair-sized tree at the edge of the pond and jutting out over it somewhat. It had a clear approach on at least two sides.

This tree's problem was that it didn't have the right kind of top. Ospreys need a flat platform on which to pile the sticks that make up the nest. They are known to accept an artificial platform as long as it has the right feel of space and height. So I strapped on my climbing spurs, relics from the old days of owl nest snooping, took one end of a climber's line and hitched myself up about thirty feet on the oak to a point where the bole was eight inches in diameter and the surrounding foliage opened up a little. Al tied the bow saw to the line below and I hoisted it up. My plan was to top the tree and affix something flat at that point as a platform.

In the position I found myself, however, I couldn't get the right leverage to use the bow saw effectively. I could have tied myself to the tree, the way real timberjacks do, but I wanted to have the option of jumping off in the worst case, and anyway I am not a real timberjack. So I let the bow saw down again and this time Al tied my power chain saw to the line. We debated briefly whether he should start it up down there and decided, for the sake of the saw, in case of a slip, it would be better for me to get it going up in the tree. I succeeded, only after some difficulty, because two hands are required to start a chain saw and I needed one to hold on to the tree. After getting it going, I discovered I had the same problem applying force to the cut as I had with the bow saw. I couldn't lean far enough back, still holding onto the tree, to push the cutting blade into the trunk. With some body contortions and by propping myself against a lower branch, I succeeded in getting into a position in which I could apply a little leverage against the saw. Unfortunately, this required that the sawdust-spitting saw chain was whizzing about four inches from my eyes, so that I quickly lost view of what I was doing.

Meanwhile Diana was dutifully photographing this piece of suicidal insanity, in between appeals to give up the whole cockamamie business. But the worst was yet to come. In my enthusiasm for the project, I neglected to take careful account of what exactly was going to happen to this eight-inch, twenty-foot long log that I was sawing away at scalp level. This is the next worst thing to sawing off the branch you're sitting on. Sure enough, it came crashing down *my* way, narrowly missing my head on its trajectory. Diana caught this lighthearted moment in a photograph.

Undaunted. Next I had to put up the platform. I remember reading in a self-help osprey platform builder's guide from ten or twenty years ago that a sturdy five-by-five lumber framework is ideal, but lacking that you can use a garbage can lid. So a few days before this, we headed across the river to the city of Poughkeepsie to scout up a stray garbage can lid. I have always thought of Poughkeepsie as more or less consisting of unowned garbage can lids but, sure enough, when we went over to get one, there were none to be had. We had to settle for a decidedly inferior product from the Esopus town dump, not a garbage can lid at all, but a kind of giant industrial washer, two feet across. That's what I wired on to the newly flattened top of the oak. To finish it off, I fixed a few preliminary branches cross-ways over the platform. Again according to osprey lore, this greatly enhances the appeal of the spot.

After that kind of work and risk, the typical provider expects a little gratitude. How did the osprey respond to my contribution to their household economy? The first spring the usual three to five osprey arrived in mid-April, but took no notice of the nesting platform. I expected that; it would take a while, I reasoned, for the possibility to hit them. Unfortunately, the same was true the following spring and each of the five years since then. Having observed them closely on the pond over these years, I am confident they are unaware that my structure is an osprey nesting platform. Osprey, like all hawks, are *watchers*. They take note of everything, nothing of any significance escapes their fierce attention. Alas, in these seven years I have never seen any of them perch on the nest tree, fly meaningfully about it, peer measuredly at it, or indeed even appear to notice that it's there. It doesn't exist.

April 24 - Strawberry blossom for first between road and pond; Female bluebird in front yard acting suspicious

The Evanescence

I was out on Burroughs Drive yesterday evening, picking up the weekly load of roadside litter, when the following exchange took place: I hear a goldfinch singing in the hemlocks; I tell myself I need to write that down now or it will go unrecorded. This is a constant for natural history notes - get it down right now or it's gone forever. I reflect that this is true for another realm of personal experience: dreams.

For many years I recorded my dreams in the middle of the night or immediately upon rising, but gradually fell out of the practice. Recently I have started to do so again and am now reminded of this parallel between dreaming and natural history.

At the corner of Burroughs Drive and Floyd Ackert Road, while bending over a pile of old beer cans that had somehow eluded my notice on previous visits, I think to myself "You better write that thought down, or you'll forget it." I did.

April 27 - First pond lily leaves on top of pond; Black racer in ruins for first; Swifts over pond for first

Thinking with My Body

We were out walking on our lane by the pond this evening just before nightfall. At the spot where the Peninsula trail cuts off to the right, I was stopped in my tracks by a lone black duck pin-wheeling out of the dusk and setting down silently onto the road ahead. I froze and with a slight motion brought Diana to a standstill. I hadn't been thinking of ducks. Thinking with my mind that is; my body had been aware of ducks all along the way.

Mallards, blacks, and wood ducks have begun nesting now in the Sanctuary. Every year at this time and often around this spot, I catch sight of a secretive female soundlessly lighting in a corner of the pond or in the middle of the lane at dusk. It means one thing. She is stealing back to her nest for the night. Year in and year out, I forget this important detail of life. My mind forgets it, but my animal body remembers, and responds correctly at that moment: freezing instinctively . . . at that place along the lane, when and where the female black duck slips noiselessly out of the sky.

Coming to know a new place has value for a nature observer, but it's not like having a decade of familiarity with one's own acre. So with the black duck. When I walk on any of the trails of the Sanctuary, I shift into a mode of consciousness different from walking in unfamiliar places. Here I am more aware of the environment while paying less attention to it. The woodscapes and vistas are familiar, I don't have to look at them to know immediately if a new branch has fallen, if the stream is a little more swollen than normal for this time of year. I see animals - deer, foxes, and owls - not because I search them out, but because, today, out of the corner of my eye, the wooded hillside to my left has a feature not there the last dozen times I've been at this bend in the road. This works in time as well as space: the same black duck, lighting on the same spot on the lane in November, would not touch the nerve it does in early April.

I don't know where this consciousness comes from. I guess that every person attuned to the natural history of his or her familiar place develops a finely detailed interior map and a sixth sense of what ought to be going on there, what ought not. After a ten-year attention span, that sense can become acute and its map detailed. After a lifelong study we might expect a Dan Smiley. Dan had voluminous records to remind him when and where to look for the next bird or blossom. He rarely used his records this way; he relied on his interior sense of what was going to happen next. Walking through the woods in mid-April, we would both catch a distant flash of rusty brown amid the fall of last year's red oak leaves. "First hermit thrush," he would venture. Chasing the bird down proved him right. Or he would look out at a March evening sky and say, "Tonight's the night for checking the salamander pools at Bontecou." And it was.

May 1 - Flowering dogwood in bloom at end of pond; First gosling hatched from goose nest

May Day

The first of May has a meaning for me that has nothing to do with the international labor movement or superpower politics. A lot is going on in the Sanctuary every year on May 1st: the second wave of bird migrants are arriving, driven by the northing sun; the trees and shrubs have already pushed the first inch of green; the pond brims with life. The weather is now constant enough to support numbers of flying insects, including the more comely moths and butterflies, and the blossoms of the deep forest step out in their summer-long parade under the developing canopy. All of these things are, of course, happening a week or so before this date and several weeks after. I have a need, all the same, for a single date which represents the enchantment of this time during the rest of the year, especially the long dreary nights of winter. The day I have settled upon is May 1st.

The image of a cheerful spring day bursting with life is compelling enough to have a little saying that captures this quality of life: "More Matter for a May Morning." The phrase is from Act III, Scene IV of *Twelfth Night* and describes some of the merry nonsense going on with Sir Andrew Aguecheek, Sir Toby Belch, and friends. I catch myself silently repeating it on days that seem to have too little of this quality and also on days like today, lest I overlook what I now enjoy.

I have had this phrase hanging on my writing-room wall for the past twenty-five years. Often it has been scrawled in ballpoint on a sheet of yellow legal paper. Last year for my birthday I was given a much finer version: Diana commissioned our friend Joan Scott, a calligrapher, to illuminate the phrase on a muslin wall hanging. Looking at it on the wall of my upstairs office reminds me of May Day all year long. Especially today.

May 2 - Yellow-rumped warbler for first at end of pond; Kingbird for first in front yard; Luminous, transparent, liquid, trompe l'oeil etc. shadbush

Companions

Ever since the geese left the nest on May 1st, they have been coming and going to and from the pond with a certain regularity, almost a rhythm. In the early morning they can usually be found paddling about somewhere on the pond, but before 10 a.m. they appear in the front yard. From there they make their way west by various routes to Valli Marsh, where I have spotted them several times at midday. Often, but not always, they reappear in the front yard toward evening. I believe they sleep on the shore of the pond. In past years I have even watched them settle in for the night on their old nest.

If they follow the pattern of previous years, these trips through the woods to distant pools and streams will become longer and more adventuresome as the season develops. We have encountered them on successive days' hikes along Black Creek from below Ackert Bridge to above Mario Valli's waterfall, a distance of well over a mile. It puzzles me why they push themselves so. As I mentioned before, they do not need to go beyond the pond for food and they are certainly not scrambling for security. As a matter of fact, considering the risk to which they are exposing the young, there ought to be some compensating benefit in these sallies. Exercise? Experience in the big, wide world? Just out for adventure? As an initiate in the mysteries of evolutionary biology, I'm compelled to look for the adaptive value of this behavior. I may not find it, it may not be there, but I need to look.

Among the animals that live within the bounds of the Sanctuary, geese are special favorites for studying behavior because I can watch them for hours and pick up lore that is hard to come by with more secretive animals. Most of this is not scientific information; it will never be found in a monograph on the family *Anseridae*, but is none the less valuable to a naturalist who wants to understand this animal. For example the style of parental care is not what we might expect: the goose covers the goslings with her wings in a winning maternal way when it rains and at night, but will fight the little ones for tasty grass morsels on the lawn. The gander is fierce in his defensive posturing around the young, but can be quite unreliable when push comes to shove. One day a Sanctuary visitor's large dog got away from his leash and made a dash for the family foraging on the lawn. Both gander and goose took off at top speed - the other way. The little ones survived, but no thanks to the Defender.

One pattern the geese did *not* follow this year is the "first-day trek," their four-mile foray down to the hamlet and back, which they habitually undertake within twenty-four hours of leaving the nest. My own behavior modification experiment may be one reason the geese did not undertake the first-day trek this spring. In late March before the nest was made I fed the resident goose and gander frequently to give them the notion that I was a resource. I did not feed them when she was setting for fear of disrupting her nesting behavior, but the day that the brood was off the nest, I redoubled my efforts, tossing them bread scraps whenever I would see them on the pond. It worked, something worked; they decided to hang around on day number two.

Success aside, purists will tsk and wildlife professionals will wonder whether a nature sanctuary caretaker is taking his job seriously if he goes around making pets of the wild animals that find refuge there. I offer the following rationalizations:

First, it is a definitive part of human nature to intervene; we are the manipulating animal. Manipulating the lives of the geese is as natural for me as reproducing goslings is for them. This is in the grand tradition of domestication, pesticide manufacture, and the peregrine falcon rehabilitation program.

Second, these geese are not truly wild (I used the word "free-living" above). They are immediate descendants not of the wild strain of Canada geese that still migrate from the deep South to Canada, but of their golf-course relatives gone feral. The latter birds have come to breed in the northern states and overwinter near by. They lack the traits of wildness of the original strain. It seems appropriate to treat them as if they lived on an extended golf course, which tradition tells them is their place.

Finally, I wish to experience other minds. By sharing with these birds a food of mine, I join with them on a level that mere study will never achieve. We become "companions," in that ancient sense, knowing the savor in the other's mouth.

May 5 - Black & white warbler(?) on Peninsula for first; No action at large-mouth bass spawning rock

Fooling the Mind's Eye

Apropos of the curious notation in the almanac for May 2nd: that evening Diana and I walked out on the Peninsula to catch the "shadow sundown," sunset except for a rain cloud cover and vapors rising from the lake. The light at these times comes from everywhere, as much from the earth as the sky. This is perfect lighting to enjoy the present stage of the spring foliage - past the mid-April mist of sprouting leaves, but not yet in full green. Most of the trees have one to two inch leaves, which are in all stages of transition from their native reds, ambers, and fuchsias to the kelly green of summer.

From mid-April to mid-May many forest leaves undergo the same passage of color that they do from early October to early November, in reverse. They are hiding (revealing) their true colors with the production (destruction) of the green enzyme chlorophyll. Details of the transition are different. For instance, nothing in November corresponds to the April mist.

These transitions take place wherever deciduous trees occur. To judge by bank calendars, fall foliage is endemic to the Northeast. The colors may be more dazzling in these parts, but not necessarily more beautiful. Watching the spring and autumn changes is often more pleasing in their more muted forms along the North Pacific coast or on Arizona plateaus.

One particular tree that caught our attention this evening was a shadbush on a cliff overlooking the pond. It serves as a "station," a biological proxy for all the shadbushes in the Sanctuary. This tree is fairly free-standing and is beamed upon from all directions. In the diffused light of the shadow sundown, it glows wonderfully. Just at this time of year the shadbush leaves have a peculiar quality. First of all we find a great variability of color. Leaves just out of the sheathe-womb are still shiny red. The most developed leaves are as fully green as shadbush leaves get, that is to say, not bright but subdued green with a dark cast of some more earthen color. But most of the leaves are in between with every magenta nuance between blood red and shadow green. The green seems to emanate from the sap-filled veins, leaving a soft wash of other color centered on the leaf surface between the veins and achieving a deceptive effect of depth and limpidity. We stood in front of the low slung tree for fifteen minutes, examining the variations among the leaves and trying to describe the quality of light that shone in them.

D: ". . . it's almost like they're not leaves. Maybe moisture or tinted haze?"

J: "To me, the thing is, you can't focus on them, the real surface is above or below what you're seeing somehow."

D: "They're transparent, you can almost see through them . . ."

J: ". . . or more like, luminous, there's a light coming from inside them."

D: "No, it's liquid, they look liquid, like pools of a stained, transparent fluid."

J: "I've got it, it's 'fool the eye,' *trompe l'oeil,* they're like those photos that change their focus as you move your head back and forth . . .?"

After all that we decided we didn't "get it;" but we had fun trying . . . and satisfaction in leaving the mystery intact for next year.

Acts around the intermission of summer -
Late spring plays early autumn,
Early autumn mimes late spring's parody . . .
This foolery can go on forever.

May 6 - Water lily blossoms almost open; Two spotted sandpipers on pond for first; House wrens in ruins, not singing; Mockingbird on telephone line

Cold Snap

It has been late November these last few days in early May. The thermometer has stayed below fifty degrees and low scudding clouds have left everything wet. The trees and herbs are struggling to get on with the business of springtime and a lull has been noticeable in the activities of animals, both residents and migrants. The prime casualty has been the May arrivals. I haven't seen the early warblers, the rest of the thrushes, a towhee or catbird, all of whom would normally be here by now. I would be alarmed to see a hummingbird for fear it could not generate enough body heat for this weather.

The insects have also been slowed. I mentioned the total absence of gypsy moth caterpillars. If it is too cold for them to digest their food, they may be holing up in thick folds of bark at the base of trees, waiting for the inevitable 70° day, like everyone else here.

A dramatic example of weather dependence are the *polistes* wasps that have been trying to make a nest in the newspaper box at the end of our driveway. During the warm spell two weeks ago they were working at it feverishly, three or four at a time. I try to discourage them from using this location, so that I don't get stung when carelessly sticking the newspaper under my arm in the morning. I dissuade them by knocking off the beginnings of their conical hanging paper nest from the ceiling of the receptacle. The best time to do this is early morning or late at night, when the air is cool. They can't warm up fast enough to catch me as I race off down the road. Removing their first efforts at nest building once or twice in the early season is usually enough. They take the hint and try somewhere else. They may be brutes, but they're not stupid.

Other insects seem to be similarly debilitated by this weather. Just pull away a few inches of duff from the forest floor and you will see a number of them bunched up there, waiting for a warm front. We humans imagine ourselves at the top of life's development, but who of us wouldn't trade, say, skill with syllogisms for the ability to crawl under the leaves for a few days until things took a more cheerful turn.

I wrote the above this morning. Even as I did, the clouds began to lighten, winds shifted again from the north to the west, the air warmed perceptibly, the energy of spring reasserted itself. This afternoon I saw the birds noted above, and was reminded again of the futility of saying anything too definite about the drama of nature or its setting in this Sanctuary.

May 7 - Small bat flying over pond, for first; Phoebe now singing around house; Quaking aspen! on lane in downy leaf; Early lady-slipper now pink, two other blossoms started; Falcate orange-tip butterfly on garlic mustard, Burroughs Dr.

A Richer Mast

Several groups have toured the Burroughs Sanctuary during the last few days and I have been showing them the sights. I consider a visitor to the Sanctuary part of the fauna, indeed a complex member of the faunal assemblage, one that feeds, metaphorically, on both plants and other animals, soil, air, and light, and his/her own images of these things. People who come here nibble on wintergreen berries, take photos of hillsides, breathe sweet air, get impressions of snakes' minds, and take away a picture of an undisturbed forest. If the visit is successful, the participant also creates a metaphor, relates this place to his or her life with an inner image. I believe making metaphors is the most meaningful work we do all our lives. Nature sanctuaries are productive fields to labor in, because they contain so many examples of interactive life and are endowed with the meaning we confer by the sacred act of "setting aside." We browse here a richer mast than do the deer.

Nature is matter and more than that, life; and nature is also message. We spend billions on cracking the secret bonds of matter; many millions on unraveling the codes of life; and what do we spend on the sense of it all? Barely a moment's thought. Nature sanctuaries are many things to many people: genetic reserves to micro-biologists, ecosystems to macro-biologists, learning labs for teachers, re-creation sources for the harassed, and, I believe, grounds of meaning for all of us.

I should say "nature" is this ground rather than "nature sanctuaries," but it is a symptom of our time that the natural world requires a safe haven, a refuge, like a political criminal.

May 10 - Red-eyed vireo singing for first; Second phase of flowering dog-wood; Bay-breasted & Tennessee warbler; northern oriole singing at house for first; Black swallowtail on lilac bush

Shuffles in the Dusk

Coming home from my lone evening walk in the hemlock grove, I heard a shuffling in the wet swale to the west of the lane, near the entrance to the Amasa Martin Trail. Shuffles in the dusk always quicken the blood of seasoned naturalists: Who might this be? I stole quietly to within a few feet of the junction of the lane and the trail, where I guessed the creature would emerge on its nocturnal way to the pond. I secreted myself in the Japanese honeysuckle as best I could without snapping a twig. It was dark enough to see the shapes of near things but not their color. I listened carefully to the noise of several small feet fumbling, scuffling through the duff around the corner of the path. It was a peculiar gait, I had trouble placing it. Foxes are much lighter of foot, deer have a characteristically precise hoof-fall, skunks usually stop every few yards. It could have been a raccoon family, but the sound wasn't quite right.

I waited with caught breath as the scrambling patter rounded the dusky corner of the trail. Two black and white heads glided around the bend onto the lane. Between them was a dark row of shapes emitting tiny piping noises. The goose family heading home to roost!

If someone asks me to describe the Sanctuary, I draw a picture, usually in words. In those moments when I describe it to myself, the image is as likely to be made up of smells and sounds like these goose patterings. And the map works in time as well as space: the wind soughing through the half-bare trees in late October is as distinctive as the musks of newly thawed soil in early March. I could keep track of rustles from this secret sanctuary and measure the progress of fall by the quality of wind sighs, the age of the spring ice by its nightly rumblings. If I kept an almanac of this aural landscape, it would be as full as a calendar of sightings. The pattering of geese feet would figure prominently.

The entire goose family marched past within two feet of my

legs. I watched them cross the lane and listened as they cumbrously climbed the rocks ringing the pond . . . the young with their continuous, inquisitive peeping; the old growling their reply that all's well in the forest. Full darkness fell around the soft sounds of them scrambling down the other side of the rocks and plopping into the pond. I stood in the bushes a while savoring this moment. These times of spying, eavesdropping, being next to, even sharing a moment with wild creatures make it worthwhile, living this far in the woods.

May 14 - Geese return to yard minus one young, now five; Starling! seen over pond; Black racers mating in ruins; Cerulean warbler singing for first at end of lane

Temporary Shelter

The muskrats have not been as evident on the pond in the past two weeks as they were in mid-April. This may be their time of seclusion for breeding. The muskrats make themselves obvious and scarce in turns during the three seasons of the year when we see them on the pond. They were certainly active about a month ago, we saw one or two almost daily swimming from one side of the pond to the other, their mouths trailing long stems of curly pondweed, which they retrieve from the bottom. This may have been the time that the males fight for territorial rights. I make this guess because of the following incident.

On April 14th while walking along the side of the pond, I noticed regular, concentric waves rolling out from a point on the water below and hidden from me. This is a pretty good sign of an aquatic mammal working half submerged on the pond edge. Of the four local possibilities - mink, raccoon, beaver, muskrat - the latter is by far the most likely. I tiptoed up to the edge and peered carefully over a ledge of rocks. One yard below me, in a little niche in the rocks at the edge of the pond, a young muskrat fussed with the vegetation around him: snipping off bits and pieces of old purple loosestrife stems, taking mouthfuls of last year's leaves and grass, and arranging them sloppily about himself. This was not a lodge deep within the rocks where muskrats typically make their permanent home, but a temporary shelter. Having lined the niche with such debris that was at hand, he curled up in it and dozed. Only then did I notice the deep, bleeding wound at the base of his tail. He nursed it with his tongue periodically, as he lay in his nest.

I was puzzled how he might have gotten such a bad wound. A

fight with another muskrat? Snapping turtle? Accident among the loose heavy rocks around the pond? The next day I asked a friend of mine, fellow Hudsonian and muskrat expert Erik Kiviat. Erik was confident that the wound was inflicted by another male muskrat as part of a territorial fight. Apparently male muskrats get involved in quite violent turf battles at this time of year. Looking at this guy resting by the pond, I guessed that he lost the fight. He was certainly doing the classic number of sitting in a far corner and licking his wounds.

I crouched down quietly on the rock and watched him for the next half-hour. Much of that time he rested with his nose buried in the fell of his rump, but would rouse himself every few minutes and clumsily rotate on the spot, like a dog, trying to find a comfortable way of snoozing on these jagged rocks. Before returning to his rest, he would lick the blood from his tail. Sometimes I had to move slightly to relieve the pressure on my feet. The gravel would crunch faintly underfoot. His head would go up instantly at any such tiny sound and I could see him stop breathing, listening for a hint of trouble, anything besides the birds and the wind.

I had a secret window into the intimate life of this wild animal. He was almost within touch, but didn't sense me, and so acted without constraint, behaving as if I weren't there. Had he caught sight or scent of me at that distance, he would have dived into the pond in a frightful panic.

Muskrats are rodents, aquatic relatives of squirrels, mice, woodchucks, and other rats. They are about twenty inches long, almost half of which is a hairless black tail, which helps with swimming. Their thick fur is rusty brown to black, depending, among other things, if it is dry or wet. Like beaver they have flat, glassy, fish-like, eyes, doubtlessly an adaptation to their underwater habitat. One eerie effect of this eye structure is that you never know if one is looking back at you.

Muskrats are more nocturnal than diurnal and, like other animals I have watched, they seem to be less wary at night than during the day. I remember once walking through the woods near my cabin in Pennsylvania quite late at night. Apparently I came between an unwatchful muskrat and his home stream, because the animal suddenly made a squealing, scrambling dash for the water, ran into me halfway there, and proceeded to climb up my pant leg. I don't know what he had in mind, I've never seen a muskrat in a tree. Needless to say we were both surprised by the encounter. The whole adventure would have been impossible in the daylight.

As I watched this muskrat resting in his niche on the edge of the pond, I noticed something about his behavior which I have observed in other animals, for instance, chickadees. He would stop periodically, often in the middle of some gesture of arranging his bed, leaves hanging out either side of his mouth, pause for a long moment, sometimes several minutes, and "rest." His mental state was not clear to me. Was he alarmed, listening for predator noises, simply catnapping, taking a break from his work, or something else? I don't know, but I have my own guess and it is none of the above.

I believe he was entering an altered state of consciousness, quietly turning inward, not just dozing or drifting off to sleep, but as if returning to center from the periphery between frazzled periods of outward busywork. I believe this because I go there myself, especially in times of stress, the demands of a too pressing everyday. This state strikes me as primal and animal-like in its felt quality. Here too is a kind of sanctuary.

This explanation made particular sense to me in watching this muskrat because he was injured. The "outside world" was impinging upon him in a special way. He had need of lying quietly, quietly indwelling. I remember well five years ago when I spent months in the hospital after a severe auto accident. Before then, I had thought a person could get a lot of busywork done in a hospital bed with all that time on his hands. Not so. I spent most of the time quietly being by myself, shrinking from the brutal over-stimulation of my body. I needed that time. - I sometimes have the image that we twentieth-century Americans are continuously recuperating from an ongoing auto accident. But we have lost the living art of pausing even momentarily in our distraction, moving a moment inward, possibly with leaves hanging out of either side of our mouth.

May 17 - False Solomon seal in bloom at end of lane; Wood pewee singing on pond for first; Bullfrog calling for first at 11 p.m.

Snappers

This morning as I walked out to the road to pick up the morning paper, I heard a rustling in the dried leaves on the rock slope above the lane. Thinking it might be a black snake sliding out of its den to sun on the east-facing rocks, I went up to investigate. Not a snake, but a young snapping turtle was scraping along the duff over the sandstone slab. This little guy - only about six inches along the carapace, adults get a lot bigger - appeared to be making a trip from one of the larger pools on the west side of the lane to the pond. He was still dripping wet and draped with the dark, stringy filamentous algae found in all slow moving water bodies around here.

We see snappers all summer long basking at the surface of the pond or snooping along underwater on the prowl for tidbits. (A good sign of an underwater snapper is a yard-long string of bubbles winding slowly and erratically about the surface of the pond.) But only three times a year am I likely to find snapping turtles on land in the Sanctuary: in the early spring and fall when young males shuffle off to find their own turf to defend; and around the first of June when adult females come up to lay their eggs in exposed gravelly places.

So the first question to pose to any land-roving snapper is: male or female? Snapping turtles are difficult to sex unless they happen to be gravid females in the breeding season. I probed the soft skin behind the back legs of this morning's turtle but could feel no eggs. This was not a surprise, since the animal appeared to be too young to mate. So I conclude the little fellow I found this morning is a male, although it seems late to be shuffling.

Snapping turtles are one of the few animals that allow me to watch them at length, simply because they move too slowly on land to get away. I've followed a solitary turtle for hours just to get a better sense of what turtle life is like. Each lumbering thrust of his leg is a lesson. One thing I've learned: how regularly they depend on their shell to get where they want to go. They seem willing to tumble over any log or stone wall confident that they will be able to right themselves unbruised and carry on the journey.

Snappers are a delight to watch, they give me the impression of making no excuses for being coarse and vile in appearance and temperament. All the books say that they are inoffensive when in their favored element, the water. My own experience bears this out. They always paddle vigorously away when I meet them swimming in the pond. I have never actually stepped on one in the water but I came very close once in Duck Pond at Mohonk, while padding barefoot through the sensuous mud of a warm shallow pool. A giant snapper had buried herself in the ooze except for the tip of her snout, which I didn't see until she pulled it sharply back into her shell. My naked toes were well within striking range when she retreated. Big snappers have been known to sever fingers and toes. Gingerly but quickly I got out of the pool.

On land snapping turtles are irascible and ugly tempered, as if still fuming over the ancestral decision to leave the water for the inconvenience of terrestrial life. Like many animals that are not swift and cannot readily hide, snappers employ immobility as their primary defense. If you happen upon one in the woods in May or June, it will pause in whatever pose you caught it and pretend that it is invisible. This is not convincing for a thirty-pound reptile two feet from tip to tail. If you get too close, the snapper may hiss at you and slowly draw its massive head back into its shell. This is not necessarily a retreat however; often enough the next move is a spasmodic thrust forward with its entire body and a resounding "snap" of its powerful jaws. The neck is long and the stabbing motion of the head can be blindingly fast. One can list many good reasons for not harassing snapping turtles, especially nesting ones, and self preservation is not the least of them.

Turtles grow continuously all of their lives, so the largest ones of a population in a certain place are generally the oldest. The largest ones I have seen here in the Sanctuary are twelve to fourteen inches measured lengthwise along the top of the shell. One reason they get big here is that they are protected along with all the other life forms and geologic features. Away from the safety of the Sanctuary, snapping turtles are subject to the same persecutions as snakes. Like snakes they seem to evoke images for many people that are uncomfortably familiar, dangerous images that need to be destroyed rather than explored.

Snapping turtles also suffer depredations from other animals, especially on their eggs. One might suppose that predators would respect the eggs of so formidable an opponent. Quite the contrary, turtle eggs in general and snappers' eggs in particular are prime quarry for the snuffling diggers: raccoon, skunk, fox, and opossum. The predators are so successful at this (the evidence is little piles of dirt mixed with crushed, leathery egg-shells on the side of the path), that I am surprised that any turtle eggs survive. But they do survive, because we see tiny snappers every September, swimming in the pond or struggling overland away from it.

Chancing upon a mature female snapping turtle laying her eggs is a memorable event. She picks a spot where the soil is loose and easy to dig and the vista open to the bounty of the summer sun. In the Sanctuary that usually means the gravelly berm of the access lane or the sandy pockets between the rocks of the Peninsula. She digs the nest hole with her hind claws and backs in to lay her dozen or so eggs. She often begins the time-consuming process at night after the first soaking rain in early June. The next morning walking along the pond I often come upon one of these craggy, slime-covered creatures half submerged in the soil. I never disturb a nesting female, but I cannot resist the temptation to look for a moment into her eye - her flat, splotchy, unblinking, eye - to remind myself of my heritage.

May 19 - Hooded warbler singing in sugar maple in front yard; Early buttercup in bloom along lane; Veery singing at Slabsides for first

This Different Light

Every day for the past few days I've noticed a water snake sunning on top of the rocky fill just beyond the false bridge on our lane. The snake has installed herself on a cozy platform looking out upon the pond.

This section of the lane between the two bridges forms the dam for the pond. The dam is rock filled and honeycombed with crevices, or at least that is how I imagine it, as I walk across the top. The prospect of becoming tiny and exploring that labyrinth is at once intriguing and terrifying. I have seen a variety of animals emerge from or disappear into this surface: insects, toads, frogs, salamanders, turtles, snakes, shrews, moles, mink, ground squirrels, mice, muskrats, and once or twice, an adventuresome winter wren. I think of the rock dam as a kind of commons for the residents that live around the pond.

This particular water snake has lodged herself in a crevice on the face of the dam. It looks like a good place for a snake to reside. By inching the fore part of her body out of the crevice, she picks up as much of the sun's energy as she needs and obtains a grand view up and down the lane and across the arm of water to the Peninsula. Having a grand view *per se* is probably not a residential amenity for a snake, but open vistas upon paths along which food or trouble come are definitely valuable. She can slip down to the water in a second to feed or to deal with an emergency from behind, that is, from within the crevice.

I have never seen the snake fully withdrawn from her shelter; usually about eight to ten inches of her head and body are exposed along a rock slab that lies in front of her crevice. It reminds me of a front porch. She lies stretched out upon a soft carpet of last year's red oak leaves in full view of the pond scene, patiently waiting for an unwary something to hop by. As far as I can tell, she hasn't left it for the past week. I wish I could transform myself to a water snake and challenge her for the spot, just to test how dear the arrangement is to her. My guess is that she would put up a fight.

I am intrigued by her bedding on this front porch. Possibly the leaves have settled here from last season's leaf fall and she is simply using them. But the leaves appear arranged, it looks like she fussed with them a little, perhaps even brought them here from a distance. If so, this would be news. I have never seen a reptile using a tool. That makes sense because I have never looked for it. Nor have I heard of such a thing reported in the literature, although animal behavior is not my field and I may easily have missed this item. I wonder now if others have looked for it.

It would be news as well if any serious animal behaviorist would discover in the lower vertebrates any mental process akin to our own: thought, emotion, imagining, even being aware - so thoroughly has the mechanistic doctrine pervaded organismic biology. One would have thought the appeal of this world-myth had run its course, dying out with its most successful image, the steam locomotive. I believe the nature-machine metaphor has endured because it allays our deepest fears: we understand how machines work because we put them together; if the universe and everything in it is a machine, then we understand it, at least potentially, and we can tell ourselves we needn't be afraid of it.

This snake is aware of her world just as I am aware of mine. No, not "just as." There are differences, no doubt deep-running differences, which I would love to investigate. And I don't have to be afraid.

I have been accused of the anthropomorphic fallacy - ascribing human qualities to non-human animals. In almost every case the accuser, consciously or not, turns out to have fallen into the opposite wrongheadedness, the mechanomorphic - ascribing mechanical qualities to non-machines. I may go to biological Hell for this, but I still maintain chickadees are more like people than Buicks.

Ever since I first noticed my water snake sunning on her porch, I have taken special pains to observe her. I circle her den when I come by and approach quietly from behind. I stand and watch, looking for clues to her state of mind. If she doesn't take note of me, I come a little closer to get a better view of her face and eyes. As soon as she spots me, she starts flicking out her tongue, testing who this might be, and begins to slither slowly backwards into her niche in the rocks. She seems by no means as curious about me as I am about her, probably even a little uncomfortable in my presence. This doesn't deter me, I always stop here and watch for her, to catch a glimpse, to share at least a few moments with this different light upon the universe.

May 22 - Dunce cap galls developing on witch hazel leaves; Lightning bugs lighting up for first; Several butterflies and moths, new to my science

The Marsh Dwellers

Black Creek arises in the apple orchards of southern Ulster county and cuts northward through the ridge and valley province, a few miles west of the Hudson. Dropping from the thin-soiled apple highlands, it flows through miles of sumptuous swamp and marsh lands before opening upon the series of falls and turns that brings it through the Sanctuary and into the Hudson at Esopus. Just before the creek enters the Sanctuary it passes under Valli Road and cascades to the lovely rock-rimmed Woodland Pool. Then it describes a hair pin around a rise of land and continues north in sequences of reaches and rushes. I am sitting on that south-facing rise of land with the creek wrapping around me on three sides. I often sit here in the evening, because it is an attractive scene and one of the liveliest in the environs of the Sanctuary. Before me lie ten acres of purple loosestrife marshland created by a beaver family many years ago. The place is teeming with life of all kinds.

For several years I did a breeding bird census on the Sanctuary lands. Our western boundary lies along the east border of Valli Marsh; that is, the marsh just misses being included in our lands, but it was close enough for me to attach this appealing area to my study plot. In this and other ways I have been keeping track of the development here, the changes over these ten years wrought by the beavers, the stream, and time itself. Many of these changes are reflected in the simple list of birds that use this marsh.

I have sat here often enough, in different seasons and different times of day, to have developed a set of "Valli Marsh Expectations," an inventory of plants, animals, weather conditions, sounds, smells, and moods that I have come to associate with this place. The great horned's somber hooting through winter nights gives way to the chiming of the peepers and squalling of redwings in March, the colorful explosion of May, the musky sign of beaver through the summer and the bright-eyed awareness of wood ducks in October. There are unexpected moments as well: a sandhill crane on a summer morning, a bog turtle hunt one April afternoon that turned up everything except the endangered bog turtle.

Birds are attracted to the edges between habitats and Valli Marsh is all edge. Besides the basic boundary conditions - soil, air, and water - that make all wetlands rich and interesting, this marsh has a mixed second-growth hardwood forest to its east, a hay field to the west, a mature beech-hemlock forest to the south, and a sizable flowing stream for a north border.

A lot is going on here at dusk in late May. The redwings alone fill your eyes and ears with their constant bickering and skirmishing. But even the red-wing racket doesn't drown out the other marsh dwellers: the yellow warblers, redstarts, yellowthroats, grackles and kingbirds, all darting this way and that in full voice. Nor do these quite eclipse the near neighbors: the whippoorwill up in the field; the wood thrush and flicker in the bordering young hardwoods; the gnatcatchers, bay-breasted warbler, and three kinds of vireos singing from the mature woods beyond; the orioles, waxwings, phoebes, and song sparrow around the pool behind me; or the Louisiana waterthrush in the wet hemlock woods across the way. Green frogs, bull frogs and peepers fill out the landscape of sound and the humble sunfish add their loud "smacks," sucking the insects off the top of the water. The excited bustle of the whole, apart from any one animal, is one of the most calming aural scenes I know.

As I sit here, not waiting for anything in particular to happen, a pair of wood ducks pinwheel down and land on the pond near the newest beaver lodge, about one hundred yards away from me. Wood ducks are good studies this time of year, not only for their handsome plumage, but also because they may lead you to their nest or secreted young, if you can follow them from a distance. Wood ducks are also the wariest of their kind. As these two settle in, ruffling their feathers, I take great care in gradually raising my binoculars, but they catch even that slight motion and bolt off in a clamor of slapping wings.

Next a male pewee on the rounds of his new territory flies up to a dead stub a few feet from my head, and sings a few weak turns of his plaintive, looping song, eyeing me narrowly all the while. Now here is a bird that tolerates fellow marsh watchers. But not for long! He spots another pewee through the trees overhead and dashes off in agitated pursuit, buzzing and clacking his bill in a furious four seconds of hair-raising chase.

I am sitting in a cloud of black flies and mosquitoes. Now is that hectic time of year when we suffer both plagues, the end of black fly season and the beginning of the mosquitoes. I keep my mind on other things, I make a mental inventory of the vegetation of the marsh and its environs: in the marsh the purple loosestrife is pushing vigorously through the pond surface under the impatient eyes of the red-winged blackbirds, who will build their nests in it; on the tussock network of the open water grow luxuriant grasses, sedges, and ferns, especially royal and sensitive fern, and an occasional blue flag; the rocky slopes around the drowned meadow support willow, poplar, and red maple trees over a ground cover of mosses and grape vines. Behind me is a beaver-felled black birch; the sap oozes out of the nibbled stub and the leaves are still green, supple, and moist. They must have chewed it down this week. This will be a good site for a beaver-watch tonight.

When I first came to the Sanctuary, the beavers that carved out this marsh had long since moved on to richer pastures above Valli Falls. About six years ago, other beavers, probably descendants of the pioneers, returned to this spot to rebuild. They did so because the poplars and birches had bounded back from the pruning of the first beaver household. The new family built a dam on the downstream side of the oxbow, to my left, which raises the water about eighteen inches in the marsh. We see them on spring and summer evenings, busy at beaver tasks.

Beavers seem to depend mainly on hearing to keep informed of doings in their pond. This makes sense for a nocturnal animal as likely to be underwater as on top. The fact that their vision is not keen makes it easy to watch them close at hand, if one has the patience. I first find out where on the shore of their pond they have been working most recently. I sit comfortably near that place just before sunset and wait quietly. Soon the beaver family, one at a time, will emerge from their lodge. If I'm lucky (this works once every five times or so), one of the animals will take up last night's task at the spot where I am posted. Beavers are not suspicious as wild animals go, so if I am quiet and they don't happen to come too close, I can get a front row seat on their busy-work through the evening hour. Their jet black front paws are mar-velously nimble and remind me of human hands more than those of any other non-primate animal.

On evenings like this the beavers born last winter join the elders in gathering their twilight meal of poplar twigs and birch bark. Young-of-the-year beavers are especially trusting and are an extra treat on an evening watch. I have seen few things as winsome as a novice beaver earnestly attacking a birch branch several times too unhandy for him. No young are out this evening, perhaps it is too early, but a large adult is now patrolling the clear bays in front of his new six-foot high lodge, still alert after hearing me tramping around his dam a little while ago.

Besides the simple beauty of this place and the busy serenity that breathes from it, one of the pleasures the scene brings me is the occasion for reflecting on ancient processes here at hand. My guess is that Black Creek used to flow directly south from Woodland Pool that lies around the corner to the right. I'm not a geologist, but it appears to me that the stream to the east, the one I call Beech Grove Branch, "cap-tured" the main stem of Black Creek thousands or, who knows, millions of years ago, drawing it by Valli Marsh from its previous northward course along what is now Valli Road, and sending it through the more erodible rock formations in the northwest corner of the Sanctuary. When the creek is running high, as it often is in April and May, the old stream bed to the west carries the overflow.

I wouldn't have been able to guess any of this had I not audited a course on geological landforms a few years ago at New Paltz College. Every scene is packed with clues pointing to the forces working upon the landscape. Some of these clues are geological, some ecological, some cultural. The more clue-finding tools I possess, the more sense the pre-sent scene makes to me, and the more fun I have ferreting out the story. Geology has some of the most effective of these analytical tools because its clues seem more hidden from common sense.

The ancient stream capture is not the end of the Valli Marsh story, however. About five years ago I noticed a puzzling change. The old stream bed was carrying more water than usual. Even in dry months some water flowed and the spring floods made the old bed impassable where it never was before. The answer to this puzzle was . . . the return of the beaver.

By damming the outflow of the creek downstream of Valli Marsh, the beavers were backing up the waters into the pool and forcing part of the creek to retrace its ancient course down the old stream bed. These busy animals were undoing with their summer evenings' labor what geological forces had taken aeons to accomplish. With enough industry, generations of beavers might turn the entire stream back to its old path. This is drama on an epic scale, sheer matter *vs* animal energy. Who will win? Alas, we have to leave before the final scene.

May 25 - Deptford pink for first at Slabsides; Starling for 2nd time in front yard; Ruby-throated hummingbird seen for first at house

Communities of Mind

I have been watching the common grackles with more than average interest this spring. They first arrive in mid-April and don't do much for a couple of weeks. Then in early May they begin chasing raucously around the pond in small, loose flocks. Now they've disappeared again, presumably off building their nests. This pattern is not unusual for a member of the blackbird family, many of their relatives act much the same way. The reason for my special attention is that a local industry is negotiating a contract with Hudsonia to prevent these birds from nesting on and interfering with their outdoor electrical equipment. It will be my job to figure out how to do this.

When I say that the breeding pattern is "not unusual." I don't mean to imply that it is well understood. The classic model for spring behavior in this family is the well-known red-winged blackbird. Redwings are among the first to arrive in the Sanctuary in the spring and, like other early birds, have to high-tail it back to more comfortable weather if a mid-March blizzard descends. Once they've established themselves however, they exhibit their familiar and poorly understood behavior. Large flocks of redwings gather in late March and swoop across the landscape, moving from one roost site to another. Here at the Sanctuary we see them leave Valli Marsh in the morning in strings of hundreds of birds, many more than could nest there, and fly due east toward the Hudson. In the evening they return, heading toward Valli Marsh where they spend a noisy hour, bickering and chittering, but not actually contesting with each other for turf or mates.

In other places I have seen these morning and evening skeins of redwings contain thousands of birds. Across the southern United States wintering flocks of blackbirds cause serious people problems. A swarm of blackbirds can make life unpleasant for anyone with a roosting tree in his backyard. A few years ago the U.S. Army, under the pretext that the birds posed a health problem, launched an offensive against large blackbird flocks on their bases by spraying the sleeping birds with detergent during a cold rainstorm. The next morning the carcasses were piled high under the roost sites. The Army had won the battle but lost the war; now they had a real health problem and a public relations debacle to boot.

An obvious question: What is going on in this pre-breeding flocking behavior of blackbirds? The intense social interaction is striking, yet quite different from the territorial squabbles that take up the red-wings' time in the weeks that follow. Another intriguing fact about this group: they are all males, not one female flies these missions. The Australian animal ecologist, V.C. Wynne-Edwards, has developed a hypothesis about demonstrations of this kind. He calls them "epideictic displays." He hypothesizes that the males are getting together to "count themselves" in some sense, to determine whether the numbers in the local population are too low, just right, or too high for the natural resources they depend upon. This count is somehow translated into a decision who will breed in that season, thus insuring that the population does not eat itself out of a living. Although the general principle of self-regulation of animal numbers is well accepted, this particular hypothesis is controversial.

I find this idea fascinating, as much for the possible explanation of the specific behavior, as for the value of exploring this poorly understood field, group communication in animals. What exchange is going on in flights of sandpipers, dozens in tight formation, that they execute extraordinary maneuvers in perfect synchrony? What do schooling fish know about keeping in step that a drill sergeant will never teach his recruits? There are many such questions.

John Burroughs was intrigued by animal communication of this kind. In *Ways of Nature* he speaks of a "community of mind and feeling" among members of other species that is absent in humans except in moments of strong excitement. We see something like it at basketball games, prayer meetings, and lynch mobs. As far as I know, these fascinating questions of group communication are being studied very little from the point of view of evolutionary biology. Wynne-Edwards's hypothesis at least addresses the issue as a legitimate question of animal ecology.

Wynne-Edwards's ideas are speculative as the phrases above betray: "in some sense," "somehow," Professional ecologists raise their eyebrows at the lack of any obvious mechanism by which such communication can take place. This "lack of mechanism" is the same infirmity of the original ideas of Darwin, Mendel, Lorenz, *et al.*

The pond grackles' behavior in this respect is not quite the same as the redwings'. For one thing the groups of grackles in early May that noisily fly from one corner of the pond to the other are much smaller than the redwing flocks in early April, possibly only reflecting their smaller population here. Also, if I am not mistaken, these grackle chases contain females as well as males. The female lacks the iridescent head plumage of the male, a distinction not easily made at a distance or in dull light. I confess I have not been watching closely enough to nail down this crucial detail. So I remain intrigued and perplexed by what's going on with the grackles, realizing once again that I will have to watch more keenly next year.

May 27 - Pondweed not taking over pond surface at usual rate; Cowbirds mating in front yard

Augury by Starling

The other day we saw a starling in spring plumage in our front yard as we walked out to Black Creek. This was the second starling I have ever seen in the Sanctuary. The first one was on May 14th. I couldn't say which one surprised me more. The first one was a shock, but the kind of blow one easily rationalizes: "Ha, here's a stray starling, probably got blown out of Poughkeepsie or New Paltz in last night's storm, poor devil." This second one is harder to explain, and suggests that this is no accident, the starlings are moving in.

On one other occasion I saw a starling out in the woods. That was on the Trapps, a sheer conglomerate cliff on Mohonk Preserve lands. Although the cliff is in sight of New Paltz across the Wallkill Valley, the bird seemed out of place there. I assumed then that he was just lost and subsequent observations confirmed that.

Starlings are, of course, common birds. In many places they

outnumber all other birds combined, but these are built communities, where human intervention has fragmented the natural vegetation. In the worst cases this fragmentation has reached the point where native birds cannot find sufficiently large, contiguous areas to support themselves. Starlings make do in these environments. Hence my surprise at seeing the starlings out here in the woods. They don't belong here any more than pigeons do; it's not their preferred habitat. *Now* they don't belong. The question is: Do they know something we don't, or more painful yet, portend a future that we see only dimly?

Starlings are a European import, introduced into New York City in the nineteenth century by a Shakespeare nut who wanted to see all the Bard's birds in Central Park. The starlings and house sparrows made it, the larks and nightingales didn't. Today he would be arrested for that stunt. From Manhattan the starlings have spread to the continent; no major city in North America is without its population of these noisy, aggressive birds. One reason they do so well in cities is that they eat garbage. More correctly they are "opportunistic scavengers," meaning they will take what they can get, what nobody else wants. In a city that is, by definition, garbage and they thrive on it.

I don't dislike any bird, but I suppose I am not doing a good job of concealing my lack of enthusiasm for starlings. Actually, I find spring starlings quite beautiful, as I do healthy specimens of other "junk" birds, blue jays and house sparrows. But starlings represent to me a way of life that I have always shunned: the citified, the super-social. This is symbolized for me by the way starlings smell. Bird-banders become aware that birds, like all animals, have distinctive odors. Black-capped chickadees smell like wet ashes, cardinals have a mild musky scent, most birds have some variation of a warm, musty, not unpleasant odor. Starlings smell like garbage, probably an effect of their chosen diet.

The ancients watched birds to foretell future events. This is the etymological basis of the words "auspicious" and "augury." I don't hold with that old superstition (I have a new set). Birds can't see what's coming any better than the rest of us. This starling in my front yard, however, gives me a twinge. Is it possible this bird knows what we have anxiously suspected for two, three years now? That this part of Ulster County is headed for Suburbia? And this omen of a starling is laying claim to the Sanctuary for starlingdom? My flesh crawls.

May 28 - Black raspberries in bloom for first by pond; Hog-nosed snake for first in hotel ruins

Spells of Cool Weather

One of the blessings of the cooler interludes in spring are the morning mists over the pond. After the top layer of the pond has been warmed by several days of seasonable weather, a cool, still spell will cause shocks of light mist to grow from the surface and will lay them over the field of the pond with great effect, another harvest of the sun. Early morning and late evening seem to be best. If the air could be perfectly still, the unclassifiable species that grow here would simply stand in their strange forms. . . but it is never perfectly still, even when we say to ourselves with conviction, "It is now perfectly still." Slight provocations stir the air though no face freshens or leaf trembles. The pond mists register these nuances better than any anemometer I know.

The effect of these tremulous wind currents on the mist fields is eerily beautiful, especially if we climb to the top of the rocks on the Peninsula and look down upon the pond. The shocks of mist are tossed about in fascinating ways by the shivering air: rising, falling, twisting, funneling, creating and destroying themselves in every direction at once. In places the motion is so complex that nothing appears to move at all. This scene occurs infrequently enough to serve as a useful reminder of the irreal, other side of everyday and gives me a new image for the old phrase, "spells of cool weather."

June 3 -Strawberries in fruit along lane; Laurel in bloom for first at north end of pond; 1/8 of pond covered with pondweed

Earth Myth: Song of the Snapper

I haven't heard a pickerel frog or spring peeper for ten days, but the bullfrogs and green frogs are respectively "harrumphing" and "twanging" with great abandon. The field crickets meanwhile are taking over from the peepers with their own peeper-like chirp. The crickets will chirp through the summer, and when they are finished in September, we may again hear a few out-of-season peepers before frost. Then an end to peeping until March. Apart from the sparrows, this is the history of peeping in the Sanctuary.

A more significant development in the economy of the Sanctuary than the rise and fall of peepers is the annual crawl of the turtles toward sunlight and a place to lay their eggs. This move is paralleled in one way or another by every other organism. The only two turtle species in the Sanctuary that I have seen lay eggs are the painted turtle and the snapper. Obviously the other turtles here - the spotted, stinkpot, box, wood, and softshell turtles - lay their eggs here too, but in what habitat and at what time of year I have yet to discover.

The first sign of turtle egg-laying activity is a few soil scrapes along the side of the lane. Although the site is probably traditional, the reptiles seem to have trouble each year locating prime ground for egg laying. Eventually they find the deep loose soil, dig the six inch pits with their rear feet, drop their eggs in, and cover the whole thing with the spare dirt. What's left is a patched hole, obvious to the practiced eye. As I mentioned earlier, such practiced eyes are fairly common here in the Sanctuary - eyes belonging to raccoons, skunks, and opossums. More often than not the reproductive effort of the turtles goes toward feeding these fur-bearers.

The best way to cultivate the skill of finding turtle-nests is to locate a nesting turtle, note the exact spot, and come back the next day to see what the finished nest looks like. Soon you develop a certain search image that you can "turn on" in early June: an irregular, three-inch, patch of sometimes damp, always slightly disturbed soil in an exposed sandy or gravelly bank not too far from a body of water or wetland. One advantage of locating the nests early on: one can keep a record, at an appropriate distance, of the success rate of turtle nests by species, habitat, and year.

To my mind, this landward movement of the turtles for propagation is mythic in significance, part of the earth myth. This part is about animals that live their lives in water and remember to return to land to give birth, where they themselves were born. It is the companion piece to the song of the salamanders who live on land and feel the urge to return to their birthing place, the water. I say this is "part of the myth," but saying it this way is more a human failing than plain fact. Actually each lumbering stride of the turtle and salamander dance, every peeper peep and spider web is the whole story, which we have verbally analyzed to its part and place.

Many other songs are embodied in the myth. We sometimes

catch, through diligent study, little snatches of the melody; but often don't recognize it as music. People of an earlier time, who studied less but were closer to the earth, may have known whole songs and even lived with a rich sense of the whole myth. There are those who believe that if everyone today had some inkling, however poor, of the earth myth, no activity which suggested the most remote possibility of "destroying life on earth" would be countenanced.

June 7 - Snapping(?) turtle scrapings on path over Peninsula; Deer fly for first

The Stapleton Method

The Sanctuary is situated in the geological province called "ridge and valley," within the humid, temperate climate regime of the Hudson Valley. All of this means opportunities abound for insects to breed three seasons of the year in the moist valleys between the dry ridges. We have come to expect and, in a minimal way, plan for the sequence of bothersome spring insect visitors. "Bothersome" describes a small minority of the many insect species that inhabit this place, the ones that bite or otherwise harass us.

Things are pretty quiet until the shad flies (actually a kind of black fly) arrive in mid-April. They seldom bite, but have the annoying habit of buzzing around one's face and flying into one's eye-balls. No problem for me. Then come the mosquitoes, whose behavior patterns are familiar to everyone. I have learned to live with mosquitoes. Next the May variety of black fly shows up, similar to shad flies in appearance but with a sharp, painful bite. I refuse to be annoyed by this species of insect. Finally, in early June, the deer flies appear and the game is up.

I should fill out this story with a bit of history. For some reason of body chemistry or metabolics, I am not attractive to insects. I have a corresponding psychological indifference to those insects that do come buzzing about my head, I just don't feel bothered by them, again for whatever reason. I don't know how much of the latter is genetic and how much practice. I have practiced quite a bit.

The practice goes like this: I watch a mosquito light on me, note carefully her shaft sink into my flesh, note the rate at which she tanks up, and let her fly away. All the while I remind myself that this is no big deal; the slight pain and itch will subside shortly; all the more so if I don't care. This is the Stapleton Method. The total effect is that I don't care and the insects don't bother me. In part, this is simply a survival technique for someone who has lived in the woods for the past twenty-five years, and, in part, a one-upmanship ploy vis-a-vis people who get physically and emotionally out of control in these situations.

The whole point of this is that my wife Diana is 100% in the other camp. Insects throng to her when we go out walking in the summer, the ratio of flying things around her head to those around mine varies from three to ten depending on the season. Furthermore, she makes matters worse by flailing about and cursing.

Very patiently I point out to her the value of ignoring them and the techniques for doing so. This education lasts through black fly season but comes to an abrupt end with the arrival of the deer flies. I have never succeeded in coping with deer flies. I turn out to be the same flailing, cursing, Fury-driven maniac as she is for the black flies and mosquitoes. My problem is the mode of attack of the deer flies: they are slow, mindless, and insistent. A deer fly lights on your face. You know she will bite if you let her sit for a moment, so you whisk her off. She flies *around* your whisking hand, immediately lands exactly on the same spot and bites. The next time you are on to the fact that whisking doesn't help, so you slap. They are slow enough to slap easily, but tough enough to endure the hardest crack. She bites you anyway. Their bite produces a brilliant, stabbing pain, but only for a few moments. If you let it alone, you feel little residual itch or sting.

It occurred to me a few weeks ago, in thinking about the upcoming deer fly season, that it is high time that I applied the Stapleton Method to this menace. I have conquered many of the other minor hazards of living in the woods - mosquitoes, poison ivy, snakebite, scratches, abrasions - through a combination of practice and will power. The deer fly problem should be no exception.

My first experiment was today's morning walk to get the paper at the end of the lane. Unfortunately, the morning was cool and breezy and only a few deer flies were about. On hot windless days, they are everywhere. I approached one of the two locations along the lane where we have come to count on deer flies, even on days like today. The first spot is under the hemlocks just south of the false bridge. I waited at my station. I felt like a sacrificial maiden. I recalled that deer flies only attack moving, preferably sweaty flesh. I pranced about, thinking up a sweat.

Finally I was approached by a solitary deer fly. She flew onto my cheek. I steeled myself. This was it, the first good test of the method. Nothing. She flew off.

I can't believe it. She is programmed to bite me, she is not supposed to have any choice in the matter. Is it possible that she sensed the drama of the moment and opted not to cooperate in this experiment? But why? If the method succeeds and is universally adopted, deer flies have the prospect of an unlimited supply of human blood, risk free. A perverse part of my understanding of deer flies persuades me this prospect is not welcome to them, they *want* to harass human beings, with energy. Life without that would be pointless, pale.

So the first experiment has failed.

June 9 - Small mulberry in garden, in fruit, not noticed before; Three or four broad-winged hawks over pond, young out of nest?

The Dialectic of Research

I had one of those encounters this afternoon which make me believe that the mature woods is infinite in its complexity, and could surprise and delight me every day with some new discovery. The incident occurred as I was strolling through the rich moist bottomlands of Black Creek where it passes through the Sanctuary in a series of pools and meanders. The space has a hallowed and hushed, cathedral-like quality, with eighty-foot beeches, sycamores, and hemlocks shading the sky and limiting the ground vegetation to lacy woodferns and soft cushion mosses. Wood pewees festoon their bittersweet songs from canopy branch to branch.

At one point in my tramp through these woods I noticed an unusual insect on the bole of a large, dying beech tree. It was a brown and yellow wasp about five inches long; two thirds of that length was a black javelin-like "tail," which entomologists call an ovipositor, an "egg-placer." This was a female wasp in the family *Ichneumonidae*, looking for the right place to deposit her burden of eggs.

If I were more of a naturalist and less a mooner over curiosities, I suppose I would try to fix the genus or even the species of this beautiful animal. As it was, rather than counting the segments of her antenna or memorizing the venation of her wings, I spent most of my time following her busy maneuvers. She would find a foot-square section of beech bark and inspect every inch of it closely. She went over the same patch of bark several times, sliding her antennae back and forth over every gray dimple of the apparently uniform surface. Tiny holes or other irregularities that she encountered seemed not to interest her at all. She was evidently looking for something, but what it was I could not discover by observation.

Ichneumonids have the habit of planting their eggs in the larvae of other insects, sometimes larvae which are buried under layers of bark. The long ovipositor is actually a drill used to pierce the bark and deposit the eggs in the unlucky host. The eggs hatch and feed off the host, usually killing it in the process. This much I know. The question is: How does the female wasp find the host larva? This wasp was searching very carefully while I was watching her, using clues that escaped me altogether. Her approach seemed tactile; she was systematically palpating with her antennae every bit of surface within her limited scope of travel. She stopped five or six times at a point on the bark that seemed to me identical to all other points that she had worked, raised her long abdomen perpendicularly from the tree, grasped her ovipositor with her two hind legs, and pulled it down along the lower side of her upraised abdomen for the purpose of poising it as bark drill. A problem immediately presented itself: her ovipositor was a good deal longer than the rest of her body. I could not imagine how she was going to raise the end of her abdomen high enough off the bark to accommodate the full length of her drill. This is the same problem I would have in trying to place my right elbow in my right palm. But she did it. Her solution was elegant and startling.

As I watched her pull up the ovipositor into its seemingly unworkable position, suddenly the second last segment of her abdomen came unhinged and parted from the one below it. A diaphanous sheath was exposed which expanded as the ovipositor was redrawn into the abdomen, but only to form a great coil visible within the sheath and outside the abdomen proper. This coil was just big enough so that the rest of the ovipositor fitted neatly along the body with the spear end freely manipulable between the two antennae.

A fine and unlikely solution to a possibly unnecessary problem. For instance, does the ovipositor really have to be twice the length of the rest of the body? To reach a host that deeply in a tree? Why not just make the abdomen a little longer or lengthen the fore legs a bit? Ichneumon evolution has decided otherwise. One possible added virtue of this arrangement is that drilling pressure can be applied to the end of the ovipositor by simply contracting the sheath, over which the wasp obviously has some control. I was not able to observe this, because she never decided to drill in any of the half-dozen sites that attracted her attention.

Her persnickety care in finding "the right spot" was fascinating. Even after she was fully in the "attack" position she fussed about, testing the immediate area with her antennae and using them to position the end of the ovipositor this way and that. After long minutes of this finessing of the drilling location, she would decide it wasn't right after all and go through the contortion of uncoiling and straightening out.

Minute examination of the sites she had chosen, or almost chosen, revealed not one iota of visible distinction between them and areas around them on either side. So I was left with work to do, things to find out. Part of the pleasure of this encounter was the expectation that the next time I watch an ichneumon fussing about her nest, I will make much more sense of the process because I will have this fund of observation to build on. I continued to watch, ecstatically, following each of her moves with the greatest care.

To no avail, however. I was left after my engrossing hour knowing only a little more than when I first spotted her. What was the process of her search? I came away guessing that she was not looking or feeling for the right spot but listening or smelling with her antennae. Possibly some ichneumonist knows this, it may be written in the basic text on ichneumonids. Rather than read the answer there, I prefer to divine this information by watching the graceful animal herself, learn her language, possibly devise a way for her to tell me in this, her own idiom.

June 11 - Young geese are showing wing flight feathers; Daisy fleabane and white foxglove in bloom along Burroughs Dr.; Several new turtle diggings in front yard

Keeping Secrets
A few evenings ago I raised a Virginia white-tailed deer in Valli Marsh. As I clambered down the wooded slope to the east of this wet-

land, I apparently made enough noise to give her a nervous start. She bounded out of the middle of the marsh in great splashing arcs. She was the first deer I saw this year in the tawny warm-weather coat, one of our favorite signs of summer.

Raising a deer is not a notable event in the Sanctuary, we do it weekly, but the time and place made this deer different. The does begin to drop their fawns around here in early June and they seem to have a predilection for doing so in wetlands: most of the fawns that I have chanced upon in the Sanctuary have been lying on raised hummocks in swamps or marshes. When this deer, nursing her fawn and especially alert, heard my clumsy footfall on the bluff above her, she panicked and tore off the other way. At least that's the story I invented on the spot.

In this part of the country male white-tails seek out does in October and November when the bucks' antlers are fully grown, the velvety covering scraped off, and in good show. I say "show" rather than "strength" or "power," because I do not believe white-tails use their antlers physically to prove herd dominance. Males of other hoofed wild animals, like elk and moose, engage in vigorous head-to-head tussles for reproductive rights.

I have heard several stories of aggressive behavior on the part of antler-bearing white-tails against humans, but only once, many years ago in the fall, did I see two white-tail males "fight" with their antlers. They jousted lackadaisically in a lock-horn position, nudging each other around a wet meadow, a little this way, a little that. Now and then they would tire of this and resume chomping on the grass, side by side.

My guess is that the size and shape of the antlers are factors, however, in a white-tail buck's reproductive success. This would be in line with what animal behaviorists have discovered about the role of "secondary sexual characteristics" in the mating of other species. Appearance is everything in matters of sexual maneuvering.

After mating with the best-looking buck, the female carries her young through the winter. In June or July she drops her one or two fawns in a secret place. I say "secret" not because the fawns are physically well hidden. Often they are in plain sight along the side of a roadway or common pathway.

The other day I resisted the temptation to slosh out to the middle of the marsh to test my guess what the doe was doing there. A combination of factors weighed against the move: I didn't see exactly where she started from, so I might do a lot of roaming through the five-acre marsh before I found her site; I would be slogging around up to my knees in marsh muck most of the way; and finally, discovering fawns, intentionally or accidentally, can be disruptive.

Does do not reject fawns that have picked up a human scent, as is sometimes claimed. Once a fawn ran up to me on a woodland path and started nuzzling me frantically, apparently mistaking me for its mother. I was so startled, I began petting the fawn's head and neck to calm it down. A few seconds later the young animal realized its mistake and dashed off just as quickly. I followed the fawn quietly at a distance and fifteen minutes later saw it nursing under its mother.

On the other hand, does become distraught when they sense some trouble around their fawns. I happened to witness a touching scene of this kind in Pennsylvania. I was biking on the forest road that ran along West Branch Creek near my cabin when I heard from the opposite bank a dreadful lamentation, a continuous bleating, as if from an injured lamb. It was a fawn that had become disoriented or lost. From my vantage about fifty yards away I could see the fawn on one side of the bend of the creek and its mother on the other, out of sight of each other. The doe was a picture of frenzy: stamping, snorting, eyes flared, her head and ears flying in all directions at once. I guessed her dilemma: she needed to run around the bend to see what was wrong, possibly help, but her instinct told her not to give away the position of the fawn with the likes of me looking on. I hopped back on my bike and rode rapidly away, hoping to help solve the problem, whatever it was.

This encounter left me with a strong impression of the many, little, terrible things that can go wrong between doe and fawn, especially with a bit of human interference.

In an unrelated adventure on the same day - it takes a certain amount of brashness to toss around the word "unrelated" in this business - I chanced upon a pair of worm-eating warblers along the Amasa Martin Trail about two hundred yards north of our house. I knew they were establishing a territory here, because I have been listening to him sing from the swamp-pools west of our lane for the past two weeks. I've paid more than average attention to these warblers this spring because of the unusual number of them. In the days when I was doing a systematic bird census, I tallied fifteen to twenty worm-eating warblers in the Sanctuary, most of them from the pathless, southern tracts of the property. In an average year, without special effort, I hear one in the woods around here and one near Slabsides. This year I've recorded at least three around the pond and several more in the Slabsides area. This kind of variability is not at all unusual, but intriguing and worth keeping in the back of the mind: "From the point of view of a worm-eating warbler, what's different about this year? Or last year? Or the last five years?" - Food. Weather. Predation. Competition. Combinations of these.

In any case I encountered a pair of them the other day in a more physical way than listening to their songs. As I ambled along the Amasa Martin Trail, I heard a bird becoming increasingly agitated. In late spring this is a good sign of a nest ahead, a sign to which hunters with a keener appetite for finding bird nests than mine are also attuned.

Habitually noisy birds like blue jays become dead quiet when one gets near their nest, while relatively quiet birds like warblers become audibly upset. The former strategy is clearly the better. No doubt the blue jays have a better sense of the value of racket.

I moved more slowly and wended through the woods on both sides of the path, navigating by the vocal reaction of the still-hidden bird. Sure enough, a worm-eating warbler popped out of the bushes (up to that point I wasn't sure which warbler it was) and tried to lead me further along the path by flitting from branch to twig, twittering vexedly all the while. I didn't buy that, so the other bird showed herself (the sexes are similar in this species, but my intuition told me this was the female) and began ruse Number Two. This involves peeping piteously and fluttering along the ground in some direction away from the nest. Birdwatchers call this "the broken wing display" and mention it in connection with the killdeer, who carries it off very well. Actually I have seen many birds do their version of the act, one of the more startling was by a ruffed grouse hen, who literally whacked me on the sneakers with her horribly distorted wing, while her chicks quietly dove under the nearest leaves.

The worm-eating warbler had her own version of the stratagem. She didn't flutter her wings much, but plopped down forward and skidded along on her belly, peeping, head flagging, her slack-twisted body clearly near the end. I don't think it was as effective as the more dramatic, wing-flailing shows that I've seen, but maybe this is the way worm-eating warblers die.

Interesting as her display was, it didn't divert me from my search for the nest. These warblers build their nest on the ground, sometimes in a ledge formation, and half submerged in leaves and grass. I once found one on the extreme south end of the Sanctuary along an abandoned jeep trail. As with most small nest discoveries, it was sheer chance. I happened to stop on my hike along the trail to tie my shoe. After a few moments the sitting bird evidently became nervous about this seeming attention so close to her and darted out of her grass-bowered nest, eight inches from my foot. If I had tied my shoe three feet away she probably would have sat tight.

Watching the placement of each footfall, I carefully quartered the area which should have been the nest site, judging by their diversion tactics. I had a clear search image based on other worm-eating warbler nests that I've found, but nothing matched it. These searches require a detached approach, in which one rises above caring whether one finds the nest or not. Unfortunately I was too caught up in the search to reach this state of mind. After five minutes of hunting around I decided I had pestered them enough and went on my way.

June 16 - Tiger swallowtail, for first; Large perfoliate blossom, not yet opened at end of lane, bellwort(?); Milkweed in bloom (Bloomsday!) on false bridge; Sunfish on nests, snapping turtle eating eggs

The Politics of Travel

I have been witness to an absorbing drama in our backyard over the past two days. My study is a small room on the second floor that looks south over our back lawn and the tip end of the pond. The local Canada geese are fond of these two sites: the first for lunching, the second for bathing, and both as links in their daily travel route. Almost every day since the goslings were hatched in early May, the troupe swims to the end of the pond, marches up the embankment to the lawn, stops for a few hundred nibbles of grass, and then down the other side, through the woods to Valli Marsh. Later in the day, or sometimes the next morning, they retrace their steps. They know the route cold, it holds no terrors for them. Or so I supposed.

Before I describe their recent peculiar behavior, I should explain a little the politics of travel that I have observed in this Canada goose family, which consists of goose, gander, and five goslings. First of all, the goose is in charge. When the chips are down and she wants them all to leave a place, they leave. In the absence of any such strong move on her part, the little flock moves about aimlessly, at least while they are feeding. On the other hand, this aimless movement seems often to resolve into a trend in a specific direction. I think this trend is the result of random deviations from randomness, rather than purposefulness on the part of any of the geese. This is what I mean: one of the goslings may move a little this way in the course of munching tufts of grass, which happens to be the same direction of a sibling busy at the same task; a third follows along (they are flocking animals); the first gets a sense of a direction of movement from the other two (which he unwittingly initiated) and continues. Soon the whole bunch are slowly but definitely eating their way in *that* direction, until a similar random shuffle turns them back *this* way . (I developed the model for this kind of progress while watching a school of hatchery trout fingerlings; other examples are around.) That's the way their day goes until the goose decides to undertake something else, such as their daily tramp to Valli Marsh.

Yesterday Diana and I independently began to notice problems in the movements of the geese. What first caught our attention was a rapid patter of webbed feet across the back lawn. The goose was racing for the pond, the little ones flip-flopping behind as best they could, their stubby little wings raised in panic. The gander marched hurriedly behind, his head held as erect as he could under the circumstances. No obvious trouble was at hand, no hawk overhead, no fox in the bushes that I could see. This behavior would not have made us take note, except that it happened several times during the day. This morning I saw it again as I sat down at my desk. What was on the other side of the lawn that was alarming the goose so regularly? Or was it alarm at all? Was I reading the situation correctly? Not knowing what he's looking at is a serious occupational hazard for any naturalist. This unaccountable goose behavior piqued my curiosity. I decided to watch for it. Watching for it doesn't require any complicated stake-out, given the location of my desk and the scene of action.

A half-hour later the flock is back. A novelty: the gander is out in front. He is not striding right along, as the goose does when she has it in mind to go somewhere. He is half feeding, half watching, his movements suggest more the mousing around mode of lunch. This is unusual. Even when they are feeding, he is almost never in front, as if it is a point of honor with him to bring up the rear, head high, ever alert for the least sign of trouble. What strikes me this time is that he is *leading* the flock away from the pond toward the path that winds down to Valli Marsh. He is not doing this in any forceful way, but with indirection . . . nonetheless, leading.

The rest of them are nibbling on grass, vaguely inching in the direction of the marsh path, following him. The goose is in the rear, also coolly feeding, no sign of agitation. I watch closely to see if I am not deceived as to what is going on here. No, the gander actually takes a step down the path to the marsh. He looks back over his shoulder. No one is following him. He takes another step. Nothing doing. They are all too busy with the grass. The random drift method of travel is not working here (if that's what he has in mind), because no grass grows on the path; none of them would mindlessly nibble that way. Going on the path means wanting to get somewhere. Nobody like that here. The gander comes back and continues eating grass.

Five minutes later, he tries again, takes a few strides down the path. This time the whole group happens to be at the west side of the lawn, close to the trail head. One of the goslings glances up and notices. He looks over to the goose. The unspoken question travels fast, in a second or two all the goslings are studying the goose. She raises her head. For a moment everybody looks at each other. Not for long. Suddenly, the goose wheels about and tears squawking back to the pond, the frantic little ones helter-skelter behind her, their oversize webbed feet slapping the mud of the new lawn. The dutiful gander hops along right behind, peering excitedly this way and that, wondering where the dreadful hazard lurks, or perhaps just wondering: What Happened?

June 18 - Common St. Johnswort; Several gypsy moth caterpillars in 3rd or 4th instar along Burroughs Drive

The Politics of Defense

The bluegills, members of the sunfish family, are now on their nests in the pond. At this time of year they leave off the seemingly aimless wandering through the waters and find their square foot of territory. They prefer sites in shallow water, one to three feet deep, with little bottom growth. The edge of Sanctuary Pond offers many such sites. The males build the nest, a circle a foot or so in diameter on the floor of the pond. The vegetation and bottom debris are swept aside and gravel and small pebbles are built up around the edges to make a slight depression. Into this depression the female then lays her eggs which are simultaneously fertilized by the male. As in many of the sunfishes (and other small pond species), the male hangs around while the eggs hatch and until the larvae grow big enough to fend for themselves.

The value of this precaution for the survival of the young is apparent to anyone watching the scene around a sunfish nest. Fish eggs are the wild grapes of the pond economy, every passerby plucks a few on his way through. Kinship makes no difference here, the male bluegill spends most of his time warding off other bluegills. He does this by systematically patrolling the perimeter of his nest, usually in a clockwise direction. He will take short, aggressive runs at anything that gets too close, but quickly returns to the nest after the warning rush. I have never seen a fish do battle when engaged in this defense, at most he gives an occasional bump with the snout. This territorial right to jostle away intruders is implicitly recognized, just as much as the license to steal a few eggs, if one can get away with it.

I guess that this kind of circling is a better ploy for the defense of eggs than standing around waiting for trouble. Several years ago, I watched a large-mouth bass, a stouter relative of the bluegill, defend his larvae against a circled pack of sunfish. His territory was on a large submerged rock at the pond's edge below the front yard. He would spot a sunny making a pass at his charges on one side of the rock and dash over to send that trouble-maker back into the weeds. Meanwhile, two or three from the other side would take advantage of his momentary absence to slurp up a few (or a few dozen) of the young bass. Back he would dash to straighten out this situation. . . a signal, of course, for the sunnies in the weeds on this side to make their next raid. This went on for the two hours I watched that afternoon. I suppose it continues until the bass larvae are old enough to outrun the sunfish. It's hard to imagine how any of them survive, even though the female bass produces tens of thousands of eggs every breeding season. The irony here is that the bass is considered a major predator on sunfish. That is a fisherman's perspective. If there is a fish god doing an accounting somewhere, the sunnies have more to answer for.

One of the great revelations that occurs while watching bluegills and bass is that they have no hands and feet. In this they are on a par with snakes and one notch lower than the birds. Take these bluegills for instance. I have watched their antics for many seasons without vision, without seeing why they behave this or that way. Until I said to myself, "They have no hands or feet." Only now do I see what a marvelous instrument their mouth is, how skillfully they use it to meet their needs. Insights like these make up for the rest of the insect-buzzed, frozen-socks life of a naturalist.

As I was peering into the pond the other day from the point on the dam where I discovered this spring's first bluegill nests, I suddenly realized I was watching a medium-sized snapping turtle smack in the middle of one of the nests. The turtle was so perfectly camouflaged against the silty, pebble-knobby bottom that I did not see him until he shifted his weight. He was tail up, his head half buried in the nest, busily grubbing up eggs. The bluegill whose nest the turtle was ravaging was hard at work making life uncomfortable for him, much as a kingbird will worry a hawk that hunts near her nest. The bluegill hovered near the turtle's head and, when the opportunity presented itself, made a sucking peck at the reptile's eye. Judging from similar pecks that sunfish have given my toes when I've been in swimming, this must have stung. At this, the turtle would snap sideways missing the evasive bluegill by a scale or two. It looked harrowing at first, but I watched long enough to realize the fish knew exactly what he could get away with.

The drama lasted until the snapper came up for air, caught sight of me three feet away, flipped over, and tore off toward the middle of the pond. The bluegill seemed to shrug off the incident immediately, reconstructed his disarrayed nest with rapid circular motions, performed some shovel work with his wonderful mouth, and went on as if nothing had happened. And what *has* happened? How many eggs is the bluegill now guarding? My guess is few, the turtle was munching away for quite a while.

What fascinated me most in the encounter was the unwillingness of the bluegill to accept help or even permit the presence of other bluegills while the snapper was plundering his nest. Several times during the incident neighboring bluegills would swim over to his nest in a helpful gesture, or so I imagined. The victimized bluegill would promptly chase them away, just as before, as if nothing else were amiss. Birds are more cooperative. If this were a blue jay having his nest raped, all the jays within earshot would respond to the call to charge the culprit. The advantages of cooperation vs competitiveness have not been fully appreciated by every animal group, and we don't have go to all the way to the sunfish to document this failure.

June 20 - White sweet clover in bloom on Peninsula; Bull frogs going strong, green frogs waning

A Feeling for Song

It seems fitting to observe the ending of spring, at least the calendar spring, with a note on hermit thrushes. They are considered by many to be America's best songsters. We can vouch for that, two or three have been singing in the Sanctuary this spring, one of them in a hemlock grove by Black Creek, just a few hundred yards from our house. This is a new treat for us, they have never before sung so late in our spring. The question is: Are they really nesting here or are these singers lone males, just testing the waters?

The way to answer this question for the science of ornithology is to document their breeding presence and the best way to do that is to locate her nest. To start, I would map his territory by playing a tape-recorded hermit thrush song at various spots in that corner of the woods and note how and where he responds to this challenge. Then I would lie in wait in one or another likely- looking spot within the territory, spying on both of them to triangulate on the point around which their June life centers. Hermit thrushes nest on the ground, which makes it easy; but they are shy and secretive birds, so finding the nest would be difficult. The procedure is intrusive; that kind of scrutiny can cause the pair to abort the nesting attempt. On the other hand, in addition to the new breeding record, I would gain the satisfaction of watching these attractive birds manage their lives for a week or so.

This nest would be historically significant just because this is the John Burroughs Sanctuary. Burroughs lived nearby for the latter half of his life and knew the birds of the neighborhood better than anyone. He says in an early essay that the hermit thrush passes through this countryside every April but never sings here. I read between the lines of this dry note a certain wistfulness.

My own observation of the hermit thrush was the same when I

first arrived here: I would see one or two hopping through the woods in mid- to late April and then they would disappear for parts north. No song.

Burroughs had a deep feeling for the song of the hermit thrush, a feeling that has rippled through American literature. For him it was more than birdsong, it was the "finest sound in nature . . . the voice of that calm, sweet solemnity one attains to in his best moments." He felt it was the woodland version of the poetic reassurance, "God's in his heaven, all's right with the world." In a letter to a friend, he writes:

> His song does not seem to me to express sorrow or a memory strung by regrets, but perfect composure and serenity. It is the most spiritual sound I am acquainted with in nature, and has that sweet plaintiveness which is characteristic of the finest music.

Frank Chapman, the eminent American ornithologist, was a good friend of Burroughs. Chapman had the mind of a scientist and the sensibility of a literary artist. I hear in his description of the hermit thrush song the influence of his friend John: "In purity, sweetness of tone, and exquisite modulation, its notes are unequaled . . . in exalted serenity of expression, these strains go beyond any woods music we ever hear."

Burroughs gave to another friend, Walt Whitman, the idea of using the song of the hermit thrush in Whitman's mystical elegy upon the death of Abraham Lincoln, "When Lilacs Last in the Dooryard Bloom'd":

> Solitary the thrush,
> The hermit withdrawn to himself, avoiding the settlements
> Sings by himself a song.
> Song of the bleeding throat,
> Death's outlet song of life, (for well dear brother I know
> If thou wast not granted to sing thou would'st surely die.)

I believe John Burroughs would be pleased to know the hermit thrush is now singing in his old haunts. The change started five or six years ago when I heard an occasional song in early May. Since then the singing has increased each year in frequency and depth into spring, until this year it seems quite possible that the thrushes are nesting on Sanctuary lands.

There remains the question of documenting this nesting for

ornithology, nailing down, once and for all, the facts of the matter. In one sense, I could do it for Burroughs and Chapman and Whitman. In another sense, I could not do it for them. I think I will not search out the nest this year.

SUMMER

June 21 - Heard an indigo bunting in early morning, first for this year; Pondweed starting to turn over; Summer solstice at 6:11 p.m

Ear to the Ground

Last week I got a call from Patrick Holmes, a technician from Columbia University's Lamont-Doherty Geological Observatory. Lamont installed a seismometer in the Sanctuary ten years ago. Patrick called to set up a meeting with me this morning: he needed help in removing their equipment from the property. This promised to be a wistful chore, sweet with old memories, the end of an era.

I have never met Patrick before today, he is the last in a series of field technicians for the seismological division of the Observatory. My association with them started in the spring of 1977, a month after I had settled in at Pond House. I came here full of enthusiasm for putting together an environmental education program and establishing the Burroughs Sanctuary as a research field station for socially useful ecological studies. I remember writing to a number of natural history museums and environmental study institutes, suggesting their use of the Sanctuary as a natural laboratory. I envisioned a network of simultaneous, interconnected studies, crates of equipment monitoring long term environmental variables, and a stream of visiting scientists camping in the unused space upstairs.

Not much of this came about except the bird and plant surveys that I undertook myself, but in May 1977 my head was full of the possibilities. Then along came the seismograph project. For the previous five years the Consolidated Edison Company, the electric utility that serves New York City, had been planning to build a nuclear power plant astraddle the Esopus-Lloyd town line. The power plant property would abut the Sanctuary on our south side.

Naturally, one met a great division of opinion around here about the value of this project. Local contractors and developers glimpsed a short-term boon, people with young children descried a long-term disaster. Three-mile Island had not happened yet, but was momentarily expected. Most people in the Mid-Hudson region wondered aloud why New York City couldn't handle the risks of generating its own power. Among the most articulate and best armored of the opponents was a pair of geologists from the State University of New York at New Paltz, Steve Egemeier and Russell Waines. Steve wrote most of the devastating reviews of Con Ed's environmental impact statements, but Russ found the fatal fault.

No one in the power plant siting business seemed surprised that the utility had chosen to build its eleven-hundred-megawatt nuclear reactor directly over a geological fault, a tear line in the fabric of the earth's rocky mantle. When a tear actually occurs along this line, we have an earthquake, a potentially serious problem for a reactor. Russ Waines traced this particular fault from Kingston south, through the Sanctuary, and directly under the proposed nuclear station. The question remained whether this was an active fault, that is, whether the two blocks of sandstone were still moving with respect to each other, causing tremors or even sizable earthquakes. The best way of deciding this question is to install a seismometer nearby, a sensitive listening device that "hears" the vibrations of the earth.

To make a long story short, I arranged with Lamont to install the seismometer in the northeast corner of the Sanctuary. This had an interesting effect on the plans for the nuclear facility. Con Ed found out about the fault and seismometer (we told them, as I recall) and immediately began to pay more attention to their alternate site across the river in Red Hook.

Not many months later, the utility announced they were regretfully discontinuing all further work on the Lloyd-Esopus site. This, despite the millions they had spent on studies. They gave out as reason the risk to the high population in the region. They didn't mention fault or seismometer. Of course, they knew before they started how many people lived around here. They didn't know a geologic fault lay underfoot, and that someone would go so far as to put a seismograph on it.

Obviously, it does Con Ed more credit to wave the flag of public safety than to admit they botched the geology.

I love this story and I squeeze it for all its worth in my nature walks through the Sanctuary. I usually start my spiel in a dusty monotone as the group reaches an open place on the Peninsula overlooking the pond. From here I point out evidence of the fault, two blocks of sandstone with bedding planes in different directions. The actual fault line is buried under the pond or beneath rock rubble on the hill beyond. I make the nature hikers believe by my tone of voice and lackluster gestures that none of this is any real concern of theirs. I watch carefully for the moment when their eyes finally glaze over.

Then I ask one person, previously identified as living nearby, if he would like to live next to a nuclear power plant. He will mumble something in the negative. I point at the fault and cry out dramatically, "Well that's why you don't!"

Everybody wakes up. I bring all this off with the zeal of the newly converted. I too used to think of geology as so much academic dust, nothing to do with me and my everyday life. Faults, seismographs, and Con Ed have made me think otherwise.

The likelihood of Con Ed coming back here is close to zero. The likelihood of *any* nuclear power plant being undertaken anew in the U.S. as of 1987 is not much greater. So I feel comfortable in leaking the word that in the ten years of operation our seismograph recorded no activity whatever at this site.

Patrick Holmes has already started dismantling the seismometer when I arrive on-site at ten this morning. I chat with him as he does his digging, snipping, and unscrewing. He is West Indian, from Barbados as it turns out. I tell him of my recent visit and we share some Barbados stories. He shows me the inner workings of the seismometer, a treat I missed when the instrument was installed ten years ago. I am particularly intrigued with the inside of the electronic "black box" that converts the geophone signal to an impulse that can travel over a telephone line. It looks like the inside of my computer. I savor for a moment the image of this hearing device lodged in the soggy earth all these years, through blazing summer days and sub-zero nights, listening to the palpitations of the living earth.

My role in the dismantling operation is to help him locate the various buried pieces of equipment (he has never been here before) and tell him what items he may leave in place. We leave a network of underground cabling and the buried shell of the instrument drum. This could be trash or a master's thesis for a future archeology student.

Why has Lamont-Doherty decided to remove this particular seismometer? Patrick explains the several reasons. Chief among them is money. The cost of doing business with the telephone company has become burdensome for Lamont. Obviously you can't run a seismometer only during banking hours. More so than most earth scientists, seismologists wait at the portals of the Great Mother for the raw material of their science. Continuous waiting at the end of a telephone line becomes expensive.

Another reason for the switch is the growing noise level in the Sanctuary. This geophone has its ear to the ground less than one hundred feet from Floyd Ackert Road. When the Lamont scientists installed it in 1977, they decided that the traffic on this country lane would not significantly affect the performance of the listening device. Every time a car went by they would get a jiggle of the graph down at the Observatory, but the few cars running by every day were not likely to mask more relevant jiggles when they came. In the last few years the Lamont people have noticed a steady increase in car jiggles. It's not worth maintaining a seismometer at a site beyond a certain level of background noise. The trend here is definitely in the wrong direction.

Without having made a scientific study of the matter, I can vouch for the increase in traffic here. Take, for instance, our walk into the hamlet of West Park for the mail, a round trip of three miles. In the early days, I often completed the hike without meeting a single car or truck. Today we are passed, on the average, every two hundred yards. The most marked difference is at night. In 1977 I would have felt comfortable pitching a tent overnight in the middle of Floyd Ackert Road. In 1987 that would be suicidal.

Patrick and I talk more about the problems of the site in the Sanctuary. I am shocked to learn this particular instrument has not been functioning for over a year. Disconnecting it is just a formality. Why am I shocked? I realize I have carried a subliminal image of the Sanctuary as my piece of land, harboring a subtle and never sleeping listener to the earth's every sigh.

The dismantling is businesslike and unceremonious. I help him pack up the rest in his truck. He makes a half-hearted promise: he might be back if this site turns out to be okay after all. He senses (I imagine) some feeling on my part about the removal of the seismometer and is doing his best to make up for it. We end our work with a friendly handshake.

As I walk back to my house along the pond I reflect: it would be hard to explain to him that the pieces left behind, the drum and the unconnected wires, mean more to me now than the listening instrument that we removed.

June 23 - Butternut and tupelo leaves changing; Family of barn swallows in front yard

Floral Semantics

A week ago on one of our strolls down the lane, Diana stopped a few yards this side of the pond overflow, sniffed the air, and asked:

"Where's that smell coming from?"

The lane which connects our house with Ackert Road also doubles along one third of its length as a dam for the pond. Along the dam at the edge of the pond runs a row of trees. It was by this row that Diana stopped and asked about the fragrance in the air. I sniffed and caught it too, faint but piquant, a familiar odor and yet hard to place in this setting.

"Smells like a chemical," she continued.

"Right, some kind of chemical." I couldn't imagine what kind of chemical might have been spilled out here. We shifted around the spot, sniffing.

"I've smelled this before somewhere," she thought aloud.

I wasn't about to contradict her. I pride myself on the acuity of my eyes and ears, but I could spend the next two weeks here and not figure out what this odor was.

"Insect repellent! It smells like one of those insect repellents we have in the bathroom closet." Diana rarely uses insect repellent, so this was a good recall.

We have three or four bottles and spray cans of the stuff that have either been left by visitors or purchased to accommodate occasional house guests who have a low threshold of annoyance by insects. One of those items is a small unmarked plastic bottle of Woodsman's Dope, which I acquired many years ago in the Green Mountains. This powerful mix is sold under the counter in Vermont general stores and is guaranteed to keep every living thing at a distance.

At home, Diana checked the various bottles and cans in the bathroom. She found what she was looking for and brought it out so that I could verify her discovery.

"Sniff this," she suggested, offering her arm with the test product sprayed on it. She was right.

The spray can was "Off," the Johnson & Johnson insect repellent. I checked the ingredients for a clue to the source of this odor in our woods. *N, N-diethyl-metatoluamide.* No help there. The rest of the active ingredients were isomers of the same thing.

The next day, ambling by the same spot, we made a point of determining if the odor was still there (yes), if it was indeed the same as the "Off" smell (yes), and what in the vicinity was exuding it. I checked the west side of the lane where mainly herbaceous and low shrubs grew. It must be a relatively rare plant, one not found on other stretches of our travels, since we picked up the odor only here. Nothing stood out. A few smooth sumac stems, young and vigorous, grew along the lane. I crushed the leaves and the stems. The bouquet was suggestive. I brought it to Diana. Not right. A little farther away, closer to the moist overflow is a small stand of spicebush. Spicebush is famous for its crushed-leaf fragrance, but not this time.

Meanwhile Diana was checking the other, pond side of the lane. She went first to the young, twenty-five-foot sycamore which droops into the waters from its perch on the rocks of the dam. It is the only sycamore on the lane and in fact one of the few small sycamores that I have noticed in the Sanctuary. Diana started by crushing the leaves and stems, but that did not produce exactly the aroma she was looking for. Yet it was there somehow. It took her a minute to discover that the agent exuding the odor was the cottony fuzz which grows on the underside of the leaf, especially along the ribs. Rolling up a wad of this and crushing it under her nose reproduced the insecticide fragrance. She had found the natural precursor of "Off."

Many plants give off their own repellents and insecticides to ward off predation. Chemists have compiled lists of these compounds. A small research industry keeps itself busy isolating and synthesizing them for commercial purposes. I do not know where Johnson and Johnson originally got their idea for N, N-diethyl etc., no doubt it was one of these raids on nature. I have a mental image of their file on sycamores: PROPRIETARY INFORMATION. Our own sycamore is not nearly so tight-mouthed about the secret.

This morning an idea occurs to me for testing the hypothesis that the sycamore aroma is actually an insect repellent. After all, it may just *smell* like one and not have the desired effect on insects. I walk out to the tree and take mental notes along the way of the number of insects that pester me, whether they buzz, light, bite, etc. A fair number. Downwind of the sycamore I test the airs to see if the tree is still giving off its fragrance. To increase my olfactory sensitivity I use a trick I learned from dogs, wetting the receptive lining of my nose. Yes, the odor is still there, a little fainter today. I pick a few leaves with more than the average amount of fuzz on them and rub their underside roughly over my face and hair.

This is the test. I walk back the same way I've come, attentive to the behavior of the insects. On the way out it was mainly deer flies who lit on my face, got caught in my hair, bit once or twice, the usual. Now I see them ahead swinging back and forth in the shadows of the hemlocks, waiting for me, the way they always do. I enter the shadow. They see me. They come for me. They buzz . . . once . . . twice . . . . That's it. Nothing! They don't land on my face, get in my hair, bite. A little ways up the lane, a couple more take a buzz at me. The same thing. The sycamore and I have beaten them!

As I come up to the front yard, exhilarated as much by the discovery as by the practical relief it promises, I begin to notice something else going on. My nose, which was clear for the exercise of detecting the sycamore's fragrance a few minutes ago, begins to congest. Hay-fever-like, I think. Unusual for me. I do a few chores in the garden, and by the time I come inside, my nose is running profusely, my face tingles, and my eyes start to water and puff.

This is the famous "side effects problem," well known to pharmaceutical chemists. I now join their ranks in supposing I can slip through the web of nature unscathed. But here is a more subtle issue: along with the chemists, I am forced to acknowledge my simple-mindedness about language. This scent is the sycamore mother tongue. Sycamores and their insect predators have developed their dialogue over millions of years. I try this language at my own risk. Nature has a bag of surprises ready for those who choose to trifle with tongues.

June 26 - Two hermit thrushes counter-singing in south woods; Staghorn sumac in hotel ruins in full fruit

Evening Illuminations

Yesterday evening Diana and I walked out to Ackert Road after a late supper. The moon was a day or so past new and the sky had a heavy cloud cover, one of those evenings in which the available light seems uniformly resident in everything. When we left our house, the atmosphere was a deep shade of gray; it was black before we returned. The air was humid, but not too humid; warm, but not so much that we noticed. The wind, too, conspired in making us not pay attention. The wind stirred the air hardly a whit, leaving it everywhere the same, and not in any way remarkable. The effect was quieted forgetfulness.

We walked to the bridge over Black Creek and only there did we notice the fireflies. By then the evening dark had filled the spaces around all but the larger things: trees and rocks and road. In between, here and there, flashed the little pinpoints of yellow light that outline the summer night without illuminating it. As we slowly accustomed ourselves to these fleeting signals, we found them everywhere; each cubic yard of evening had at least one twinkle in any ten-second period, the females in the grass below winking at the males in the air above.

The total effect throughout the space above the stream was pyrotechnic. With the speed of thought the dead quiet air leaped to life, not only from the flicker of fireflies, but with the thousands, perhaps millions of the other insects around who were not showing us their lights.

Once again, living things redefine a space and time fixed by matter. I was at peace with the world made of moon and wind and cloud, and feel a little overcome with the sudden luxuriance of life.

July 3 - Acadian flycatcher(?) heard at Black Creek, would be a Sanctuary first; Vernal pool at end of lane now completely dry; Raised fawn for first on large marshy island in Black Creek

Oxymoron

Many people take a hot afternoon in high summer as their image of life. Not me. I can find little going on in the forest at these times; even the plants shut down under the stress of great heat, holding their breath till evening. This is the opposite of mid-winter when most activity takes place during the day. Everyone old enough to remember is familiar with the lifelessness of a cold winter night, but a person must be quite naive to see how dead a mid-summer's day can be. This is the kind of naiveté that good naturalists cultivate.

This week's night and day offer a striking contrast in the quality of light. The excessive moisture in the air fills the daylight space with a bright glare, a thin, dazzling haze reaches from sky to earth, obliterating the sharp lines between objects at the horizon, reducing the visual diversity. This same character of the atmosphere has the opposite effect on the night-space, it fills the air with a soft luminosity, making distinctions in the dark.

July 7 - Purple milkweed in bloom by pond

What's in it for the Dragonfly

Yesterday while stretching my legs in the front yard I happened to notice one of our large dark dragonflies, perhaps a darner or biddy, flying back and forth across a muddy puddle left by the recent rains. I was surprised to see her dibbling with the end of her abdomen in the puddle, the dragonfly way of laying eggs. I smiled to myself. "Poor thing, she doesn't know that this puddle is going to dry up in two days, a week on the outside. An inadaptive stunt . . . very inadaptive." "Inadaptive" is the nastiest name a biologist can call a natural event.

Normally, adaptively, dragonflies drop their eggs in more permanent water bodies, by preference the pond, although I have also seen them work the quiet backwaters of the creek and the larger seasonal pools. The egg-laying dance step is unmistakable: a slight, delicate rocking motion forward and downward, with a looping dip of the long abdomen into the water. If you know dragonflies, you will recognize this gesture wherever it happens, whether there is a pond, a summer day, or even a dragonfly.

I have heard that dragonfly eggs hatch quickly when laid and the aquatic young, the larvae, avidly eat their way through the other small swimming animals until the following spring, when they crawl out of the water and metamorphose into flying adults. In the case of the seasonal pools, I've always assumed that the larvae quietly wait out the dry season in the soggy soil underneath, though I have never checked this out. In the case of the mud puddle in our driveway, I said to myself, this isn't even worth thinking about. If she were a robin or a raccoon, we could chalk it up to inexperience. A dragonfly, however, has only one season to reproduce. She better get it right the first time.

A moment later I caught myself up short. How could I assume that she didn't know what she was doing? Worse, why did I assume that I know better? I've learned very little about the life history of this animal, either from personal observation or books. I don't even know its name. What chutzpah! It *is* worth thinking about, this mud-puddle egg laying, it's worth watching and inquiring. She knows something, find it out.

July 8 - Pointed leaf tick trefoil in bloom by Slabsides

It's a Beach!

We have not seen our spotted sandpipers this summer since the first few days after their arrival in May. They usually disappear for a month or so, probably to breed. This year's absence seems longer than usual. In mid-summer we generally spot them again with one or two fledglings. The family reclaims the pond in skittering flight from rock to rock, scolding and pumping their tails, like young ballet dancers in a huff about being watched in practice.

I wonder if the low water level in the pond has something to do with their absence. This is a reasonable conjecture in light of the discovery I made last year concerning their feeding habits. The lane to our cottage, which doubles as the dam for the pond, has a small bridge made of railroad ties. The ties span the eight-foot-long, sloping rock sluice that allows water to flow out of the pond. For years we noticed that a sandpiper, sometimes two, would shoot out from under the bridge when we strolled by on our walks. And for years I assumed this meant that the sandpipers were nesting somewhere underneath, in the structure of the bridge or the overflow. It seemed like a good place to nest for a sandpiper, an aquatic insect eater.

Many's the time I squatted down on the bridge, reaching under, gingerly probing this or that crevice for the familiar feel of warm pebble-stones in a dry grass basket. No nest. One year I actually crawled into the eighteen-inch clearance between bridge and dam and checked every minute nook and cranny of the sluiceway. Nothing. They were better hiders than I was a finder. I credit most birds with that, that wasn't the problem. What vexed me was that I *knew* that their nest was under there somewhere and, if I only had the sense of a spotted sandpiper, I would find it at once.

I labored under these misconceptions until late last summer when I grasped the correct interpretation of the whole situation in a flash of insight. Diana and I were walking slowly on the dam a few feet from the bridge. A sandpiper flew out from under the bridge. I stopped in my tracks:

"It's a beach! It's not a nesting hole at all. It's a beach!"

"What's a beach?" D asks.

"The sluiceway, the overflow, under the bridge . . . don't you see? They're using it like a beach . . . they nibble on stuff that comes over the dam . . . stuck onto the dam . . . insects, larvae, eggs, whatever . . . like sandpipers on a beach . . . picking up stuff the waves bring in, run back, run up, nibble, run back . . . like on a beach."

She had to admit, it was a perfect insight, appropriately inarticulate, into the behavior of the sandpipers. They weren't nesting there at all, in fact they nest off in the woods somewhere, as I quickly found out in my Peterson's nesting guide, when we got back to the house. We have started them so many times from under the bridge because they are using it the way sandpipers use a sandy shore. Sanctuary Pond has no sandy shores, but it has a beach and our sandpipers found it.

July 9 - Still singing: red-eyed vireo, wood thrush, pewee, occasional phoebe, bullfrogs and green frogs enthusiastically so

More Things in Heaven and Earth...

Since the pondweed folded under the surface of the pond three weeks ago and lies unavailable at the bottom, the goose family has turned to the grass in our yards. They have spent whole days there passing from the back to the front and back again, alternately eating and resting. I am drawn to speculate how the *end* of the pondweed cycle relates to the needs of the geese, as I previously speculated about its beginnings.

Last April, as I was watching the gander tip up to feed on the early shoots of curly pondweed, I wondered if this aquatic plant might be growing at exactly the rate to meet the needs of the developing family of geese, the plant's most visible consumers. Unreflectingly I rejected the idea as too far-fetched. I didn't even bother to work out the notion further, to examine the rest of the linked life histories of these two organisms. For example, how about the pondweed dieback, the sudden sinking of the floating mass to the bottom of the pond?

Here's where the pondweed-goose connection loses credibility. The perfect ending would be a die-back of the pondweed in mid-July, when the geese fly away from the pond for the season and no longer need it. A semi-skilled theorizer can easily fabricate more complicated relationships to explain what actually happens: that the pondweed dies back in mid-June. One might suppose that the June timing accords with the need of the geese to get off the pond and exercise their legs by tramping through the woods in search of newer food sources. A story more plausible from the point of view of the pondweed would relate this die-back to the plant's own strategy to regenerate throughout the neighborhood by means of seeds and vegetative tissue carried by the roving geese.

As easy as it is to spin out such theories, it is even easier to laugh at this sort of tale-telling that seems only to satisfy our human need for wholeness in the world. We stop laughing when we realize that more complicated, more mysterious, more holistic relationships than this are in fact unfolding in the woods and ponds around us.

July 10 - Geese eating gravel on driveway; Peppermint(?) on lane

Release

For the past four or five days the temperature has been in the nineties and the humidity not far behind. On days like these every organism lives for keeping cool or at least minimizing the unpleasantness of being hot and sticky. The geese remain close to the pond, the snakes keep to their dens, even the insects stay out of this sun, and Pussycat stretches out full length along the sill of a north-facing second story window, asking only not to be disturbed.

Diana and I have our own devices for coping with this stress. We each have an electric fan playing over our scantily clothed bodies while we sit at our respective desks, she in the bedroom, I in the upstairs study. We eat little, mainly cold cereal and salads, and shower frequently during the day or take a quick dip in Woodland Pool across Black

Creek. We leave the house at mid-day as little as possible, shifting business and pleasure outings to early morning or late evening.

The last few days we have adopted the habit of walking out to Ackert Bridge at dusk or even well after nightfall, to watch the fireflies and savor the special quality of night after a too-hot day. I wear my bathrobe and sandals for these outings; that's what I have on in the evening. Diana wonders whether this might be a little risqué; it is after all a public road. But I go out in the morning for the paper the same way. I haven't been arrested yet. After a day or two, she's doing the same.

Again this evening we set out at dusk. As we stand in the front yard admiring the full moon rising over the eastern ridge, a sudden thunderstorm piles in behind us. The rain starts - large, heavy, summer-thunderstorm dollops of rain. Diana runs back inside. Going in for a rain coat, I suppose. No! Out she hops a moment later - in the altogether! A great idea! Off comes my bathrobe, we gambol around the yard and skip down the lane in the buff . . . watched with approval by the rest of the naked fauna.

July 12 - Geese practicing flight; Fringed loosestrife in bloom; Stinkpot turtle sunning in pond

Takeoff

The goslings are now only slightly distinguishable from the adults in size and plumage. They continue to grow slowly but have fully gained their flight feathers, as have the adults who molted their feathers a month ago. Still in moult is another adult who has attached himself to the family group. Not quite attached himself, because the gander has drawn a ring around the foraging family about twenty-five goose-lengths in diameter and vigorously excludes the newcomer from the circle. The outsider appears to be at least three weeks behind in his moult schedule relative to the parent geese. This makes me wonder whether parent geese synchronize their moulting with the development of the young. One more theory with a sample of two.

This interloper (possibly a hatchling of this pair from a previous year) lives a harried life on the lawn. He clearly wants to eat with the family group, geese naturally congregate. Also his genes may be telling him that fall is coming on, time for banding together for migration. On the other hand, the resident gander's genes are still instructing *him* to make distinctions between "us" and "them," and he carries out his orders ruthlessly. In the course of an afternoon of nibbling over the lawn, the outsider inches closer and closer to the family group, which is usually spread out over a dozen goose-lengths. The gander keeps a vigilant eye on this development as he does upon the family's environment altogether. At a moment whose rightness is clear to him alone, he decides that enough is enough and charges the intruder, head thrust low and forward, wings akimbo, honking horribly. I have never seen him actually make contact with the newcomer, but I have found sizable tufts of down and contour feathers in the front yard this week, which are probably from these assaults.

The goose family regularly returns to the pond for roosting at night and more recently, afternoons as well. Here they do their wing stretches and their "flying in place." Here also they venture their first, tentative sallies down the length of the pond - half flapping, half pattering - in a buoyant ruckus of juvenile honking. In a day or so they will be airborne, if only briefly, and a day after that they will clear the trees at the north end of the pond. That's the last we'll see the family this year. Mid-March next year we shall set up our annual watch for this productive pair, with our eyes, ears, and a sense of the new life year.

July 16 - Two yearlings, one with spikes, at north end of pond; Robin eating bush honeysuckle berries

The Book of Birdsong

At nine in the evening I slip outside for a moment. The dusk has fallen and the quiet air is clear except for the looping, melancholy song of the eastern wood pewee by his nest in the woods beyond our front lawn. After the days of mind-clogging heat and humidity, the air is light and sweet, the soft blue of the clear sky holds just enough light from the long absent sun to give the wooded ridge across the pond a pebbled look . . . trees maybe, or something else, it's hard to tell for sure. The pewee sings again . . .

"Whooooooooooooo meeeeee? Yeeeess you!"

Along with the wood thrush he loves dusk best for asking his eternal question and coming up with the right answer every time. He seems to be singing later than usual these days in appreciation, I imagine, for the new softness of the air. He is still singing, now, while I can just . . . and now cannot, make anything of the shapes across the way. But it is late and his singing begins to trail off in a slurring fashion. As if he drops one heavy eyelid, raises it . . .

Whoooooo . . . ? Whooooo . . . oo. Then the other . . .

Whooo. . . ? Yeeees? . . . Whoo. . .

Finally both eyelids fall together and the book of birdsong is closed for another day . . . a long pause of perfect stillness . . . before the crickets open the nightbook of insect music, and bear the burden to the break of day.

July 17 - Green diatom scum on pond surface; Ten wood ducks at Woodland Pool

Educating Deer

The other day I was walking along the Peninsula, when I heard the unmistakable "thumpity-thump" of deer hoof-falls ahead of me. I was about halfway out on the Peninsula trail at the time, where the ridge of land narrows and, looking down, I can see water on both sides. I stopped in my tracks.

The deer is trapped!

I had him pinned in the upper end of the Peninsula. The neck of the land spit is too narrow here for him to run by me. If I pursued my path, he would have two choices: hide in the vegetation in the wider part of the Peninsula ahead or dive in the pond and swim to the other shore. White-tailed deer are capable of both escapes. I had two questions:

When will he perceive that he is trapped?

Which escape will he choose?

The first question occupied me. I walked slowly, quietly forward on the path, with all senses alert to fix the moment, "when."

My brain was whirring, running over what I knew of "trapped deer" psychology, trying to imagine his own state of mind and taking bets with my different answers to the question of "when." I've had ample opportunity to watch these handsome animals for long periods of time, both at my Pennsylvania cabin and here in the Sanctuary. I think of myself as a minor expert on deer psychology. I do not give deer much credit for being "smart" in the conventional sense. All of the hoofed tribe, as a matter of fact, seem to lack insight.

Why? For one thing, deer are preyed upon by other animals, more than they are predators. Their eyes at the sides of their heads are designed for sweeping the horizons for possible danger. The forward-pointed eyes of predators, like foxes and humans, are built for fixing on a single object in front. Thus deer are at a disadvantage in concentrating on anything, physically or mentally. I imagine their interior landscape as an involuntary pell-mell of ominous apparitions rather than any careful assessment of their immediate situation. This is clear from watching them. When they move, they walk gingerly, lest anything hear them. When they stop to feed, their heads bob up constantly to check every real and imagined noise. If the forest becomes too quiet, it makes them nervous. They live on tenterhooks; even sleep is no reprieve, it's their most vulnerable moment.

You might suppose that this anxious state of mind would make deer wary. In some situations they are, but not consistently. And this costs them dearly. An old hunter who lived near my cabin in Pennsylvania once showed me how to make any deer stop in his tracks, even though he is running away. The trick works every time, and it is in this inquiring pose, looking back over his shoulder, that thousands, who knows? millions of deer have taken a spear, a bullet in their left side.

As I stalked this deer on the Peninsula, I was reminded of one situation in which a deer seems to make a calculation of risk: I am walking along a path. I see a deer ahead off to the side. She has seen me from a distance and is watching. If I walk carefully forward, without changing direction or pace, without turning my head, or giving any outward sign that I am aware of her (such as hunching my shoulders in a sneaking posture), the deer will often let me pass within a surprisingly short distance of her. I have walked within five feet of stock-still deer in this way.

I guessed from the sound of the hoof-falls ahead of me that the deer on the Peninsula knew I was behind him. I was curious whether he would employ this standing-still device. Would he try it *before* or *after* he knew he was trapped?

And when would he figure out that he was trapped?

My cynical side guessed it would be late in the game. He would be pressed almost to the tip of the Peninsula, with water on three sides and a human of unknown intentions on the fourth, before realizing that the only thing left was to jump in the pond and swim to the north shore. This would be no disaster for him. We often see deer wading through the shallows munching on emergent vegetation, and once or twice I have seen one swim from one side of the pond to the other, apparently just to get there.

My generous side, remembering the deer's statue trick, guessed that he would sense his tight situation sooner, perhaps by the time he reached the widest part of the Peninsula and try to hide there.

While making these calculations, I tiptoed quickly along the path, not wanting to miss any crucial decision on the deer's part or frighten him further with my footfalls. After twenty or so yards of cautious hurrying, I heard a splash toward the end of the Peninsula. I couldn't believe the common-sense explanation of this noise and ran headlong down the path looking this way and that to make sure he wasn't hiding behind some bush. No deer on either side. As I neared the tip of the Peninsula, I swept the scene with my eyes, still expecting to find him perched on a rock, quivering with indecision. Not here either. Nothing except deep waves rolling from the middle of the pond. I scrambled out to the point of rocks and looked to where the waves led. Nothing.

Sum-up: The deer heard me coming before I knew he was there, ran directly to the end of the Peninsula, jumped in, and swam to the far shore, up and away. I never saw him. He made his decision before I started thinking about it. So much for deer psychology.

July 18 - No Canada geese yesterday and today; Phoebes feeding young in nest above front door

Surface Tension...

The pond is going through its typical summer cycle. The latest development is a layer of algal scum on the surface. This light greenish slick is not itself algae, but the natural vegetable oils which are dispersed when the algal cells called diatoms break down. It looks like outboard motor pollution to the casual observer.

A careful observer, however, can distinguish an oil slick caused by vegetable matter from the mineral oil slick seen on power-boat lakes. The former breaks into angular fragments when touched with the finger, the latter sticks together better and comes apart in swirls. The difference is that mineral oil has greater surface tension, the chemical bonds between its molecules are stronger than in the vegetable oil.

Diana sometimes takes over the nature walks when I'm out of town and likes to surprise the participants with scraps of technical trivia such as the above. She collects these tidbits on our own strolls around the Sanctuary:

"But why does it make the pond look like that?" i.e. sleek and smooth.

"The oil slick makes a tighter weave," I explain, as we take a rest from the lingering heat of the early evening on the high rocks above the pond. "It holds together better, so when tiny breezes come, they don't ripple the surface easily. The same with other disturbances, like earth vibrations or animals swimming below."

"But if the wind blows. . . or a fish jumps, the water ripples."

"Sure, but it's the lack of the little squiggles that makes the pond look glazed over."

"The glaze doesn't last long," she notes.

"No, I guess not. It evaporates or something. Gets eaten by bacteria maybe. I don't know. A lot is happening right on that layer."

"You know what this smoothness reminds me of?" D recollects. "Mid-December, just before the ice forms."

"Yeah, that's right." I think about this for a minute before responding. "There's no oil on the pond in December, it's not a chemical slick. I think it's a physical slick. The forces between water molecules become stronger just before the surface freezes, so the surface tension increases, and you get the same effect."

In early December we watch for this pond glaze because it means the skin of ice will form in a night or so, and then, if the weather favors, we can go skating in a week.

As I sit watching the pond with Diana on this steamy late afternoon, lost somewhere between the far woods and its reflection in the oily slick, I am momentarily put in mind of that other, structural slick at the opposite end of the year. Transported for a few seconds to mid-December, I shiver involuntarily at the change of climate. Chilly recalls like these are welcome on the hottest day of the year, even if generated only by abstractions like surface tension and molecular forces.

July 19 - Partridgeberry now in fruit on lane; Fragrant bedstraw in bloom on lane

...Underneath Calm

A week ago in the evening I heard a cicada-like buzzing around the pond. The song was a little softer, more musical, and longer in duration than the music of the seventeen-year cicadas. Since then I have heard still other calls during the day, edged with the more strident rasp that is common around here in late July and August. All of these are probably cicadas of one kind or another. In a few days the evening katydids will join them, as the musical mid-summer insects take over from the spring singing birds.

Of the many kinds of cicadas, the most famous are the periodical cicadas (genus *Magicicada*) which come in thirteen-year and seventeen-year forms, corresponding to the length of time they spend underground sucking on the roots of trees. One of the larger broods, Number Ten, erupted in June of this year. That brood does not extend to the Mid-Hudson Valley, its range is west and south of here, covering much of the Mid-Atlantic and Midwest states.

I remember well the brood of 1979 which did occur here. Diana and I were bicycling through the Marist Monastery property a couple of miles north of the Sanctuary on a pleasant late spring afternoon. We stopped to rest and propped ourselves against a large sugar maple. In a few moments we realized we were along the route of a mass insect migration from the soil to the upper trunk. Ghost-like nymphs, almost two inches long, were crawling around us and upon us to reach the bark. There they shed their last skin before adulthood. I *knew* of periodical cicadas, but never before did I *take part* so directly in their life changes. The trees above were beginning to ring with the buzzing song of those already transformed.

After they emerge as stout, winged adults, the male will sing, the pair mates, and the female will lay her eggs in twigs near branch endings. This incision often kills the twig from that point out, giving the characteristic "singed" look to cicada trees. In a few weeks the eggs will hatch, the nymphs drop to the soil around the tree, and burrow underground for a certain number of years, as prescribed in their specific name, *septendecem* or *tridecem*.

Many people express amazement at this feat of animal timing, as well they should. But it is no more astonishing than the million other documented or guessed at performances of plants and animals that have a clock somewhere about them.

Using our eyes as much as we do to discover our environment, we normally picture life in a spatial landscape. But time is life's measure as much as space. Unfolding from both of these are the dimensions of vegetation, climate, geology, pedology, history and so forth. The cicada emergence is a good example of an event in many dimensions, all placed in the imaginative compass that gives it meaning. The emergence of the gypsy moths in April is another; the arrival of the phoebe yet another. In fact all the events in my calendar are that complicated, that simple.

I don't have to wait another seventeen years for the cicadas. Whenever I pass the Marist Monastery or even bring the picture of it to mind, I imagine the thousands of cicada nymphs underneath the sweeping lawn, sucking on the roots of the maple trees. I love to picture them stopping momentarily in their seventeen-year meal when a heavy human foot thuds overhead, and, with a shrug, turning back to the dark night of their preparing.

July 20 - Lone Canada goose on front lawn, the others apparently gone; Phoebe riding deer's back at false bridge!

Deer/Fly/Phoebe

Today I took a walk on the Peninsula, the usual combination of reconnecting with the spirit of the place and picking up the weekend garbage. As I arrived at my shadbush station, the point where the vista across the west bay of the pond opens up, I noticed a mature doe standing by the false bridge. I stopped and looked at her through my binoculars, expecting nothing in particular. I was shocked by the image in the glasses. The doe caught sight of me as I came around the shadbush, her head was erect and pointed toward me. All perfectly normal for the circumstances. Perched on her rump was a phoebe.

The deer was motionless, intent on me. The phoebe was doing what every phoebe does on a perch: keeping a wry-necked lookout for the right sized flying insect to snap up in mid-air. The difference was that this phoebe's work space was the deer's back, picking off one by one the cloud of biting insects swarming around her rump. Now and again the bird would dig into the deer's pelt to retrieve his prey. The deer twitched her skin involuntarily whenever the phoebe would do this, but paid no further mind to the bird. Her attention for the moment was riveted on me. Once, after a particularly vigorous skirmish with a fly in which the phoebe fluttered back and forth a moment along her spine, the doe unglued her eyes from me and arched her head over her shoulder to peer askance at the phoebe, who was once again perched comfortably right above her tail.

It was an outstanding moment. I wish I had a telephoto shot of it, as much for the oddity of the encounter, as for the particular quality of the doe's expression, a mixture of bewilderment and alarm in face of a possible conspiracy.

She looked back at me and made one of those four-legged shifting motions that betray anxiety in a deer. Just then the phoebe spotted a large fly near the deer's head, darted over and snapped it up with a smart clack of his bill, right at her ear. It was too much for the doe, she wheeled abruptly and dashed into the woods behind. The phoebe settled into his more usual perch in one of the sparely leaved white ashes bordering the pond.

I have never before seen a phoebe using a deer as a perch. I asked several of my naturalist friends: they hadn't either. I looked into the literature, the closest account was a field note from California, having to do with magpies picking ticks off of mule deer. Evidently the deer were cooperating, standing quietly for as long as it took one or two birds to work the ticks and flies out of their hair. The deer would even rotate their ears forward so that the birds could clean behind them.

This account raises the question that intrigues me today: Was the deer I saw collaborating with the phoebe? Or merely tolerating his presence at a closer range than she normally does?

Most people have seen pictures of African oxpeckers, sitting on the backsides of water buffalo, pecking away at the flies and ticks in their hide. In this country some species of blackbirds, especially cowbirds, and the introduced cattle egret hang around livestock and even perch on their backs on occasion. But these birds appear to be using the cattle as mere meadow beaters, snapping up the insects that the cows stir up in their passage. This is not true cooperation, no willing participation on both sides for mutual gain. The cows simply tolerate the birds perched on their backs, and do not seem to gain anything in the exchange. Ecologists have called this kind of interaction "commensalism," one party gains (+), the other neither gains nor loses (0). In the case of the phoebe and deer, I was presumably looking at mutualism, a (+ +) interaction between them.

It's fun to compare what I learn in firsthand observation with what I pick up from books. In this case I got more than I usually do from the literature search. In any case this scene raises knotty questions about who is accommodating whom. Since I have to guess, I would say the deer are the slow learners of this evolutionary lesson, despite the fact that they may have more to gain from the exchange. My shred of evidence for this conclusion is the ten seconds of observation on the Peninsula. All theories aside, I consider my ten seconds to be privileged viewing, a window on the living, evolving process.

July 21 - Katydids singing for first; Wood thrush and pewee only evening songbirds still at it

Bloodroots

Yesterday at Slabsides I noticed a few leaf shreds of bloodroot, all that remains of the April bloom. The leaves are now pale and prostrate, tattered by a passing summer. So different from the vigorous sea green leaf of early spring, the leaf that enfolds the cold naked flower in its soft palms at night.

This gesture of leaf toward bloom puts me in mind of a poem about another bloodroot years ago -

Not often a soft evening
Moment empetals my stamen soul
From the noise of expecting
Remembering and the cold of stars
Dreaming in its dark
Perfume and aware as a flower
Of life. Not often
But now.

July 27 - Bracken fern practically all withered; Barred owl shrieking in South Woods

Sonata for a Subtler Mist
Statement

This early morning as we walk out to pick up the newspaper, Diana pulls me to a stop near the overflow bridge and points out a light mist over the north end of the pond. We stop and watch it for a while.

It takes us a few minutes to discover that this mist is different - subtler, more ephemeral, less yielding to close examination - from those we explored in April and May. Today the vapors seem to arise from one corner of the pond near the north end marsh and spread toward the center. They are lighter, lower, less substantial and sometimes vanish if one of us turns away to talk about them. Still naive about these appearances and anxious to find out how they originate, we walk through the woods to the point above the pond where the mists arise. Here we find the phenomenon has disappeared. After some maneuvering back and forth along the shore, we discover that we see these light vapors only if we lower ourselves to the level of the pond surface and stay some distance away. The closer and more directly downward we look upon the pond, the less we see.

Development

Last night's soft rain and the cool morning (temperature in the low sixties) have chilled the drafts of forest air that tumble down to the pond. The point from which the mist radiated was a patch of lake that caught the morning sun's rays. This newly warmed surface, evaporating a little faster than the surrounding areas of the pond, generated vapors which were cooled by soft draughts of forest air falling into the pond. The vapors condensed into puffs of mist. These same slight movements of air propelled the mists out toward the center of the pond where the air was warmer. Here the condensate re-evaporated.

Recapitulation

We see now that the mists are not moving out toward the center, but are propagating in that direction like waves across the sea, creating and destroying themselves in a swirling dance of cool and warmth. This is pure movement in the absence of anything moving, anything we can point to. We are watching a temperature ballet.

July 28 - Agrimony in bloom on lane; Mostly green frogs calling in pond, few bullfrogs left

High Crows

A couple of days ago I picked up a long black feather on the Peninsula. It had recently been attached to the left wing of a crow near its body. In ornithological jargon it was one of the secondary remiges. The shaft bore no telltale marks of beak or teeth. I looked around for other feathers, possible evidence of some struggle or even death. I saw none, so I concluded that this feather had fallen out in the normal process of moulting. Many birds, including crows, moult in late summer after the nesting ordeal. For a moult feather, it appeared to be in good shape.

As I continued ambling along, I began mindlessly making like a crow, flapping my left arm, the feather inserted between my fingers. As the arm whooshed down on a power stroke, the feather vibrated lightly against my fingers with a fine buzzing sound. The physical sensation was pleasurable, similar to a gentle pulsating electric shock. I recognized the buzz as the sound I hear when a large bird flies by where I am sitting quietly.

My arm and hand stopped in mid-flight with the sudden image of ten thousand tiny pulsators massaging a crow's body every time she takes to wing. All these years I thought crows, especially March crows, were exuberant because of the *visual* thrills of flight. But now I know: crows live aloft in a full body buzz.

July 29 - Yellow wood sorrel on lane; Pointed leaf tick-trefoil in bloom

"Salamanders! Do They Bite?"

Over the years I've made a low-key study of nature watchers who are not paying attention. I see them every week here in the Sanctuary. They've come to stroll and notice and be here, but they are never quite here and they are clearly not noticing. They move up and down the trails swiftly; but in a fog, their eyes burrowing into the path before them, their minds out at sea. This kind of semi-consciousness must be recent in human affairs. Not many centuries ago it would have been fatal to walk around so oblivious of one's environment.

I speak with some authority, because twenty-five years ago I was one of them. When I returned from three years in western Europe in the early 60s, I brought back exactly two images of native fauna from the eastern hemisphere. One was a deer carcass hanging in a German butcher shop, the other a nondescript brownish bird in a bush on the Canary Islands. My interest in the latter centered on the speculation whether this was one of the famous "Canaries." I decided no, on the evidence that it wasn't very yellow.

Apart from such lexicographic questions, I simply wasn't curious about animals. I can't remember a single wildflower. Not that I wasn't strolling in the wilder places there: I remember long walks in the forests around the university town of Göttingen and through the barren hills above Las Palmas in the Canary Islands, where I retired for a winter season. No fine feature of those natural environments survive in my memory because they weren't there for me.

Being attentive in the woods or "keeping a sharp lookout" as Burroughs used to say, brings with it the same banes and boons as meditating, doing mathematics, or any other exercise that requires focus and constancy: one fails with discouraging frequency, but one improves with every failure. One trick I've used is to walk out in the woods with a goal: "I am going to find a scarlet tanager this morning." Then every flitting patch of color in the trees and every snatch of song is part of the game. You may see several different kinds of flycatchers and hear many variations on the bullfrog song before you step back inside, realizing you lost the tanager and won the day.

My years of indifference to the natural scene are behind me. Today, as one newly evangelized, I never fail to point out to field trip participants how little they are taking in of the world around us. I will stop somewhere along the trail and suddenly ask people what they are hearing. Nothing. Let's be silent for a moment and listen. How many birds are singing? "One." Someone else will venture: "Three." When we stop to count, we often find ten or twelve. No one heard them. Or I will ask everyone to close their eyes at some unlikely point along a hike and guess the number of different kinds of plants in their last visual field. "Five?" "Ten!" "Fifteen?" They haven't forgotten, they never noticed.

"How many salamanders have we passed on the trail since we left Slabsides?"

"Salamanders! Do they bite?"

What are we to make of this indifference? I believe it is a question of *interest*. I see what interests me. My first memorable lesson in this kind of relativity came several years ago when Diana's son, Eric, casually mentioned that Beethoven's string quartets were okay, except that they all sounded the same. I was thunderstruck! That was exactly my opinion of his favorite Punk Rock heroes. Neither of us had heard each other's music because we weren't interested. The same inattention is in play along these nature trails.

Most Americans persuade themselves through mechanical tricks that they live independently of the natural world. So they're not interested and it doesn't exist.

"Of the insects you've noticed today, were more walking or fly-ing?"

"   ?"

I recently added an item to my lore on natural unawareness: the role of *duration*. Many people do not hear random, environmental sounds that are short, lasting less than, say, one-tenth of a second. I first noticed this one day when our telephone was malfunctioning, calling us with one brief blip of sound instead of the continuous rhythmic ring-ing. No one in the house heard it, unless they happened to be sitting at the phone. This insensitivity, which I believe affects vision as well, is probably a healthy response to the din of abrupt and irrelevant static that afflicts our modern lives. However, it is maladaptive for a nature watcher, because many of her signals are brief and isolated: bird calls, meteors, seed expulsions, tail flicks. I wonder if this threshold insensi-tivity applies to other stimuli as well, tactile and olfactory. I'll have to keep my eyes and ears open for that.

July 31 - Long-horn grasshoppers mating in front yard; Broad-wing hawk carrying garter(?) snake over pond; Poison ivy profusely fruiting on chestnut oak in front yard

Knowing Where Deer Stand

As I sit here in my upstairs study overlooking the back yard, a handsome doe is munching slippery elm leaves about twenty feet from me, unaware or at least unconcerned that I am watching her. I know this deer; she is *our* doe; she has inhabited this place at least as long as I have, probably longer. We recognize her from year to year by the unusu-ally slim and graceful slope of her nose, and from season to season by the particular set of scrapes and scratches on her hide. She seems to spend much of her time within a quarter mile of our house and usually brings around her two fawns late in the summer. She is the doe upon whose back I spotted the phoebe a few weeks ago.

It is entrancing to watch her eat leisurely a few feet away. She doesn't waste any time as she moves through the four foot high shrubs, sniffing quickly each twig or leaf that comes within nose length, decid-ing at once whether it is palatable or not. Her mouth moves rhythmi-cally, mechanically along the foliage of the small, bushy slippery elm at the back door, first down one side and then the other. Sometimes she nibbles one side, pauses, and leaves the other, catching the scent of some finer delicacy and following her nose to it.

Deer have no teeth on their upper jaw. This fact is not obvious in watching them eat, unless one looks closely. This doe doesn't snip the leaf from the twig as a rodent would, she takes it in her mouth and pulls it off with a little tug. The physical evidence of this slight gesture of pulling is almost invisible in the case of these leaves which are so easily removed, but the mark is unmistakable when a deer has been eating more substantial stems. Most of the stem is cut cleanly; the remainder is torn away and shows a little frayed edge. Noting this sign is the classic method for identifying deer browse, separating it from the foraging of members of other mammalian groups, like rabbits or rodents.

Watching this deer eat, I have an idea for enhancing my skills as a deer sign interpreter. When looking at a deer-browsed stem and noting which side is cut and which torn, I can say to myself, or to other people: "The deer was standing here, on this (cut) side of the plant, because the lower jaw has the cutting teeth."

Then I berate myself: "What a trivial piece of information! Why in the world would anyone want to know on which side of a plant a deer was standing when she took a bite?"

But now I stop again to clarify my thought: "Why would anyone want to know what a deer eats or how she eats or when? Why find out anything about a deer?"

"Because she is a comely, graceful animal in a world that needs each embodiment, every gesture of grace and comeliness."

August 3 - Orioles not in evidence this nesting year; Algal bloom on pond, heaviest I've seen; Grey tree frog hanging on front door, late at night

Katydid Ardor

The katydids have been chirping for two weeks and show no sign of losing enthusiasm. As usual among singing animals, it is the males who sing to attract females. They are at their best on warm, humid nights when their rasping "KA-TY-DID" song reaches a high point of volume and frequency. "Frequency" has two senses here: the musical pitch of the individual syllables and the rapidity with which the syllables follow one another. In both senses the song of the katydid changes with the weather.

My friend Dan Smiley performed an experiment many years ago at Mohonk to measure the effect of temperature on katydid singing. Over a series of late summer evenings, Dan recorded the air temperature, while his wife, a musician, noted the musical pitch of the call of the nearest katydid. Compiling his data at the end of the summer, Dan showed a good correlation between the two variables: the warmer the evening, the higher the tones of the katydid song.

A person can satisfy himself of the truth of this in a rough way by going out on an unusually warm or cool summer evening and comparing the tones heard with one's recollection of a typical katydid concert. One doesn't have to have absolute pitch to hear how a katydid becomes a basso when the evening air temperature drops into the fifties.

The other frequency effect is even easier to detect. On a warm sultry evening these insects deliver a clean, crisp "KaTyDid." As the temperature drops through the seventies and sixties, the phrase becomes more drawn out and slurred until, it gets down to about 50°, when one hears an agonizingly slow "ka......ttty......ddid," and finally "ka.......tttty........," at which point the weather kills the song altogether.

This makes sense when you know that katydids make their songs by rubbing together the sides of their forewings, which are fitted with rasp-like edges. Insects are cold-blooded, that is, tend to take on the temperature of their environment. The warmer the evening, the better the muscles work and the more vigorous the song.

Since vocalization is an important feature in their lives, you might guess that katydids hear well too, both males and females. Experiments have borne this out and added the following bizarre note to our insect lore: a female recognizes the song of a male of her own species, *only as long as* they are both at the same temperature. In other words her discrimination of sound varies with the temperature in the same way as his song does. This makes evolutionary sense too - a female should recognize a male of her own species no matter how cold or hot it gets, and the more selective she is in that recognition, the less likely she is to make a mistake, that is, choose one not-of-her-kind as a mate.

In real life, however, what could go wrong? It is hard to imagine a situation in which a male and female sitting on the same branch could be at *different* temperatures, apart from the mischief of some perverse entomologist, who might transplant one there from his refrigerator. Entomology aside, the above discovery is worth studying: male and female katydids, at least, need to share a certain degree of warmth to achieve union.

August 7 - Tiger swallowtail on lane, wings fringed by bird? Solar earth-image at sundown; Sour-gum on lane turning crimson

Earth Image Sun

This evening, as we walked out upon the warm land, I glimpsed the Sanctuary's setting sun through the still, drooping white pines that protect the banks of Black Creek. The ball of the sun was a beautiful gold orange in the swelter of this settling August day, but momentarily across its perfect circle stole two tatters of cloud that crudely counterfeited the dark shapes of South and North America over the gold. I pointed it out to Diana and we smiled together at the astronomical confusion. Only a moment later, after both sun and earth image had slipped below the far ridge, did I reflect how fortunate we humans would be if this apparition were permanent and we had a daily reminder of the daily connection between things.

August 8 - Three unlikely singers this afternoon: mourning dove, phoebe, and titmouse, all young males?

Sour-gum Christmas

This morning on our way to fetch the paper we check on the new things at Ackert Bridge: evening primrose and an immature ruby-throated hummingbird amid the purple loosestrife. On our way back we stop at the pond's solitary sour-gum tree. I noticed a couple of days ago that our sour-gum, *Nyssa sylvatica*, a squat, conical tree at the edge of the pond, was beginning to turn its lovely, understated shades of vermilion and lemon and claret. Sour-gum along with Virginia creeper and bracken fern are the heralds of autumn, trading off another month of photosynthesis for the oohs and aahs of everyone tired of summer. Even now a few of its leaves are beginning the long transformation that will end with leaf fall in October. The effect today is a sprinkling of crystalline reds and yellows, spattered on a tree of green. We debate anew the quality of these colors:

D - "They're like glass . . ."

J - ". . . transparent somehow . . ."

D - " Look, when I hold this leaf up to the light, it changes colors . . ."

J - " . . . no, the *colors* change . . ."

D - ". . like those plastic things filled with colored liquids you swirl around . . ."

J - ". . . or a wash of water colors . . colored lights . . ?"

D - "I know . . it's a Christmas tree!"

And it is! So we sing a festive carol, celebrating sour-gum Christmas in the middle of summer.

August 11 - Many freshwater clams opened around pond, raccoons?

From on High

Tonight I steal out to the front lawn after dark to catch the Perseid meteor shower. I move one of the lawn chairs to the middle of the front yard and sprawl out on it, alternating my gaze from the southwest to the northeast quarters of the sky. I have forgotten from which compass point these meteors typically appear.

The moon, a few days past full, now rises over the ridge east of the pond and washes out the southeast sector of the sky. I hope the meteors aren't supposed to come that way, but I am prepared for anything. Forcing my recollection of the newspaper account of this annual spectacle, I conclude that it is the southeast where the meteors arise and I may miss seeing them because of the brightness of the moon.

I am not much of a star-gazer. Astronomy holds little excitement for me. At most the heavenly display serves as a useful field for metaphors; I wrench little moral lessons from it as the need arises. For instance, the ancients looked at the night sky, one of our best daily reminders how disordered the universe is, and saw there the orderly constellations, pictures of people and animals engaged in complicated activities like hunting and weaving. This is my metaphor for our deep, pre-rational need to *make* the world make sense.

I try to catch one hour of the Perseid shower every year to refresh another image important to me, the picture of the essentially random course of events in the universe. Meteors are good symbols of this; they happen anywhere, anytime. Attempting to predict their appearance would be insanity. The annual summer showers are only a slight concession to order in this chaos, a modest increase in frequency, a vague expectation of place.

My hour with the Perseid shower is the annual confirmation of my theory of the universe: that it is out of our hands and thank God for that. For me, an unregenerate scientist, this gesture is equivalent to the affirmation that a Newton or an Einstein draws from a successful experimental verification of his prized physical theory.

I sit comfortably for an hour or so, the katydids drowsily sing their slowing song to the cooling of the night. Nothing falls out of the sky. I am beginning to wonder if the experimental apparatus has broken down. I do not for a moment entertain the possibility that my theory is flawed. Then three meteors appear in quick succession, brief streaking lives from nowhere to nowhere. Two of them come out of the northwest. I go to bed justified, content.

August 17 - A single green frog singing; Red oak acorns now falling; "Our" doe brings her fawn out of the woods; Nighthawks migrating south in evening

Roundelay Lullabies

Drifting off to sleep tonight with the katydids chirruping comfortably, I drowsily reflect that the bullfrogs seem now to have stopped their harrumphing for the season. And fortunately, just in time, the round is now taken up by another songster, the katydids . . . one of a series of Sanctuary singers to slide me off to sleep . . . but the thought snaps me back momentarily:

How many lullabies do I have in a year? I need to count them:
 - First, there's the great horned owl, from January to March,
 - then come the spring peepers peeping well into May,
 - followed by the mid-summer chorus of bullfrogs,
 - who now pass the round to the katydids . . .
 - four so far . . . so far four . . .
 - a good square number . . . and so slide off again, dreaming of the smooth fittingness of things in this world . . . and number five.

August 23 Virginia creeper turning pink along lane; Grackles back again after summer absence; Fall web worm tent at Slabsides; Whirligig beetles in Black Creek

Early Fall Pool

This evening we pick our way across Valli Marsh and stroll to the bridge over Black Creek on Valli Road. The air is quiet and our eyes come to rest on the subtle colors in the ponded creek above the bridge. The waters, nut brown with tannins, stream lazily beneath us, trailing kelly green duck weed from pools farther above. The creek is bounded on both sides by fields of purple loosestrife, now in its prime. Beyond this fringe and up to the hilltops, the scene is filled with the vital green of summer. But right here, within the bowl of the pond, the slacking summer sun casts a pale, variegated light over the changing elms and maples.

The more we look, the richer becomes the scene in subtle tints and shades of coming autumn. The red maples border the picture above with crimson tips, and withered thistles lay a base of brown at our feet. Flecks of gold dot the spaces in between. Only after we stand at the bridge and gaze a while do we note the most subtle color here, the one that creates the feeling of this place, washing it with a dark bronze glaze. This shade comes from the silky dogwoods, nearly finished with their season's work.

In the foreground of this transition scene are the dotted colors of fall blossoms: touch-me-not yellows and oranges, white umbrellas of climbing hempweed, and standing off to the right, a tall pink hibiscus. A tangled web of rufous orange in the shrubs across the pond becomes more intelligible when I pick a strand of the same parasitic dodder from a nearby dogwood.

This is the most colorful picture of the fall so far. It may well be the most pleasing that we see this autumn. Doubly so, because all of it is mirrored in the still pond. The scene is pure calm.

But not for long. As we stand at the bridge for a few long moments, we catch some movements around the old beaver lodge in the middle of the pond, long out of use and bearded in loosestrife. A stick pushes this way, the loosestrife shakes from behind. Maybe a new beaver is working to refurbish the place. Through the binoculars Diana catches a glimpse of his wet, black coat glistening on top of the lodge. He's not alone here, minutes later we see a raccoon swimming across the pond, her fluffy tail sailing high in the water. Way above, the swifts ride herd on the high-flying insects, while the dragonflies snap up the ones close by. In between, the goldfinches bounce from treetop to treetop, singing their "Potato Chip" song. Before our visit is over, a hummingbird buzzes by, visiting the *impatiens* one by one, and a big snapping turtle bobs up on the far side of the pond.

We leave shaking our heads that such a placid scene of foliage can be so full of animal energy.

August 30 - Imagined a raven calling

Raven Calling Me

Early today as I stepped outside the back door to look at the morning, I heard the call of a bird high and far to the north, over the town dump. I couldn't see anything in that corner of the sky; the large chestnut oak in our front yard blocked my view. It was a raven's call: a low, hoarse, gargling croak with a strong undertone of derision. I know it quite well. The problem is that ravens don't live around here; they don't migrate through; they don't even wander about these parts by mistake. Ravens are birds of the north and the west. In New York they are most common in the Adirondacks, but they have been sighted increasingly in the Catskills in recent years. A couple of dubious records exist (one of them mine) from the nearby Shawangunks. All the same, I stick to my story: there aren't any ravens around here.

An isolated population of ravens thrives southwest of here, along the Appalachian ridge and in the Allegheny Mountains of Pennsylvania. They nested around my cabin there and that is where I first became acquainted with them, if only at a distance. I loved to watch them in March, gamboling with each other in the brisk, buffeting winds above Lyman Lake. I once found a raven nest, but decided not to investigate further. I was content to visit once or twice during the spring and smile at their attempts - raven, the trickster - to persuade me it wasn't there after all.

I've renewed my acquaintance with ravens on our trips to the Pacific Northwest, an area that increasingly attracts us since we discovered it seven years ago. Ravens are common on the Pacific shores, but that commonness does not diminish their beguiling appeal. In fact the native peoples of that region have given the raven a central place in their creation stories, a sympathetic gesture I would like to know more about.

I don't know ravens the way I know chickadees. I've never had a raven in hand or studied its behavior for hours. I've not played tricks on them to watch their reaction. Nevertheless, I feel a kinship with ravens. So it's possible to hear a raven calling, even though there are no ravens in this Sanctuary.

August 31 - All frogs silent now; Virginia creeper at height of color; Horse nettle in bloom in back yard

Black Creek Dervishes

Last fall Diana and I noticed for the first time a colony of twenty-five or so whirligig beetles that thrived in a little backwater pool below the Ackert Bridge. We marveled at their state of agitation, and how it varied from minute to minute and from day to day. The whirligigs buzzed around the pool under the bridge until November.

About two weeks ago we saw the tight little cluster of beetles again for the first time this year, not in their usual corner, but out in the center of the stream. We didn't understand the significance of this difference until it rained at the end of August. After the stream waters swelled a little, they returned to their side-pool of last year. Apparently they choose to inhabit a portion of the stream that is not too turbulent, but through which a certain amount of water flows. During the August drought, that kind of flow can only be found in the middle, the side pools are quite stagnant. After the rain the center of the stream rushes too much, but the pools near the edge take on the right quality. At least that's my current theory.

The whirligig colony keeps us coming back to watch and reflect on the fascinating changes in their energy level. Sometimes the beetles are quiet, swimming together in a tight elliptical formation in the stream. They are probably taking advantage of the same fluid dynamic principle of reduced resistance to flow that Canada geese use when they fly in formation. In these low-energy states they sometimes retreat to the side of the pool for a few minutes at a time and clump tightly together on a stick, maybe resting.

More commonly they adopt a looser, more active swimming formation, which is visually pleasing. In this mode a basic elliptical or circular pattern is maintained by the group, but individuals take liberties within the pattern: One will suddenly shoot crosswise through the formation or spin backwards with the current for several feet only to make a dash back to the group just in the nick of time. More spectacularly, another will dart out of formation, circle the group in a wild dervish two or three times, and shoot back into the middle. The total impression is energetic weaving, on a temporal as well as a spatial loom.

Every once in a while an explosion of energy occurs in which all of the beetles do their excursion at once. The pattern here is chaos, a few moments of pure insanity. Then quickly they return to their entwining mode, as if the phantasm that caused the flurry were a fleeting one. On rare occasions they continue this motion for minutes at a time, wildly flailing about in a looser circle for no reason that we can discover.

If these beetles are feeding while they shuttle about (which I've never been able to verify, despite close observation), some of their behavior makes sense. Holding a position in the current of the right speed allows them to prey upon food items carried downstream without being swept away. Even the extraordinary sally across and out from the pack could be explained as a dash for a particularly inviting morsel.

This leaves unexplained the wild flurries that the whirligigs occasionally indulge in. This behavior may simply be random craziness - there's a lot of it in the world, no need to invoke a special principle here - or an instinctual reaction to an environmental change: a shifting current in the stream or the quick tack of a trout 20 feet away. It may even be a group mating ritual. But I don't think so, I don't believe any of these explanations is the right one. I see their behavior as normal animal exuberance.

I was so intrigued by the to-and-fro of these little beetles that I conducted a little experiment. I scooped one of them into a jar and took it home. The beetle performed dazzlingly, racing through the same kinds of hydrobatics that we saw in the creek. It polished off most of the fresh insects that I tossed into the glass jar. The whirligig seemed relatively content, and rested occasionally on the leaves that I put in the jar for that purpose. It never made a serious attempt to get out of the jar.

I used this opportunity to look at the whirligig body closely. It is quite flat vertically but has an egg-shaped cross-section for speed through the water. The fore legs are long and oar-shaped and are used for rowing over the top of the water. The two pairs of hind legs are much shorter, but also flat and paddle-like. All of the legs end in a small claw, probably for holding on to vegetation when they are not swimming, which is not often. In front of its barely visible mouth is a mustache of bristles, which may help in detecting prey floating in front of it. Perhaps the most curious feature of this insect is his two pairs of eyes, one above and one below the water, each adapted to its medium.

After a day of watching this beetle, I felt it probably had its fill of experiments. I wanted to find out a few other things, so I brought it back to the creek and exchanged it for another whirligig. I was surprised to find I had latched on to a different character altogether. This beetle never stopped fighting, spent most of his energy frantically crawling the walls of the jar, and came close to making it several times. It ate nothing that I so laboriously collected, but did manage to bite me once. It never rested.

Some biologists, especially those studying insect behavior, believe that animals have no individuality; their behavior can be explained in terms evoking a machine - "mechanism," "device," "conditioning," "drives." These biologists have constructed elegant and powerful demonstrations of this insight, which they have assumed from the beginning. I have little sympathy for such a philosophy of nature. I suspect their view springs from a messy need to have the world tidy. I know that their assumption is wrong on the level of vertebrate life forms, like birds and mammals, because I have had my eyes open in that world for the past fifteen years. I am beginning to open my eyes in the world of insects.

September 8 - Spicebush in fruit in woods by Valli Marsh; A single bullfrog call on pond!

Advent

This morning the air is clear and bright. High, thin cirrus clouds set off the blue of a true fall day. Some people look up on this kind of day to scan the length and breadth of the heavens, not for the pleasure of the experience alone, but in the vague expectation of some wonderful advent. Good things must drop from skies like this.

I have refined this expectation to the point of bringing my field glasses out on such mornings, finding a patch of sky empty to the naked eye and peering into it with binocular vision as deeply as I can. I am looking for anything that might appear from that region, but especially for hawks on their annual soaring migration from north to south. This is the hawk migration season, they sometimes fill the air on days like today.

Across the eastern part of the continent, the hawks of mid-September are mainly broad-wings, the smaller, chunkier relatives of the red-tailed and red-shouldered hawks. In this season they mount mornings from their breeding territories in mature forests to ride thermals of air from the warming land. The broad-wings form themselves into funnels of hawk energy, called "kettles," which rotate slowly southward.

When I peer into the sky in mid-September, I am looking for kettles. Every once in a while I see one, but not for a moment do I stop expecting to do so.

Reason laughs at this expectation, that a soaring hawk might be in that tiny, random patch of sky, much less a gyrating kettle of them. Usually the laugh is on me; occasionally the laugh flies back in the face of reason. Today, I spied no kettle of hawks. Instead I spotted a solitary turkey vulture, probably not even a migrant, but some local resident up for a morning soar. And a good day for it, too. But then, every day is a good day to laugh at reason's expectations.

September 15 - Various warblers passing through; Blue-stemmed goldenrod on Valli Rd.; First fall osprey on the Hudson

The Return of the Birds

After June the number of birds in the Sanctuary rises dramatically as the result of successful reproduction, while at the same time the number of *obvious* birds, the ones we see and hear, decreases dramatically. Walking through the woods on a hot August afternoon, you might guess all the birds have left, if you use present evidence only.

This disparity between what's here and what seems to be here makes sense in terms of bird behavior. Some of the birds, the breeding males, make themselves noticeable in May and June to defend their territories and attract mates. After the breeding season, *all* the birds have one strategy: to feed, grow, and live through the summer while attracting as little attention as possible. They excel at this.

Now in September, we begin to see the birds again, little family groups squabbling through the forest, the first small bands that will grow to large flocks for migrating or staying for the winter. Again behavior: we see them because they become bolder and more social in their search for food. They need to fatten for the coming ordeal, whether they cope with winter by fleeing or persevering.

These cool mornings I see more and more small mixed flocks of warblers, chickadees, kinglets, and creepers. Yesterday I heard a catbird mewing in the white cedar by our front porch, the first catbird I've noticed in months. In the afternoon I saw two handsome warblers working in the boulders along the pond, two of the "confusing fall warblers," that seem all alike. Over the past week the blue jays have been making themselves noticeable in their raucous manner, and this morning I watched a small flock of cedar waxwings flitting around the dead maples on the hill above Slabsides, fattening themselves on summer's last, lazy flies. All these birds are signs of comings and goings, as well as coming and going themselves, like everything else in the Sanctuary forest.

September 17 - Phoebe sings one last song near house; Monarch butterfly flying through, first for fall; Hairy woodpecker calling at house, very few this year

Fall Whimsy

This morning, in the middle of a heavy downpour, I heard a spring peeper, a tiny frog, calling from the temporary pool west of the lane opposite the pond. A *spring* peeper in a *vernal* pool . . . in the middle of September. This is no more strange than the other halting springtime things happening now: birds sing, territorial brawls flare, the pools half fill with rain again. It's as if the earth, returning to her equinoctial axis, becomes mindful of that other time and dreams whimsically of going back, starting summer all over again.

Some of this whimsy has been labeled. For instance, the fall singing of birds is ascribed to the young males practicing for next year and the autumn rains that fill the temporary pools have been mapped by ecologists. No doubt some frog expert has an explanation for the spring peepers peeping in September. Me, I have a different take. I prefer to think of all this confusion in terms of an equinoctial wind, whistling energetically from March to September, not through the summer, but across the other dimension. Peepers know what I mean.

September 22 - On Ackert Rd: Witch hazel in bloom, fly amanita and sulphurous polyporus mushrooms; Wooly bear caterpillars moving north across roads; 20 tree swallows migrating south

The Summer Sun

Now that the season of high sun is officially over in the Sanctuary, I pause to muse upon my way of being here: sun worship. I am like the Africans in Jung's autobiography, like ecologists in professional journals, like bathers who savor the warmth of the mid-summer sun, all reflecting somehow on life.

Tomorrow morning at 9:45 the sun will pass the equator for the second time this year, finished now with it's major work on our half of the globe and moving away into the southern hemisphere. This transit is one of those obscure events that we all know about, but would never identify with precision except for the observations of astronomers. The crossing of the equator has life and death implications for the woods and ponds in our zone and eventually for us. This is a global event that needs to be recognized and celebrated locally . . . which I do, here in my little patch.

AUTUMN

September 24 - Seen in migration: kestrel falcon, monarch butterfly, and 3 tree swallows; Winter flock of chickadees & golden-crowned kinglets below Julian's Rock; Mink swimming in west bay of pond at evening

The Mustelid Mind

Yesterday evening while Diana was fixing dinner, I wandered out to the Peninsula under the pretext of exercising my role of overseer. In fact I simply wanted to be there for a few moments in the dusk. Sitting on the ragged rock edge overlooking the west bay of the pond, I picked out of the gloom a dark, cat-sized shape moving rapidly. He skittered along the rocks below the lane, slipped into the pond, swam quickly to my side, popped out, shook himself briskly, and disappeared as suddenly into the talus jumble at the base of the Peninsula. I was looking at a mink, an animal that acts under no pretexts.

When I first caught sight of this motion, I thought "muskrat," because that is the most common aquatic mammal in the pond, although I haven't seen a muskrat here since early summer. But the rapid, direct progress in the water and on land were those of an aggressive predator. In this pond that means a mink. Only every two or three years do I have the pleasure of watching a mink working the pond. More often I see his tracks in the snow among the bankside boulders, always dipping into the water where it is open, his trail - this is the best sign of mink - frequently splotched with the blood of his latest victim.

It may seem strange that I jump to the conclusion "mink" after only a second or so of watching shadows. Strange only to a someone with little experience in identifying animals. This was a "gestalt" identification, the workaday tool used by experienced naturalists and, in fact, by most people who get beyond primary dependence on field guides. It is very different from the field guide method in which one or two diagnostic clues are used as a litmus test of the animal in question. Gestalt is an intuitive process in which many of the relevant, and some irrelevant, factors - shape, size, color, movement, time of day and year, geography, habitat, and the sequence of the last five hundred animals seen - whirl together in the mind and out pops: mink.

This facility develops over time and after attention to many minute details, even those that seem unimportant at the time. A passionate interest in the subject pushes the process along. One of the finer developments of this art is hawk watching: experts on mountaintops unerringly pick apart families, genera, species, ages, sexes, and physical condition of raptors who appear as specks on the farthest horizon. These identifications are intuitions based on extensive experience in what these creatures look like as specks.

Gestalt identifications are a great source of frustration for novice naturalists picking up the tricks of the trade from an old hand. What made that flash of red-brown in the April woods a hermit thrush? What makes this black separation of pondwater a mink? Alas, there is no royal road to this knowledge.

To fathom the mind of mink even a little would be worth the extra time out on the Peninsula. The whole weasel family (*Mustelidae*), of which the mink is a medium-sized member, serves as a living metaphor for ferocity. They are rapacious and seemingly insatiable killers, death on four paws. Weasels are one of the few animals that kill beyond their food needs; they seem to enjoy it. Chicken farmers have horror stories of nocturnal visits of weasels which leave only carnage behind. I can believe these stories, after watching a mink patrol the pond. All of his movements are quick and efficient, designed to make a difference in the world. Unlike vegetarians such as woodchucks and muskrats, I never see a mink mope around the pond, stare absently at the sky, or doze off in the middle of chewing. Unfortunately he rarely remains in my field of view long enough for me to get a detailed impression of his inner state. I've often thought if I could watch a mink working through a whole day, I would finally gain some insight into the modern business mind.

September 27 - First osprey on pond in autumn

Surprise

Walking into my downstairs office this afternoon, I was surprised to see the sun describing a particular angle across the chair, desk, and wall of the room. No need to be greatly surprised, the sun cuts this same angle each late September and early March. I was still obscurely registering summer as I walked into the room, and this reminder of autumn brought me up short.

Every year the sun traces a pattern across the sky that tells the week of the season as well as the time of day. Plants and other animals are more observant of these signs, or less distracted, than we are. Their life rhythms follow these sun angles and day-lengths. Our rhythms have become more attuned to the wall calendar and the alarm clock. Most of us have become functionally illiterate in that archaic language. I know I have. So when a certain low angle of light in my office cuts across that part of the chair and this much of the desk, some ancient knowledge in me knows: not that the date is September 27th or that the clock says 5 P.M., but that it is time to migrate. . . and surprises me.

September 29 Flea working on dead newt along lane; Many squirrel-cut oak twigs in woods; Doe and fawn in back yard, both now in winter pelts

Children of the Hof

This afternoon Ed Dunn from the Bruderhof brought nine of his third graders to visit Slabsides and tramp through the Sanctuary. I met Ed several weeks ago when he was hiking through the property with part of the same class. They stopped then to chat with us on the way through, negotiated an impromptu fishing expedition, and arranged for today's guided tour. That was Diana's first meeting with the Bruderhof children. It brought her to the brink of tears.

Der Bruderhof (literally "Courtyard of the Brethren"), otherwise known as The Hutterian Brotherhood is a religious intentional community with two local centers. They practice voluntary simplicity in lifestyle and openness in human dealings. This combination does wonders for the kids. The community supports itself through farming and manufacturing wooden toys. Like most such communities, they have a tendency toward institutional closedness: they maintain their own schools, their own style of dress (much like the Amish or Mennonites), and do not involve themselves in the life of the wider community. On the other hand, they have an open-door policy for strangers: you may come and stay there for no charge; nor will they pay you for the work they ask you to do. They prefer the barter economy to the cash system of exchange. In return for allowing them to fish in the pond the other day, we got a jar of their raspberry preserves. For the field trip to Slabsides, a pint of delicious grape jelly. I think we made out well.

I first came into contact with the people of the Brotherhood while I was working for the Mohonk Preserve. They would come spring evenings to the Duck Pond campground, where I lived in a small ranger's cabin, and sing hymns until dark. I found their music affecting, but I was suspicious of their offspring. Any closed society devoted to an aging god would yield, so I believed, only repressed children. I was quite prepared to see muffled fury in the faces of their kids. But that's not what I see. These are the happiest, most cheerful, most open children I have ever met.

I joined them for this afternoon's trip at the foot of Burroughs Drive. Ed brought three boys and six girls for this outing. I remembered all the boys from the fishing trip. One wispy little towhead had charmed Diana with his pell mell eagerness to tell his story. He could hardly form a whole phrase, much less a sentence, his thoughts came so fast for his poor tongue.

I always give a nature walk group a head start by introducing them to some relatively uncommon item of forest lore - a deep woods flower, a faraway bird song, one of the rarer insects - and asking them to keep a sharp lookout for more. Today I showed the Hof children an oak apple gall, and dissected it to reveal the wasp larva within. I have been finding a few oak apple galls around the woods the past few weeks, but not so many that the hunt would become boring for them. I was mistaken on both counts. Not only did they come up with a few dozen galls of six or seven different sorts in the next half hour, but their breathless enthusiasm grew with each fresh find. The rest of the day became a treasure hunt for new and more exciting galls, which they dutifully brought to me for my identification and approval.

I have much to learn from these children about being in the woods. They catch on faster than older people, more gracefully. I suppose all children do; that may be the defining trait of children. Even if

I can be redefined - I always assume I can be redefined - I still have a long way to go. It's not something they have gained, it's what I've lost.

It took almost an hour to make the half-mile hike to Slabsides. When we arrived, one of them asked me how old the building was. They were so bright and inquisitive about the natural world, I thought I would let them dazzle me with their mathematical skills. I started:

"Slabsides was built in 1895. And this year is. . . ?"

A short pause before a tentative, "1987?"

"Right! So how old is Slabsides?" I beamed at them confidently.

Blank stares all around. Ed looked a little fidgety. Was I assuming too much for third graders? I offered a little help.

"Well, how many years between 1900 and 1987?"

They seemed barely more comfortable with this calculation than with the last, but then Ed came to the rescue:

"Children," he always addresses them as Children, "can anyone count from 1900 to 1987?"

A few of them took on this challenge with the telltale faraway look of intense mathematical concentration. One winsome little blond girl buried her head into the logs of Slabsides and processed in sequence each finger of her right hand with the thumb and forefinger of her left. This was the long way to the right answer, but maybe the surest under the circumstances. After a few minutes of this and more prodding of the like, Ed came up with the number. Great relief shared by all.

I was amazed that arithmetic seemed such a lightweight matter to them. It was all right that nobody could subtract 1900 from 1987. On reflection I thought this indifference may be appropriate under the circumstances: if your main dealings are with God and your neighbor as human being, subtracting 1900 from 1987 simply doesn't amount to much.

I brought the Hof children into Slabsides and made an elaborate speech about its being a museum, etc. etc., and that's why they must stay behind the cordon just inside the door. This is a damage control precaution I take with every group. They dutifully accepted this constraint as long as I was explaining the general features of the cabin to them. But when I began to point out artifacts farther and farther across the room, one by one they slipped under the cordon. They made this move not with devilish eyes, but mindlessly, like air molecules out of an open bag, as they became absorbed in the old plate over the fireplace or the gnarly feet of the side-table that Burroughs himself made. Pretty soon they were wandering all through the cabin with the same delighted wonder with which they scouted the forest an hour before. The only way I got them on the porch was to promise the story of "How The Nuclear Power Plant Got Bonked by the Big Old Fault."

Assembled on the steps outside, I gave them an animated version of the history of the Lloyd-Esopus nuclear power plant, which I have already related in the *Almanac*. The story is not an easy one for third graders and I watched carefully for signs of comprehension. Their eyes were fixed upon me, their mouths half open in frank astonishment. I thought we were doing well, until one of the brighter-eyed boys asked me if the "nuclear power plant was bigger or smaller than *that* one," the joe-pye-weed growing next to the porch. I still think we did well.

The outing closed with a hike through the hemlock woods of the Fennell Trail and back to their van. Again they frolicked along the mossy fragrant aisles of these woods like sprites on a holy day. When the girls began softly to sing their devotional folk ditties, Ed promised they could sing on the drive home, if they were quiet and listened for now. The afternoon was turning nippy and the talk was of hot chocolate waiting in the school kitchen. Before they piled in the van, they thanked me liltingly in unison for the afternoon's outing. I promised I would invite them back when I set up my bird-banding operation. This evoked an appreciative ripple. While Ed was helping to load the bus, the little blond girl sneaked back and whispered in my ear:

"Please make it on a school day."

October 2 - White ash leaves turned to shades of rust; Indian tobacco in bloom in back yard

Early Autumn

Early autumn is my favorite season, as much for the quality of contagious excitement in the air as for the color changes and the renewed activity among the napping summer animals. Biologists employ a word from the German language for the migratory restlessness that energizes many animals this time of year whether they are moving on or not: *Zugunruhe*. I feel *Zugunruhe* too, I feel it every early autumn. This is one of the many little signs that let me believe that humans, at least those in my genetic line, were wanderers of early autumn.

The Sanctuary world abounds in stimuli that might explain this high level of energy. The air is bright and electric in the lungs; more so on days like today, when it rides high pressure waves from the balsam Catskills. I want to gulp this air, buffet my insides with it, push it back and forth through my bronchial tubes. The winds of early autumn raise my awareness of air, the spirit stuff of life.

The colors of the hillside, today, are better, in my opinion, than they ever will become this year. Many people look forward to the full flush of autumn, when most of the deciduous trees are well along their path of color change. This "height of color" of the Sunday supplements occurs about the second week of October in the Mid-Hudson Valley, depending on the elevation and other more nebulous factors. But by then the best part of fall is over for me.

I see few colors now on the hillsides around the pond, but they are flashy: here a flaming red maple, there a flushed sassafras, a few lemon birches, and in other corners, scarlet creepers twining up chestnut trunks - all set in a matrix of deep summer green.

Swallows, butterflies, and especially hawks travel south in great numbers on afternoons like this one. I delight in looking up from some dull chore and seeing a hawk - it could be a sharpshin - volplaning from a height into the canopy. A spark then flickers in my breast too. I wish I could compose a song, write some epic poem in praise of early autumn, so fond I am of this season.

October 4 - Red-backed salamander in woodpile; Six inches of snow!

Power Failure

We wake up this morning uneasily conscious of a day full of high energy. It has been raining heavily during the night; lightning and thunder flashing and crashing above. The rains of the past few days now combine in streams around us. The sounds of rushing waters come from all sides: from the dam overflow, the woodland rivulets, the old stream diversion across the pond, and above all from Valli Falls to the west. The falls are normally inaudible, but they become a dull rumble during the spring and autumn rainy seasons, and now fill our western soundscape with roaring.

As we lie and watch in the poor pre-dawn light, the rain slowly begins to change, becomes harder and sharper, glints against the night light by the kitchen door.

"Sleet! That's sleet out there!" I announce to Diana, pointing over her shoulder to the mess outside. "What next?" Next, peering out from the coziness of our bed, we watch the hard driving sleet evolve to a wet snow, which masses in soggy clumps on the trees and shrubs.

Getting up, I think aloud, "You know, this is the kind of day we lose our electric power."

But I have speculated after the fact.

"The lights went out ten minutes ago," Ginnie, our weekend house guest, cheerfully greets us from the kitchen. Ginnie is Diana's oldest friend who lives in Brooklyn. She hasn't had this much fun since the blackout of '65.

The snow gets thicker and faster as we talk over morning coffee. "Looks like there's four inches on the ground," I estimate. Diana and Ginnie have already put on their first layer of sweaters, bracing themselves for the duration.

"There's not much chance this snow will hang on for a whole day," Diana predicts.

"But the damage by that time could be bad," I finish her thought. Many of the trees, still fully leaved, are bent double or broken. I wince at the image of our electric power line, strung through a narrow corridor of trees to Ackert Road. It may be a long time before we get our power back.

This is the first snowstorm of the season, in fact the earliest snowstorm here that I can remember. We sometimes have flurries on brisk days in late October and often spitting snow on raw November nights, but we rarely see snow piled on the ground much before December 1st. This blizzard today is having the same damaging effect on the vegetation as the late spring storms, which are a regular feature of this climate. The leaves collect the wet snow and bear down the trees with a massive weight they were never designed to carry. The result is broken limbs, fallen trees, and downed utility lines.

Residing in a nature sanctuary usually entails living back in the woods somewhere. In our case it also means hanging on at the end of the line for utilities such as electric power and telephone service. The upshot is that in the event of damaging storms we are the most likely to have our service interrupted and the last to have it restored. Because of storms like this we lose one or both services, on the average, six or seven times a year, mainly in the winter. When the damage is widespread and serious (as it surely will be today), four or five days may pass before we are reconnected to the electric power grid. We have gone without telephone service for weeks at a time.

We are old hands at coping and have alternate resources always at hand: a wood stove, a propane range, kerosene lanterns, battery operated radio. The telephone is not as easy to replace, so we simply do without and trust nobody needs to talk to us. Long outages in the depth of winter have not been that uncomfortable for us. In the old days we met them with a sense of cozy resignation. "In the old days" means pre-computerization, before we became dependent on word processors for our daily work. Now I become edgy if I am forced to be without my computer for a few hours.

Diana, Ginnie, and I sit around the dusky dining room table, reminiscing over the old days. The storm swirls around us. A new thought occurs to me. "You know what?" I start slowly, "I wonder if the phone is out too."

I check that possibility. Correct.

Today, this is a major problem. "I'm on call," Diana reminds us. One of her duties as Director of the YWCA Battered Women's Services is to take an occasional shift on the twenty-four- hour hotline. This is her weekend. Domestic violence emergencies in the area will go unanswered until we fix the phone or make other arrangements.

Enough of talk, my tasks are well defined. I need to check the power line for downed wires, locate the break in the telephone wire and fix it, then cut some wood for the stove. I put on my slicker and pac boots, grab the binoculars, and trudge out into the heavy weather. The falling snow has warmed to rain again. The going is slushy, but the air is still bracing and wintry. The scene is incongruous: not winter, not fall. Instead of the stark, black sticks of tree trunks poking out of the snow, I see bright swatches of mauve and vermilion, crimson and canary shining through the weighty white masses.

Branches are down everywhere, our entrance lane is closed off with drooping elms and red maples. These are young, opportunistic trees that bend into the opening in the canopy caused by the lane, and for that bold, graceful gesture are the first to crack under the weight of unexpected snow or ice. I am delighted to see asters and goldenrods in vigorous bloom poking through the slush. The fall colors appear more subdued this morning, but the difference seems to be in the storm-light rather than the pigments. I see the snow has made one or two long-term changes in the foliage: the leaves of the white ash trees along the lane have been brought down in numbers by the wind, and the cascade of Virginia creeper over the high rock of the Peninsula has itself been washed away.

I start walking the power line. From our house to the road the electric cable and poles are defined as "customer property." We are responsible for repairing any break occurring in this section. For a major storm like this, a break in our line could leave us weeks without power. I want to know what's in store right away. Our electric line is so finely enmeshed in forest vegetation that I expect every major storm to bring it down. That has never happened and it hasn't happened today; our line is whole.

On the way back home I check the telephone line. I have a different motive here: if I find the break I will fix it. The twenty-four volts that push the telephone signal along will give my finger a little buzz, if I grab the wire wrong; very different from the forty-eight hundred volts of the electric line. Foolhardy as I've become in my old age, I wouldn't dream of trying to fix a broken power line.

To say that the telephone line installation does not meet company standards is an understatement. The wire droops over the lane and the Amasa Martin Trail with the help of one dilapidated pole on top of the ridge between them. From there it straggles across the ground, haphazardly supported by occasional bushes or securely tied to fallen branches. The line used to cross Black Creek underwater (without being designed to do that), until I remounted it on bankside trees. From the creek it passes to Valli Road through a pole stand of red maple, tacked or tied to the least vigorous looking trees. The connection to the main line at Valli Road appears to be the work of a raccoon. Needless to say, this line goes out of commission with fair regularity.

The same circumstance that makes our telephone line so unreliable - that it runs for a half mile through the woods - makes getting it fixed almost impossible. Legally this is New York Telephone's property, but practically I am responsible for it. Scores of telephone linemen have come out here in the dozens of outages we've suffered in the past ten years and I have listened to all their excuses why it is virtually impossible to fix the line on that particular day. These excuses run from technical discourses tricked up with telephone jargon to frank admissions the lineman is not feeling up to it today. On more than one occasion, the underlying hang-up has come to light: they are afraid of snakes and believe that every bush and rock in these woods has a resident copperhead just itching to sink its fangs into a New York Telephone man.

I have learned to counter this concern with a ploy of my own: before the repairman gets out of his truck, I run up and find some way of inserting into the first minute's conversation the information that no big snakes hang out around here, no sir. None of the linemen have ever told me they don't believe me; they don't have to.

The rain has stopped now and the wind is picking up, a brisk winter wind that stings the nostrils. Early autumn is a melancholy period and now the sweet-sad smell of a season out of season compounds the wistful quality of the day.

I find the line break at a familiar spot, the second ridge west of the house, the top of the Black Creek bluff. This is the highest point on the line and bears the stress from both sides. I have patched breaks at this ridge of rock so often, I come here first when the telephone goes out.

This combination of no break on the power line and a readily accessible break on the telephone line is the best of all possible utility emergency scenarios. I go back to the house for my tools.

"Everything under control now!" I announce to the womenfolk who are huddled together on the sofa in the cooling living room.

"Is the phone working yet?" Diana is worried.

"In a minute." I lumber into the kitchen, being careful to get some mud on the floor.

I carry to the line-break a knapsack full of screw drivers, wire clips, vise-grip pliers, and twenty feet of lamp cord. I also bring a spare telephone handset that has no other function in my life but this. I verify that the company side of the line has a dial tone. Good. Then I paste the various scraps of wire together in a fashion that would make a member of the Electrician's Union wince. Fixed.

Back at the house I haul out my axe, maul, and wedges from summer storage behind the chain-saw box. Our house is heated primarily by woodstove, but the fall has been mild so far and we have relied on the new oil furnace back-up. Since the power went out six hours ago, the inside temperature has dropped 25°. Diana and Ginnie are now wrapped in down comforters in the living room, talking about their inner selves. The portable radio says that eighty thousand households in the area are without power. It's going to be a while before we hear the hum of the refrigerator. I go out to the back yard to split the few chunks of wood that I have managed to collect this fall.

While loading the split wood into our woodshed, which is a separate part of the kitchen, I notice an unusual number of yellow jackets in the area. Earlier this summer two colonies of yellow jackets built nests within our cottage. Both colonies gained access to the house through the shingle siding between the first and second floors. The wasps worked their way into holes there and built their nests between the ceiling of the kitchen and the floor of the guest room above.

I have been complaisant toward the wasps through the summer. I persuaded Diana that they will not interfere with our life, although the throng of them that hums outside the kitchen door on warm summer days seems formidable. At worst they have made breakfast in the lawn chairs a little tense with their visits to our cereal bowls. My philosophy of let-live prevailed.

Now for the first time they are inside the house. Over the summer we could hear from our bed little murmuring noises, like the purr of a small cat. But no wasp, apart from accidental strays, invaded *our* space. In retrospect, that was the deal I made with them: stay on your side of the wall and we shall live peaceably together. Today I see they have broken the pact. As a material symbol of this breach, they have punched a hole in the ceiling of the kitchen, a tiny opening an eighth of an inch across, but large enough for them to squeeze through one at a time.

My first thought is to patch the hole with plastic tape. In doing this I can feel that only a flimsy shell of paint remains on that part of the kitchen ceiling. They have completely eaten away the substance of the wallboard. The ticky-ticky sounds we heard all summer were them hopping around on the paint, the only layer between their nest and ours.

Predictably the scotch tape patch fails. Twenty minutes later I find five yellow jackets buzzing through the kitchen and ten more milling around the hole in the ceiling, now enlarged. The wasps seem tense and energized, as if sensing their own violation and its inevitable retribution. What I do next does not improve their state of mind.

I have to stop the flow of bodies into our living space or give the whole place over to them. I am aware now how fragile the partition is between us and them. If the foot-square patch of paint falls with the whole yellow jacket nest, we will move out sooner than later. The situation requires quick action; the wasps are emerging faster and faster. My plan is to place a two-foot-square piece of plywood over the spot. Then nail it in, rapidly and resolutely. The wasps already flying around will not notice or, at any rate, will not take it amiss. That's the plan.

In order to do this, I need to have better access. I clear away a spider web from that corner of the ceiling with the wide swish of a broom. But I have seriously misjudged the irascibility of yellow jackets. At this vague motion of the broom toward their nest all twenty of them in the kitchen go for me at once. I am not dressed for a wasp blitz. I do not have enough hands to flail them away. Angry wasps are nailing me left and right on the face and neck. Three or four dive at the top of my head. They work their way into my hair to sting my scalp at will. These are the worst, I cannot pick them out of my hair. The pain is intense, but not so bad that I don't reflect how adaptive this strategy would be against furry enemies like raccoons and bears. Altogether eight or ten of them get me.

Undaunted, I pursue my course; I still intend to dam up the hole and save our home for human life. All of it in the next five minutes. But I see now that I need help. Despite her evident misgivings, I manage to talk Diana into holding the hammer and nails. I will rush up and clap the plywood over the hole in the ceiling, she'll run behind and nail it shut.

My left eye is beginning to swell closed from one well-placed sting on the eyelid, so we must move fast. I make a dash for the hole, but before I am halfway there, the circling wasps get the idea and start for me again. I retreat quickly to the hall and try to rally Diana's weakening resolve.

"We have to move more quickly . . . in one swoop . . . both of us . . . together."

"You're crazy!" This is not a new thought for her.

"What do you want to do, give over the house to them? C'mon! In one big swoop."

"Forget it! I'm not going to do it." She's going to do it, Diana never says no to my schemes.

"Whaddya mean `Forget it'! Forget living here? We gotta do it, so c'mon! In one big swoop . . . into the kitchen . . . ready?"

"Forget it! I'm not going to do it." She's not going to. I can't believe it. Where is this obstinacy coming from?

In the end, we don't do it. Beaten, I watch from the shadows of the hall as the wasps cruise triumphantly around the newly won kitchen. I vow under my breath that they will rue this day. We close off the kitchen from the rest of the house and leave the outside door open, abandoning the room to the wasps until tomorrow and whatever bright idea that day brings.

In short order the sun appears and the other lights come back on. All of fall's glory on the far hillside is restored. The furnace kicks in. As I sit in the living room licking my wounds, the irony is clear: despite the absence of the sun and its man-made surrogates, this has been the most energetic of days. The day is not yet over.

October 5 - Full moon tonight, flying squirrels rustling in the treetops

Hosting the Elders

Today is the semi-annual Slabsides outing of the local Elder-hostel retreat. Every spring and fall seniors come from around the country to the Holy Cross Monastery in West Park for a week of lessons in birds and scriptures, dancing and origami. My part in the week's curriculum is to show Slabsides and give a nature walk around the woods.

This is an appealing, if distracting, exercise. These people are tried and true learners, they are here because they have retained or regained their zest for finding out about the world. They also have a lifetime of lore to share, about nature and living. However, as field trip participants, they are somewhat undisciplined.

I bring them to a station where I begin shedding light on the scene in front of us. Half of them promptly find something more compelling across the road. Two or three others will be put in mind of a story from their youth and tell it to their neighbor, usually at a fairly high volume since many of them are hard of hearing. By the end of the walk they are strung out in twos and threes for over a half a mile, chatting about breakfast or what a nice young man I am.

The pay-back is that these seniors appreciate the gift that I offer here. They let me know this in a thousand different ways. They value good moments (and resent bad ones) more keenly than younger people, perhaps because they are now counting more closely. I relish their company as I would an inexplicable movie of me, made thirty years hence.

The tastes of these seniors are different from those of younger audiences. They seem less interested in spotting nature's rarities than fixing their attention, one good time, on something well known. They have more to gain from looking with more widely opened eyes at another robin in the grass in front of them than "bagging" ten rare warblers by dim glimpses into the treetops. They also have less patience with convoluted theories of eco-science than with the earthen common sense that forms the substance of environmental concern. These attitudes accord with my own and give me comfort in the past, if not hope for the future.

Like children these older Sanctuary visitors have a clear eye for metaphor, which the rest of us in the noon of our days have to squint to achieve. As if dawn and dusk allow the eye of the mind to see how shadows relate everything. They appreciate my offer to nominate witch hazel, which blooms in November, as the Institutional Flower of Elderhostelry.

Two comparisons urge themselves upon me today:

1) These people, who only yesterday heard of the Sanctuary and of Burroughs himself, are more attentive and attuned to this place than were the attendees at Slabsides Day last Saturday, supposedly members of the flock.

2) In another era, insight and information about our common heritage would flow from these greyer heads to mine. I would be glad to have it this other way, hearing from their lips stories of the great men of our village and of the woodlands our heroes roamed. They would know the meanings of these things and I would need to learn. They are the elders.

October 9 - Katydid with skeletonized wing along lane; Grouse drumming in evening

Does Katy...Did?

I have been paying close attention to the last gasps of the katydids this fall. A couple of times I thought the weather had finally cut off their evening mating songs: ten days ago when we had our first hard frost and earlier this week with the freak six inches of snow. For a day or so after these hard knocks they were quiet, but another warm afternoon would bring out one more hanger on.

In the heat of the katydid breeding season the males start singing only in the later stages of dusk. Now at the end of their time I sense in these afternoon outbursts a certain urgency. It's clearly now or never for a male katydid that wants to leave any of his genes in the next generation. I have no idea if these considerations are compelling for an individual katydid, or if the afternoon is simply the only part of the day still warm enough to muster a "katydid."

Spotting a katydid yesterday on a small red oak near the lane, I suddenly understood another pressing deadline for these insects. Katydids are perfect mimics of leaves; they are about the size and shape of birch leaves, bright *green* birch leaves. One has to look twice when katydids are sitting on live twigs in late summer to separate them from the rest of the foliage. As fall unfolds, as leaf after leaf assumes its own color, the katydid loses its disguise shade by shade. The katydid I saw yesterday was on one of the last red oaks to change, but even this tree was beginning to brown. I wonder if anything like apprehension circulates among the neurons of this green leaf-like insect watching his natural cover disappear beneath him, as his cleverly designed body becomes his own worst enemy. I believe I have noticed that the katydids are seeking out successively later-turning trees to sing on.

The katydid I found yesterday on the red oak was remarkable in another way: part of his wing appeared to be skeletonized. One often finds leaves in late summer from which all the soft green tissue has been eaten, leaving only a framework of ribs and veins, the "skeleton" of the leaf. This leaf damage is caused by lepidopterous insects called skeletonizers. The trailing edge of this katydid's right wing appeared eaten away in exactly the same way that a leaf is skeletonized. The puzzle is: How did this happen? Is this an accidental deformation of this particular katydid? Is it indeed an affliction at all or simply another strategy on the part of the katydid to look like a leaf? Does the katydid do this to himself? Or has he engaged the help of a guest "skeletonizer" with which he has evolved this mutually beneficial relationship? If so, how much of his wing can the katydid afford to have nibbled away, before the benefit, which is to prevent him from being eaten, disappears? There are many other "if so" questions about katydids, many more than "if so" answers.

October 18 - Katydid singing in an orange maple; Pileated woodpecker drumming at Ackert Bridge

Autumnal Slush

I walk back into the South Woods this afternoon for the first time since last week's damaging snow storm. Ostensibly I am checking some tree work being done in that corner of the Sanctuary. The pleasant amble along these well-known paths is made unfamiliar this week with a blanketing layer of half the forest's yellow-orange and russet leaves. The leaves here in the deep woods completely hide the ground and form a colorful, comfortable pre-winter slush to wade through. I feel I could slosh through these leaves for days on end. Every autumn spends a moment holding an equal number of leaves below and above. This is the moment. I slosh on.

October 20 - Spicebush in Amasa Martin swamp still green; Beaver house in pond above Woodland Pool plastered with mud, ready for winter

Laying in for Spring

My favorite season of early autumn is now over. Some high points remain: the sugar maple that fills the view from my study window is still passing through its harvest transitions - lime to lemon, then faintly pocked with apple blush. These spots blended a week ago to a day-glo orange that gave me a jolt whenever I looked up from a surfeit of thinking. This same tree gave me a worse start a few nights ago when I glanced out by the light of the bathroom window and saw the woods on fire! So it was. Not with combustion heat but with the warmth of autumn. Yesterday the winds took most of the leaves off this tree and left it looking threadbare. Now only a few dirty red leaves dangle at my window, reminding me of the blazing days of a week ago.

Many people find autumn a melancholy time, a sad-sweet season of colorful dying. Some living individuals do end with the fall, insects that overwinter as eggs and annual plants that start next year from seed. But color is not a sign of dying, leaves color and fall so that the tree can bound back alive in the spring.

Every temperate organism has a strategy for passing through the desert of winter, when water is locked up in its frozen forms. The strategy of deciduous trees is to drop the leaves that have served them as surfaces for food making and cooling over the summer. The sun is now traveling too low to make food efficiently and the tree could not afford to lose water to cool its surfaces in the winter drought, even if it needed to. The tactic for this strategy is to plug the arteries leading to the leaves, and the device is a thin layer of obstructing cells at the base of the leaf stem. As these cells cut off the flow of water from the roots, the food-making chlorophyll is no longer produced, the green color disappears, and the true colors of the leaf, which the chlorophyll has been masking all summer, are manifested. These obstructive cells become more brittle through the season and soon the right gust of wind breaks the leaf off the twig, and adds it to the forest compost system for next year's growth.

Autumn is not the end but a laying over during winter and a laying in for the new life year next spring. The sinking sun itself promises this much. Some individual organisms die and we, as self-conscious creatures, are accustomed to consider the end of individuals as THE END, but whether insects and flowers share this sense is unclear. Certainly the forest itself would not say so, if it could verbalize its interests: eggs and seeds and you and I are all one with the cause.

Winter would be a disaster except for this retrenchment and laying in, the falling of leaves and dying of mated katydids. These apparent setbacks are bright signs of renewal: this sugar maple will bud out next spring *because* it yields its leaves this fall. We celebrate the vernal equinox in October. Nothing is what it seems, everything is ineffably somewhere else. My favorite season is now by.

October 23 - Tupelo leaves gone, but one; Little brown bat in house

House Guests

Last evening while I was carrying firewood into the house a little brown bat flew through the open back door and into the kitchen. I believe it was a little brown bat, *Myotis lucifugus*, because of its dark brown color and its size, larger than a pipistrelle and smaller than a big brown bat. Bats, who are otherwise navigational masters, sometimes fly in doorways by accident. They love to free-wheel around the outside of houses in the late evening, when lights from windows attract numbers of flying insects. If a juicy beetle flies in an open door, the bat may follow in the heat of pursuit. Twenty years ago at my hermitage in Pennsylvania I used to hear the "flick, flick" of the bats circling the cabin, brushing their wings on the corners as they passed. It felt good to know they were there.

Yesterday's bat flew around the kitchen for a few minutes obviously uncomfortable in his suddenly diminished maneuvering space. Diana closed the interior doors and I whisked up a towel to cover him once he tired and came to rest. In my foolhardy youth I used to grab bats barehanded, but they have sharp little teeth and a remote chance of carrying rabies. Nowadays I use a floppy piece of cloth to scoop it up and carry it outside. This one lit on the side of our polished wood pantry, hanging on to I don't know what, exhausted, confused, and visibly panting. We peered for a moment into each others' eyes and I was reminded how evil-looking bats are at close range. No wonder they've been treated so poorly in folk literature. As I took my eye off of him to adjust the towel, he flew out the door and into the night.

This hapless bat is only the latest of a long line of animal visitors we have had in our house. Not counting the four of us, we have only one official house animal, Pussycat. But it would be hard for a completely objective observer to make these distinctions. An unbiased eye would count many more ants or crickets in season than people or pussycats, and, if called upon to name the year-round possessors of the place, this observer would have to say: spiders.

Season by season this is how the house list runs: spring brings its horde of small red ants to the kitchen, who quickly find every crumb or dab of spilled anything. The ants pass control of the kitchen over to the crickets in mid-summer, who this year ceded it ever so briefly to the wasps in early fall. Mice we have with us throughout the year despite Pussycat's best intentions. The little rodents seem to make a special effort to insinuate themselves into the nooks and crannies of the place in the late fall. Winter is mosquito time inside, as late spring is out of doors. Our domestic December mosquito population is as predictable as the June population in the woods. The mid-winter mosquitoes are not biters. Their impact, as they whine about our heads in the middle of the deep winter night, is purely psychological.

These are the regular house guests. We also host the occasional visitor and as a group they are more entertaining. A few years ago in the late fall I noticed oddments disappearing from the kitchen apparently in the middle of the night: nuts, forks, packets of sugar, scraps left on the table. I solved the mystery one night when I was awakened by a wooden clatter from that part of the house. I stumbled into the kitchen, and switched on the overhead light. In the far corner at the base of the wall the honey spoon was trying to wriggle sideways into a two-inch hole in the wallboard. Rubbing my sleepy eyes, I finally realized the spoon was not leaving on its own, but was being worked through the hole from the outside by a small furry face. When I showed up, the face paused for a moment in its labor and a single beady black eye measured me from the other side of the hole. I rescued the honey spoon and went back to bed, imagining that my new house guest was a wood rat, delightful, intelligent animals that have the kleptomaniac habit and are becoming quite rare in the Mid-Hudson Valley. Over the next few days I got better looks at the thief, who turned out to be a Norway rat, a less engaging rodent. We still hear Norway rats rummaging around the basement from time to time, but they mostly keep to themselves.

Another visitor/thief from downstairs has proven to be more persistent. This summer small, mouse-like droppings began to show up in Pussycat's dinner dish. Occasionally we would hear brief, furtive crunching noises from that direction when we were in the kitchen. Hard to imagine that Pussycat would tolerate a mouse nibbling on her dinner. She often crouches hours on end at a hole in the wall or floor, patiently waiting for one of the little beggars to make an unlucky appearance.

We finally got a look at the culprit, a long-tail shrew. He would pop up through the drain opening in the kitchen floor, dash over to Pussycat's dish, laboriously climb in (these shrews are only five inches long, half of which is tail), grab one pellet of Meow Mix, crawl out, and chug back to the hole in the floor. The round trip took about ten seconds and would be repeated every two or three minutes for a half hour while the feisty little animal was feeding.

The first time I saw this, I was amazed that the whole business had escaped Pussycat's attention. I soon got a clue what was going on: one day I watched her step back from the bowl as the shrew dived in on one of his raids. Shrews are known to be scrappy fighters, but this was over-reacting, I thought, until I also remembered that shrews have a disagreeable odor, probably exude some kind of musk when they are excited or threatened, and Pussycat was stepping back from experience rather than cowardice. I interceded on our cat's behalf by removing her dish to another room. Shrews have short memories, short life-spans, and short activity ranges. He never found the new feeding spot, although I'm sure he patrols the kitchen regularly.

We know faster ways to get rid of pesky intruders, but I prefer not to kill animals if I can find a less extreme way of keeping them out of our space. This forbearance has been sorely tested over the past few years by raccoons. Although this house is as porous as an old house can get, it did not come with holes large enough for raccoons. We made them. The in/out holes in the basement doors that I designed to be convenient for Pussycat are also ideal for medium-sized raccoons. Late fall and winter seem to be prime visiting times but we've had raccoon visitors all through the year.

Raccoons can be inadvertently destructive if they lose their bearings and cannot find their way out of a house. I like to discourage them from the beginning. I will relate one story of my experiments in "discouragement."

Two or three years ago I awoke one night to the kind of clattering and crashing that I have long since learned to interpret as a raccoon visit. Drowsily I put on my bathrobe, trudged out to the kitchen, and turned on the lights. By this time the animal, a fair-sized adult, had heard me coming and followed the raccoon climbing instinct. He clambered up on the refrigerator. Not seeing any branches, he made his ascent by way of the kitchen table and oak buffet, knocking off most of the utensils sitting on them as well as everything on top of the refrigerator.

Slowly I began to collect myself, focus on the alternatives. I could open the kitchen door to the outside and shoo him out that way. This would minimize the short term damage. But knowing raccoons, if he got off that easily, he would be back tomorrow and next week and so on until he got the message. I needed to sacrifice the next few minutes to insure peace over the weeks ahead. He had to know that the Meow Mix and half a tempeh burger and whatever other *benefits* he enjoyed in the kitchen in the last few minutes were not worth the *costs* he would incur in the next few minutes. I wanted him to do his own version of a cost/benefit analysis the next time he paused a moment outside of Pussycat's doorway . . . then shuffle back into the woods. Onward with the economics lesson!

I ran into the living room and snatched up the 19th-century seaman's swabbing broom that Diana bought a few years ago in Lunenburg, Nova Scotia. The broom was a four foot birch limb shaved backward at the end to form a bristle head. It was as rough and scruffy as the raccoon himself. The plan was to chase him around the house for a few minutes, shouting and stomping, rapping him on the behind with the broom as the opportunity arose. He picked up the idea quickly and started racing from room to room. 'Where is the chink that got me into this hellhole!'

I flailed behind, cursing hoarsely, and jabbing him in the rear whenever he stopped long enough to search for a way out. We made quite a ruckus together. Now the whole household was up standing on their beds, wondering how all this would come out.

What happened next enhanced forever my opinion of Pussycat's physical courage. She was watching the chase from the safety of the dining room table, carefully unengaged in all of this potentially dangerous nonsense, her usual disposition toward nonsense and danger. However, as the mad scramble passed from Diana's massage room to my office, across the dining room floor and directly under her, Pussycat took a snarling leap off the table and onto the back of the scurrying raccoon. Hard to say who was most surprised at this, Pussycat herself probably.

Everyone survived. The raccoon soon found his way out and never came back that summer - due to an unexpectedly high cost/benefit ratio, I presume. Needless to say, Pussycat's personal stock went up after that night. She still shrinks from tough-minded mice, but I no longer sneer at her for it.

Not least among our housemates are the local snakes. They visit dependably through the year. I have discovered milk snakes in the basement during all but the coldest months. More surprising was the sizable (4 ? feet long) black rat snake that found its way into the kitchen shortly after I moved in here. She was looking for mice, who were busy with the spiders, that were working on all the flying biota smaller than the phoebes, who sometimes fly in the front door on the lookout for a nesting ledge.

The most uncanny snake was the mystery slider, which we heard slithering around in the hollow walls and ceilings of the place for several weeks one summer, presumably patrolling for mice, but who knows? This sliding in the walls by day and night was spooky. We never saw that snake, but felt that it had us somehow in mind.

Apart from the millipedes and flying ants in May, the luna and polyphemus moths in July, the peepers and gray tree frogs on the windows in August, and the cluster flies all the rest of the year, that pretty much covers the wildlife in our cottage.

November 4 - Temperature in mid 70s, small bats flying about pond; Wood frog singing; Grouse drumming

Out of Season

This evening is exceptionally warm for November, exciting all the tactile senses. It is a night made for adventure. When Diana gets home from work, she suggests we take an after-dark walk to Ackert Bridge.

The air is soft and sensuous as a summer evening, made more lush by knowing this is November and not June. The nearly full moon rises as we walk along the lane, brightening the forest all about and dimming further our uncertain sense of time. Breaths of warm air caress our cheeks from miles or months away.

Times like these beg for foolery, so fool we do, skipping down the lane and singing songs of childhood, made up along the way. The illusion is so good that we expect fireflies at the bridge and are surprised when they fail to appear.

On the way back to the house, Diana confesses:

"It's funny. I don't like to leave the house when I'm settled in, but once I'm out walking, I hate to go back in."

We shamble about the front yard, waiting for an inspiration, some way to enlarge upon the languorous evening. Diana brightens:

"I know, we could have dinner out here on the picnic table."

We often eat a late meal here on the front lawn in spring and summer, but always under a fading remnant of daylight. Moonlight dinners have other connotations. How many Americans have walked out of their house and had a full-moon dinner in the middle of the woods?

"Let's do it!" I am enthusiastic. "Our first moonlit dinner."

Tropical air piles wildly out of the southwest while we eat our soup and toast. Our senses are drawn into the bright-lit nighttime scene of the front yard. The world seems crackling with electric activity, the wind-tossed leaves rustle against the sensitized surfaces of a night out of season.

This rush of warm air keeps the temperature in the 70's well into the evening and we find it pleasant to linger over dinner in our shirts. Diana comes up with another idea:

"Let's sleep out tonight, Sweetie."

"Great idea!" We'll do it.

Diana slips out the mattress and sleeping bags from the truck camper and arranges everything in a grassy part of the lawn that affords the best view of the moon, now climbing in the eastern night-sky. This moon is bright. Lying on our backs, we find ourselves squinting at the lunar radiance as we might at the full summer sun.

A small bat flits overhead and a moment later I feel a drop of moisture on my cheek; the first time in my life I've been smitten by bat droppings. We laugh at the earthy novelty.

"You know what?" Diana begins. "We only see the *real* sky at night. It's hidden by the daytime brightness of the sun." We watch on, looking at the real sky.

The clouds change gradually from high, racing fragments to low, thick masses, but all of them are translucent to the bright night light and create a rich variety of lunar halos.

"Where do they come from?" D asks about the halos.

"Ice crystals in the clouds. They refract the moonlight as it passes through them."

"So it's freezing up there!" She marvels at the incongruity. Despite the tropical evening here below, these nearest clouds are traveling in sub-freezing streams of air.

The shapes, colors, and tones of the halos unfold second by second in the rapidly moving display above us. Sprawled out under our sleeping bags, we watch and say little more.

The quieting wind hushes the leaves to a whisper. In the fields we hear crickets now and from Amasa Martin's swamp a peeper or two. Foxes bark at an unimaginable distance. Providing a ground under these night melodies is the distant rumbling of Valli Falls, carrying seeds and spores and eggs to downstream pools. And with this living music in our ears, we drift off to luxuriant sleep.

November 5 - Green heron flying over pond; Chickadee roosting in flying squirrel tree

Plenty

One of my favorite spots to hang out in the Sanctuary is the topmost rock in the sawtooth ridge of sandstone that makes up the Peninsula. From here I can look down on both arms of the pond and watch ducks and bass, muskrats and mink going about their business unawares. I can also look out over the canopy of the nearby forest, across the bottomlands formed by Black Creek, and all of the movement of life that thrives here. Sometimes I lie back and let my eyes sweep around the horizon. Of all the lookouts in the Sanctuary the Peninsula ridge gives me the best sense of "big sky," the expansive feeling of spaciousness one gets everywhere on the Great Plains.

Plant life here is spare. It's a tough place to live. A few yards below the crest of the ridge pockets of windblown clay and silt have collected, enough to support a few white pines and chestnut oaks, survivor species that loom over the rocks. But up here the wind and rain allow little soil to stay; water runs off this stony slope as it runs off pavement. A few crustose lichens cling to the bare rock, but not much else survives in this harsh micro-habitat . . . except black birch.

Black birch is called an opportunistic species because of this ability to flourish on sites where most plants fail, places like a road cut or the top of the Peninsula. Here the birch seeds fall into rock cracks packed with a few cubic inches of dirt, take root, and tough it out over the next few years of drought, baking sun, hard freezes, and whistling winds. In some cases the sapling appears not to be bedded in any soil at all, so small and hidden is its base of support.

The lack of soil makes for puny trees that have trouble producing seed. In good years and in good soil fall is the time of year when the female flowers of birches mature on woody cones, or strobiles. These strobiles are brown, about an inch long, and made up of numerous tiny three pronged scales which enclose the winged seeds. After the leaves fall, the whole cone begins to disintegrate, letting the wind take the scales where it will. We find seeds sprinkled the length and breadth of the pond ice, when we skate in late December.

Scant soil also means small moisture reserves, so these trees are under continual water stress. They remain small and are always older than they look. For instance, one of the larger birches on the ridge-top is about eight feet high with a five-foot spread, less than two inches in diameter at its base, and has twenty annual rings. This particular tree is rooted in a protected crevice behind the highest point of rock on the Peninsula.

Sitting on this point of rock, I notice how well furnished with seed cones this black birch is despite its poor footing. How many potential birch trees are on this small tree? I decide to gauge the number of seeds it has produced this year.

I estimate the number of strobiles on the tree by the process of successive mental halving: cutting the tree in half with my eye, halving that half, and that, and that, until I end with a manageable piece whose cones I can easily count. The total for the tree is 1,100. I then pick apart a couple of typical strobiles and come up with a average of 120 seeds per strobile. Multiplying the two estimates tells me about 132,000 seeds have grown on this scrawny, eight-foot black birch. This year. Just for the sake of coming up with a number, I assume this is an average year, that the tree is similarly productive in other years. Barring disasters, the tree should remain fruitful for the next ten years at least, during which time it will produce well over one million seeds.

What do I make of all these dry numbers? The message is that mother earth is teeming with seed. Her womb gushes forth plenty. It's frightening to dwell on.

November 8 - Four wood ducks over pond; High-bush blueberry around pond now turning scarlet

Living the Arboreal Life

This morning Diana and I have decided to do our morning meditation in the front yard, facing the rising sun. In the warm summer months we often spent this quiet time sitting in picnic chairs turned toward the eastern hill. Today is warm again; the air is soft and hazy perhaps for the last time. And so, for one last time, we sit outside before breakfast, close our eyes, and quiet our minds amid the heady, sensuous odors of autumn.

The sounds of a fall morning surround us: chickadees and woodpeckers natter somewhere in the air above while the ubiquitous "potato chip" birds loop their querulous cries from tree to tree. We barely hear the hushed flip-flapping of the doeskin leaves on what kind of trees? . . . perhaps behind us. But the sound itself is unlocatable, like a soft rainfall pattering all about. Nothing is where it seems or what.

We open our eyes again and peer about at the world of yellow goldfinches and quaking aspens rooted in the old hotel ruins . . . Diana begins slowly:

"Look at that tree" nodding at the shagbark hickory on the other side of the lawn, "it knows exactly how to be . . and just does it. No 'Who am I?' or 'Why all this?' Why can't we be like that?"

We talk some more and get up to look at the aspen leaves that have been drumming soft accompaniment to our meditation. I show Diana why they are flapping so gaily: the stem, flattened vertically, allows the leaf to flutter freely back and forth in the faintest of breezes, thus "quaking" aspen. A faint breeze comes up now and D holds a leaf pinched between her outstretched ring and little fingers, letting the air play with this new extension of herself. The minute quivering of the leaf delights her and she urges me to try. Just then the wind dies and only the topmost leaves of the aspen continue to wave a little. We stand with leaves tucked between stretched fingers and watch the skies patiently. Slowly a slight stirring, the air freshens, and one by one the leaves around us begin to tremble. Our leaves begin to shiver too, back and forth, tugging at the skin of our clasping fingers with the tiniest impulses, this way and that. For a moment we are quaking aspen trees.

November 9 - Fifty+ juncos in front yard; First heavy snow of season; Snowy tree cricket song on Peninsula

The Voices of Trees

A week ago as I was walking along the lane by the pond over-flow, I was brought up short by screams coming from Black Creek, screams of young children. They were not cries of terror, but shrieks of merriment. I stood on the bridge for a few moments guessing where the children were and who they might be. I had difficulty locating the screams: they came to me up the draw only intermittently, when the wind blew strongly and the wind-song itself half succeeded in drowning them out. This fact should have been clue enough, but I still strained to make sense of it all. Only on my way back, again at this point on my path, did I solve the mystery.

There were no children scampering along Black Creek, there were not even screams, despite the evidence of my ears. A hundred feet downstream from the overflow a dying red maple had fallen against a tall, thin white oak and was scraping off patches of its bark with every passing buffet of wind. The screams came from this rubbing contact of the two trees.

The voices of forest trees are one of the constants of forest life, so much so that we no longer hear them. For being "dumb" life, trees have a great variety of voices:

a) crashing, when part or whole hits the ground;

b) rubbing, one branch or trunk against another, which pro-duces all sorts of wailing, whining, moaning, and groaning. . . and gay yelping as I now discover;

c) soughing in the wind, which also comes in many forms: sighing and murmuring, whistling and whispering, susurrus rustling;

d) interior creaking and ticking of trunks bending in the wind; and finally,

e) the sucking noise of trees whose bark is breached in the spring.

This is a partial list of tree music that I've heard and registered. The questions remain: What have I heard and not registered? What haven't I heard at all?

November 13 - Lone turkey track on Fennell Trail; Skim of ice on temporary woodland pools; Flock of 25 dawn geese over pond

Dawn Geese

At dawn we are awakened by the muffled ruckus of Canada geese who set down last night on the pond, a resting place on their long way from the far North to the far South. Lying in bed, I hear them take to the air and I estimate that twenty-five of them now wheel above the tree tops and circle for height, experimenting a little with directions before they strike out again southward.

We rarely see these late visitors to the pond. They set down evenings, when we are making too much noise ourselves, or late at night, when we are asleep. We become aware of them, if at all, only as they leave at dawn through winter mists over the open pond.

These are different geese than our companions of spring and summer, who trust us to feed their young. They are also different from the earlier migrants that we see forming neat, purposeful arrowheads across the October afternoon skies. These winter visitors come to us as twilight skeins of honking, rather than flesh and feather. I call them dawn geese.

November 22 - Ice completely covered pond this a.m. for first

Birds of the Night Ice

Eric, Diana's eighteen-year-old son, and I worked this afternoon on the woodpile. I sawed and he split with the ax. We wanted to bring in enough firewood for the coming week, when neither of us will have much spare time. Eric is home for a month from his school in Massachusetts to do an internship at the YWCA Battered Women's Services.

After we stacked a good-sized load in the wood stall next to the kitchen, we turned our attention to the handle of the sledge that cracked the other day. I showed Eric the time-honored method of getting a broken wooden handle out of a steel tool, by reaming with a drill until the head slips off the way it went on. This sledge was particularly well attached, it was dark before we got the new handle affixed.

We walk down to the pond in the twilight to put the noise of sawing, splitting, and drilling out of our ears. Last night was exceptionally cold; a skin of ice now covers the pond from edge to edge, an unexpected sight in late November. We decide to test the ice at the south end, where the winter sun is shaded by the surrounding forest and where the ice will be thickest. Eric bets that the ice won't hold me, and I half agree with him. November ice shouldn't hold a bird, but of course I try it anyway. Holding on to the wispy black birch branches hanging over the end of the pond, I inch out over the ice. I feel the surface give slightly under the tentative weight I apply to my forward foot, but the ice does not break. This is encouraging, so I slide out a few more inches. No cracks. Another foot . . . two feet. Nothing. The ice holds. It would be no great disaster if it didn't; the pond is a few inches deep here; I would get a boot full of wet muck at worst. Directly in front of me the ice darkens, and I guess that it becomes significantly thinner at that edge. I reach the toe of my boot over the color change and three or four craze marks race out from the point of contact. I guessed right; this is as far as I go tonight.

I consider myself a bit of an authority on crashing through the ice. What I lack in theoretical grasp, I make up for in drama: One warm March afternoon twelve years ago, I was walking across the ice of Mohonk Lake to take the weekly temperature readings at the point of maximum depth. I was carrying about twenty-five pounds of electronic gear and thermometer cable. As I passed a south-facing headland of rock, I felt the ice underfoot get a little rubbery and in a flash I was in the water up to my neck. The time scale of the event allowed me to be shocked rather than frightened. I summoned the presence of mind to put the gear I was holding back up on the ice and slide it to safety. Then, gripping I don't know what, I hoisted myself out of the icy waters and walked back to shore. This experience has given me a certain perspective on thin ice accidents: when the ice breaks, the victim has as much control as a falling stone; but getting out is easier than it looks.

Back on our pond Eric and I check the state of freezing. Leaning back from the dark ice, I punch a small hole in it with my boot. The piece I knock out is about one-quarter inch thick. Eric, who is considerably bigger than I am, manages to dash a hole in the heavier white ice that was whipped up here by last night's cold wind. This piece proves to be well over a half-inch thick. We marvel at one night's work.

The sky has darkened now without a moon, but a few stars define the corners of the half-mile sheet of ice in front of us. We quietly watch the night sky's silent descent.

While we watch, vaguely, from overhead, comes an eerie tinkling, a silvery, continuous knell. Birds? This delicate music comes not from any one corner of the sky, but all over at once, the kind of experience that begs to be verified. I turn to Eric. Yes, he hears it too. I listen for the telltale passage from one side of the night to the other, but I cannot detect any such movement. I still think they are birds, a flock somewhere overhead, perhaps pine siskins who often call tinklingly to each other in flight. But why on a November night and why so difficult to locate or track? Eric does not think we are listening to birds, but he too is at a loss to name it. As surprisingly as the music comes, it goes.

We return from our rapt attention to the surrounding night. We chip off pieces of ice and skitter them down the lake into the dark. They pass from our eyes, but not from our ears. As the little shards of ice whiz over the length of the seemingly endless pond, they send back a jingling sound, ice on ice, a pealing from some tiny world to which the whole pond reverberates. Is this the sound of our birds? No, not quite right. Too mechanical, too directional.

Eric and I talk about the feelings this night engenders. Eric confides he has an overwhelming desire to take a running start from the side of the pond and whoosh out upon the ice, as far as it will take him. He knows it would not be far. All the same. I admit I have no such need. I am content to *listen* to thin ice. I tell him the story of my Mohonk plunge through the ice, probably not for the first time. We hark again to the mystery sound. Not now, not yet.

We return to work on other corners of our ice patch, the one we are allowed to stand on for this night. We break loose heftier pieces of ice and sling them across the surface of the pond, experimenting with the uncanny sound effects. Eric is better at breaking the ice than I am. As he drives the heel of his boot into the edge of the ice mass, the shock travels down the half-mile pond and back, ringing hundreds of tiny ice bells at once, a marvelous chime of the whole lake shivering under one small blow. Is this the song of the birds? Closer, but no.

Taken by the spirit, Eric does a little dance on a flagstone-shaped piece of ice made slick by the water from the holes he has kicked around it. I hum the show tune that goes with 'the ol' sof' shoe'. It feels good to keep moving as the cold air seeps down from the hills around us. I show him my "Hey, Ab . . . *bott*!" slipping and sliding routine from an old vaudeville comedy team he's not likely to have seen. He can't believe I used to do this when I was alone in the woods in my cabin in Pennsylvania. It's true, I did.

After this moment of hilarity, we are suddenly quiet and once more the spectral ice birds breathe by. We listen again intently, our eyes fixed on each other in surmise. But the birds do not reveal themselves more clearly now than before. Perhaps this is the wind playing with the ice (although it seems windless), perhaps it is our own laughter vibrating in sympathy with the pond (although we are now silent), perhaps they really are birds of the night ice, as I imagined. We don't know.

November 25 - Most of ice on pond melts with light rain; Mists dancing over ice film, waves waltzing under

Mists, Over and Under

This morning, while driving out along the lane in a hurry, I noticed a late fall mist riding toward me across the pond. Despite some appointment that I was already late for, I took the time to get out of the car and watch a little more closely by the side of the pond. The fragments of mist were parading across the water in formation, like a company of soldiers, each squad buffeted from behind by an easily imagined puff of air. I watched rank after rank materialize at the far shore, march across the pond, and disband into the rocks below me.

Then I noticed something else. The night had left a paper thin film of ice extending from the near shore a few meters out. As each imaginary squad of mist filed from water to ice, a companion wave passed under the film, sending a slight kink in the sheet in perfect lock-step with the mist above. I tried to picture how this kink would look to a fish below: it should appear as a moving band of hazy light. Very mist-like. So the fish also have their mists to watch, mists that may distract them, cause them to pause a moment as they speed by, pursuing the business of fish.

November 30 - A warm moist day, the woods are full of jays and crows

A Corvid Note

I have a vague impression that jays and crows, members of the family *Corvidae*, are more than usually present on warm, moist days that follow a span of wintry weather, days like today. I have distilled this impression from hundreds of such days. Like everyone else who watches the natural world around them, I have thousands, millions of vague impressions like this. They do not come from the written almanac as much as from countless daily, hourly observations . . . when I look up from cutting wood or pause a moment before getting in the truck and notice, for instance, that the woods are full of jays and crows on this warm, moist day.

It happened again today. I saw more jays and crows this morning than I have seen in the past two weeks put together. They are everywhere: crows streaming overhead in long, raucous files; gangs of jays in the sumacs, like corner bully boys just itching to beat up on somebody; both groups badgering an imagined owl in the hemlocks across the pond; all of them screeching at the top of their lungs.

Where do the corvids come from on days like this? There are only a few possible answers: 1) A warm day in December engenders them. Implausible. 2) The southerly flow of air brings them tens or even hundreds of miles from more pleasant climates where they are this raucous every day. More plausible. I'll bet published studies exist on this sort of short-term migration. 3) These birds are here the whole time and until now were not stimulated by the right combination of temperature and humidity to make all the fuss and racket they are making today. This seems probable. The only question remaining is: Why should only a *few* answers be possible? Why only possible answers?

December 7 - Three different flocks of winter birds between house and road; Pond completely frozen this morning, except for 50 foot patch

Wind, the Broom

Last night the combination of sinking temperatures and brisk winds painted a curious design on the surface of the half-open pond. As I stand above it on the Peninsula, the waters appear to have been swept in tight circular arcs, by some assiduous pond sweeper, whose broom had a freezing touch. The burnished effect is overwhelming to the eye:

thousands of tiny, momentary whirling motions caught for a day; millions of minute gestures of tidying. The sum of it is tumultuous confusion.

The wind is the pond's broom; the effects are visible at my feet. The wind is the forest's broom and the mountains' broom, too; I imagine these effects above and around me. And the world's broom; I can barely think that.

I am grateful, gazing now down at the pond, that I can't see the work the world's broom does.

December 9 - A warm, moist winter day, no crows or jays; Accipiter dashes through the front yard

Hawks at the Bird Feeder

Today Eric and I finished bucking the logs in the back yard, making them ready for the wood splitter on Sunday. Late in the afternoon, with the yellow winter sun hanging over the Black Creek bluffs, we took a break and shared our Paul Bunyan fantasies, playing the real off the imagined. He started swearing in French-Canadian and I bellowed toward the house for a 'stack of flapjacks an' plenny of 'em'. We tossed a few maple rounds back over our heads to get them out of the way. More hot cursing and bulging muscles in tattered tee shirts.

We've both seen woodsmen's carnivals, where professional lumberjacks compete at tricky and energetic timber-felling tasks. His favorite is the precision chopping contest, in which an upright the size of a telephone pole is cut down so carefully that the top of it drives in a peg thirty feet away. Mounting the log I had just finished cutting, I re-enacted the speed chopping work-out, in which a row of mountain men astride three-foot diameter logs whale away until one of them chops clean through. It was a sight to behold! For a few blazing minutes the air was filled with skull-sized wood chunks, the setting sun flickered against them flying above the woodpile.

Back to work. But we could barely move around the last logs now, we had become so brawny with the tall timberjack tales. As we were marveling over our new muscles, a hawk flew by. I stopped Eric in mid-sentence and pointed. It was an accipiter, a sharpshin or Cooper's hawk, a young one, I guessed, because of the light brown streaking all over its body. This bird was doubtlessly a feeder watcher, too. And our front porch feeder birds were no doubt watching him. As a matter of fact, I looked up at that moment because I heard the chickadees roused to sudden excitement. As I raised my eyes, the hawk came swinging past the front door, glided silently across the yard, and pitched into the hemlocks across the pond.

The local winter bird hawks - kestrel falcons and accipiters - take regular whirls at our feeder birds. As a hawk wheels into sight, a chickadee or titmouse will spot him and give the characteristic, high, piercing warning cry. The whole porchful of birds dashes into the bushy white-cedar. The hawk's only chance is to intercept one of them between the bird feeder and the bush. Maybe the bush is too close to the porch, because I've never seen a successful snatch at this feeding station.

The story was different at my cabin in Pennsylvania where I saw several birds nabbed next to the feeder. The bushes must have been too far away there. The most dramatic grab occurred one late-winter afternoon as I was standing in front of my cabin, feeding chickadees sunflower seeds from my hand. Suddenly, as if at an invisible signal, all of the birds around me screeched and darted in all directions. Before I could look around to see what the problem was, a hawk, almost brushing my still outstretched right hand, shot by me at full tilt, and, in one sweeping gesture, knocked a hapless chickadee out of the air, picked the bird up from the snow with his talons, and darted into the woods. I hardly had time to let my jaw drop in astonishment, so sudden and explosive was the move, so quickly was it all over.

I have been eye-witness to several other attacks of the same kind. They are a regular if infrequent part of forest life. You have to be out in the woods a good deal to witness the marauding of top-of-the-food chain predators like hawks and weasels, but it's worth the time, if only to give you an awed sense what slam-bang lives they lead and how desperately their survival is measured in centimeters and milliseconds.

December 11 - Waves working a hole in the ice of the pond

Natural History of a Woodpile

This morning we started splitting the wood we've collected over the last three weeks, using the log-splitter from the rental shop in Port Ewen. In the early morning Diana and I lugged the smaller logs around, later in the day Eric came back from New York City to help me finish it off. Depending on the amount of wood to split, we always make a bit of a ceremony out of the event.

In my early years at the Sanctuary, I cut all my own wood from our lands and stuck pretty much to logs under ten inches in diameter for reasons of handling as well as splitting. In those days, any splitting was done with an ax or with a maul and wedges. Recently, under the pressure of other obligations, I've gotten more of my wood from outside sources, or, as happened this year, from outside woodsmen who worked inside the Sanctuary. These arrangements have meant larger logs that require heavy-duty power splitting. This year was the extreme case: after we bucked all the logs, the back yard was covered and in places stacked high with tire-sized rounds of oak and maple.

Wood-splitting of any sort is not easy work. Even with a gasoline engine expending most of the energy, a great deal of monotonous lifting, positioning, and stacking of wood is required. This is hard on the lower back - and boring. Happily, the work supplies the very relief it needs with a steady stream of woodpile flora and fauna. Keeping an eye out for the life in this stack helps us to plug away through a log-splitting day.

First, I will say what we haven't found today. We haven't uncovered any of the vertebrate animals that we frequently do when we lift a log or jumble of logs that have lain together on the ground for weeks or months. Usually we spot one salamander in this pile, a quick red-backed or a fat marbled salamander. I find it hard to believe they spend winters in so exposed a spot. On the other hand, I must confess my experience with salamanders this fall leaves me less confident than I was last year how and where they overwinter. Garter and ring-necked snakes are other cold-blooded vertebrates that we've uncovered in past years while rolling away a log, but none today. Early December may be too late in the season for them.

We've seen no white-footed mouse nests today. Come fall, these little woodland rodents love to build nests in the labyrinthine passages of a tightly packed wood pile. The first clue to their presence is a frantic dash for safety by the mother from a suspiciously dense cluster of grass, hair and wood fragments. This is a real leave taking; she doesn't look back. She will not fight for her young, nor will she endanger herself with some feint, as a grouse or killdeer will do. Somehow she knows that more will come like those she is leaving behind, better save herself for another litter.

We turn up no shrews or moles in our work in the woodpile today. I believe these small mammals are not over-wintering in the stack like the salamanders or nesting like the mice, but are simply on their way from here to there. One year I surprised a long-tailed weasel working in our jumble of wood, or rather he surprised me . . . my impression is that weasels *live* in a state of surprise. I do not look for weasels in the woodpile.

Another surprise are birds. Sparrows and other ground-feeding birds will secrete themselves in woodpiles on cold, windy days. I think they roost there overnight. I've seen house and winter wrens in the wood too, but we see no birds here today.

So far, it sounds like a pretty dull day, but this is not the case. What the woodpile denies us in vertebrate diversity, it more than makes up for in all other kinds. Insects in all of their forms provide us with a lively show. One of the first maple rounds broken open on the splitter disgorges carpenter ants all over the ground, the machine, and us. These are large, black, wood-loving ants that play as much havoc with local frame houses as termites do.

Carpenter ants are oily and ominous-looking. They often serve as models for monsters in C-rated science-fiction films. Here they are less threatening. They rouse and stretch themselves slowly into the abrupt opening around them, waving their antennae and looking startled in the dim way that over-wintering ants can look startled. A moment ago they were nestled deep inside a moist, rank log; a wrenching thud; suddenly sky and biting cold air; there is no way back. The trauma of birth.

In the course of the afternoon we open another half-dozen rounds filled with carpenter ants. Each time they tumble out over the scene in bemused confusion. We brush them off our clothes as they land. As slow as they are, they still have a sharp bite. Most of the logs have only the wingless workers and soldiers, but one or two contain the winged, reproductive castes, males and females. In warmer seasons, we've seen these take off in mating flights. Eric wonders aloud whether that business still goes on in cold weather like this. His answer comes in the next carpenter ant log, chock full of eggs.

We find other ants in other logs: a smaller black type with wings and a red variety, both species unknown to us. All of them seem stunned to be so roughly visited in the middle of their long winter night. Eric uncovers new treasure in a half-decayed wedge of sugar maple.

"More winged ants," he announces.

"No, termites! Look how pale they are and fat-waisted." They are easy to confuse with winged ants, but termites are not hymenopterans like bees and ants, they are in the order *Isoptera*. Termites belong to the guild of decomposers, recycling dead and dying plant material back to simpler chemicals that can be used by new generations of plants. In the tropics where living plants turn over rapidly, they are an even more important component of the woodland ecosystem.

"I saw this study a while ago," I tell Eric, "that showed termites make a lot of the methane in the atmosphere, digestion products from wood . . ."

"Termite farts?" He doesn't know whether to believe this or not.

"Right. Very powerful in the chemistry of the atmosphere, the balance of things, it's true."

We pause, pleasantly diverted from the tedium of wood splitting to acknowledge the global significance of termite flatulence. Truly the good of the earth hangs on small matters.

In the course of the day we find several cocoon-like pupal cases buried deep in the wood. We inspect the niches from which these larvae fall and find they are at the end of long passageways snaking from the bark deep into the interior of the wood. We guess that the insects, whatever they are, make use of natural fractures in the wood to gain entrance, and are exposed by our work because the wood splits along these fractures. Most of them are dark red to brown, an inch long, and have loose threads straggling from the pupal case, like moths. Also like moths, the pupa has wing-shaped surfaces over its back, and writhes under our exploratory handling. We wonder if these are indeed moths, some variety that overwinters as pupae deep in dying trees. The best way to find out is to isolate the pupa in a protected enclosure, as near to its natural conditions as possible, and see who emerges next spring. But the press of today's duties allow us no time for engrossing experiments like this.

By far the most abundant of the insect forms that we meet in the wood are the beetles. Beetles in all of their life stages have an affinity for bark and interior wood, particularly the wood of dead or decaying trees. A glance at the index of a field guide for beetles gives a hint of this trait: wounded-tree beetle, flattened bark beetle, ship timber beetle, metallic wood-boring beetle, long jointed bark beetle, bark gnawing, powder-post, and sawyer beetles. Most of the beetles that we uncover as we work are in the form of egg, or of larva, the intermediate stage between egg and adult. Larvae come in all forms, from fat, sleek grubs to wire-like worms to paper-thin wraiths that slide between bark and tree.

We see a good assortment of them today, but we can identify only a few. Beetles are one of the most common of the earth's life-forms. Every time I see a list of living things, the ante goes up on the number of beetle species. The guess now is more than a million and some will say this number is much too conservative.

The taxonomy of our beetles today is simpler than for the rest of the world: we find bark beetles and deep wood beetles. The latter bore tunnel galleries deep into the sapwood and heartwood of the tree, passageways no wider than the larva. These channels are filled with the digested residue of their chewing, called "frass." We open chocks of wood so riddled with this tunnel work they look like they have been blasted with a shotgun at ten feet. If the insect chewing is recent, the tubes of elastic frass might still be sticking out the passageways.

"It feels like rubber and smells like fungus," he says with a wry face.

"They come in different colors, too," I add, looking over the last few specimens, "cream, dead white, brown and violet." We take a motorman's holiday, splitting a promising specimen into thin shingles. No beetles.

We see many other forms of tunnel work, usually passageways that slowly widen from narrow to fat as the larva feeds and grows in girth. Every different size and shape of tunnel in each tree species is probably evidence for a separate species of beetle, but our classification system becomes even vaguer here.

Our most exciting find of the day is the beetle "sunburst," a design etched on the sapwood under the bark of sugar maple. We expose them again and again while splitting these chunks. The heart of the sunburst is a short, conical passageway that ends in a chamber an inch or so high and a half inch wide. From this chamber minute tunnels ray out symmetrically in graceful arcs. The whole foot square design reminds us of a primitive icon of the sun. I tell Eric my interpretation of this design: "Some adult insect has eaten her way to this point in the sapwood and laid her eggs; the adult moves on or, who knows? - maybe dies there as a nesting substrate for her young; the young hatch and eat diametrically away from the nest, making the sunburst."

"Sounds good," Eric concurs.

This image and its explanation raises a possibility I've never thought of: beetles exist whose entire life cycle, from generation to generation, takes place within the protective layers of long-lived trees. They never breathe fresh air, never see the sky. Upon reflection it makes sense that such insects live and thrive; I just haven't imagined them before. But the image gives me long pause from the drudgery of splitting: buried inside the hundreds of dead and dying sugar maple trees on these hills rising all around us are thousands of bark burrowing beetles who know nothing of the sun except what is spelled out in their racial memories, in their molecules. This secret is expressed in the very act of entering life: the sunburst gallery. Only on one level is this a reproductive pattern. On another, this is a dark celebration of the sun by animals that never see it.

We resume work on the chugging log-splitter. We see the work of many other bark beetles, tracery of all sorts on the sapwood. Each pattern is distinctive, many suggest a message we can't quite decipher. They invite divination, but we have no time. This pile has to be split before supper.

Underneath the logs and rounds that have filled the backyard for months, we find other phyla and classes of fauna. Fat, pale, juicy earth worms and slimmer, quicker red worms wriggle uncomfortably as we suddenly remove the lid on their world. Sowbugs and centipedes and pale larvae of unknown lineage crowd in the same space. We begin to wonder what can be so appealing about spending one's life under a log. We promise ourselves to think about it at some future leisure moment.

Pallid versions of green shoots lie twisted in mats under these logs alongside of insects and their kin. Fungi of all sorts thrive here too, in the soil and on the wood. We have been studying an assortment of fungi all afternoon, simply in watching the rounds break on the splitter. White, black, purple, orange, green, and blue fungi of subtle delicacy have passed through our hands, to ooohs and aaahs of our appreciation. Flat crustose fungi, which seem no different from the wood except for their color; scaly or powdery fungi attacking the inner bark; black fungal strings that appear to run the length of the tree; green, leafy fungi that may have gotten on the tree by subterfuge; slime molds that cover sticks well advanced in decay; flesh-colored bracket fungi that seem like ears listening for the end; black and purple gelatinous molds that look like the end itself. All these change agents pass in succession as we carve the wood from pies into slices. The fungi have a more radical breakdown in mind than we do. If given the time, these fungi will reduce our woodpile to the airs, waters, and minerals whence it came fifty or one hundred years ago. Fungi head up the forest recycling team.

The most intriguing fungal form that we find today - is it a fungus at all, we're not sure - are irregular, black, pencil-thin lines etched into the heartwood of many of the older ashes, maples, and oaks. For any particular cross-section of wood, the line appears as a closed loop. We discover with a little fooling around on the splitter that the loops close in three dimensions as well. Which leaves us with an irregular surface of black, paper-thin fungus enclosing a volume of wood that looks no different from the wood outside the surface. The mystery remains, the wood-splitting goes forward.

Many well-intentioned people believe they are doing nature a favor, minimizing the damage to "life" by cutting only dead trees. I used to believe that myself, until I started cutting on my own and watched who crawled out of the wood. Cutting and burning one perfectly healthy tree kills one perfectly healthy tree and a handful of commensals. Cutting one desperately diseased tree, or worse, a long dead tree, and putting it in the stove wipes out thousands of plants and animals that have finally found the tree useful. Life never had it so good as it does in a dead tree.

Today we split about three and one-half cords, much of it brimming with life. Throughout the day we made a half-hearted effort to put back the pupae that fell out of their woody niches and stack the chunks chock full of carpenter ants so that the black, slimy creatures were not hopelessly exposed. But we don't dare measure our accomplishment for the day in number of lives saved. We pause in our work well after dark and sit wearily debating what to do with the half a cord of rounds still on the ground, a few hundred or possibly a few thousand more lives. We decide to give them a temporary reprieve, not, alas, for their sake, but for ours.

December 14 - Aerial "hoppers" still flying, south side of house, but no more dragonflies

Dragonflies Not Revisited

While sitting in my upstairs study this warm afternoon and looking at the sun-drenched back yard, I spot one or two of the flying insects whose habit is to ascend vertically a foot or so and drop suddenly along the same line. They seem to do this continuously, once per second, for as long as I watch them. I found them dancing in the backyard by the thousands earlier this fall, rising and falling out of synchrony. This behavior may be related to mating, rather than feeding or maintenance. I imagine a female lodged in the grass, eyeing the proceedings narrowly. I don't even know the name of this insect.

Flying insects out my window do not normally engage my rapt attention, mid-December cases are an exception. I can't remember when I last saw a flying insect *outside* the house. We support a healthy population in the artificial atmosphere inside the house throughout the winter.

I can think of physical reasons why flying should fall out of favor in the wintertime. For one thing, flight requires a light flimsy body with a high surface to weight ratio, exactly the configuration that favors high heat loss as well. Moving rapidly through the air causes more heat to be lost, because no insulating layer of air is allowed to form. Maintaining body heat is the great challenge that winter poses to all living things. In view of these heat-loss problems associated with flying, it's a wonder anything is left to fly through the December air.

As I reflect on the steady decline of flying things since August, I remember a resolution I made in early May upon spotting last spring's first dragonfly. I wondered then why I spend so little time noting the disappearance of the plants and animals in the fall, whose first appearance in the spring I document so carefully. Things come and things go, but comings are much better attended in my calendar than goings. I remember promising myself at that time that I would watch for the last sign in October of each of the types that appeared in May, singling out the dragonflies for special attention.

October and November have come and gone. I remember now one other thing: I bet myself in May (in that under-the-counter, self-defeating way) that, come November, I wouldn't have the presence of mind to deliver on this promise. I didn't.

December 18 - Fox track along entrance lane; Ice again covering pond, thick enough to walk on; Barred owl at end of lane

Poof!

This afternoon, I patrol the northern perimeter of the Sanctuary: by Slabsides, down Burroughs Drive, and along Ackert Road, the north border of the property. All seems well. That's my essential role here - to check and see that All is Well.

Turning into our lane, I am stopped in my tracks by a light crashing among winter branches above and to my left. By the time I wheel and look, the owl has winged his way across the road, dodges around some hemlock boughs, and lights in a large dead oak one hundred yards away. The two possibilities for a large owl in the Sanctuary are great horned and barred. When the bird flew away from me, I couldn't see the characteristic marks of the head and underparts to decide between them. As it lights in the oak and spins its head to look back, I recognize the round earless head and uniform grey-brown plumage of a barred owl.

Barred owls are the first of their family (the *Strigidae*) that I came to know at my Pennsylvania cabin where I first took interest in things of the woods. The barred is certainly the first owl I *heard* there, as opposed to the first one whose voice fell upon my ears, which no doubt happened much earlier than that. This owl may also be the first one I saw there, although this detail is lost in the daily doings of twenty years ago. Partly for these reasons I think of barred owls as more accessible, less secretive than the other big owls of the eastern woods. Their common call is characteristic of them, the easiest one to teach learners of bird calls: the "eight-hoot," ending with a dropping "aw" sound. "Who cooks for you, who cooks for you all" is the English language version.

These robust forest owls will sing their melody back and forth to each other over a piece of midnight woods for hours at a time, conveying God knows what messages of food, risk, hope, or sadness. The barred owl may have given rise to the expression, "Not worth a hoot," among (so I imagine) New England shopkeepers, who saw fit to say a thing once, and thought the night was a proper time for decent folk to be abed. I long to see the study in an ornithological journal which discloses the complex informational content of these exchanges, perhaps some elaborate pricing system for all the goods of the forest, prices that fluctuate with the market of the night.

Barred owls have a rich repertory of other sounds: squeals, grunts, clacks, screeches, chucks, and yowls. I have a feeling that I haven't heard most of them, the bird surprises me with its new voices so regularly. The most striking of their calls is a barked shriek, "Ker-YEOW!," which, if it explodes near you in the night woods, is guaranteed to tighten the skin on your scalp. I have never succeeded in calling in a barred owl with my imitation of their hooting, as I have great horned, screech, and saw-whet owls. I did once engage the severe attention of a female barred owl, who came and silently perched a few feet away from my head as I picked her three chicks from their nest, one at a time, and banded their legs.

Since I am far enough away not to be a threat, this owl across Ackert Road has momentarily lost interest in me and is examining the forest floor below his perch. I know another way to get the attention of owls and I decide to use this trick on him. I purse my lips and suck in air, emitting a squealing squeak that reminds me of baby mice whose nest has just been opened. Apparently it reminds owls of something like that, they are irresistibly drawn to the sound. At this, the barred owl turns sharply toward me and cranes forward, angling his head this way and that to verify with his eyes what his ears are telling him. His neck thrusts toward me, but his talons grimly grip the branch. He doesn't need a verbal language to express his inner dissonance; his entire body conveys the conflict: get the mice, avoid the human. I relieve his tension by saying "Poof!" and off he flits, deeper into the hemlock woods, where an honest owl doesn't have to study to separate the mice from the men.

WINTER

December 22 - Winter Solstice, 4:46 a.m.; the ice is not quite here; Pair of brown creepers around back yard maple

Forest Librarians

This afternoon I spotted from my study window a pair of brown creepers in the back yard, one working the maple, the other on the slim red oak behind it. Brown creepers are not rare birds in the Sanctuary, but they are uncommon enough that I take notice when I happen to see one climbing a trunk. Their quiet businesslike habits make them not nearly so obvious as the noisy chickadees, titmice, and nuthatches. In the wintertime I see a creeper here about once a month, usually because one will tag along with a flock of chickadees and their rambunctious kin. Seeing two brown creepers practically on the same tree is unusual for me. My bird memory may be getting mushy, but I can't remember having two of them in the same field of view before today.

Brown creepers are small (five inches from beak to tail) and dainty birds, with finely streaked, bark-colored backs and white bellies, well camouflaged for their principal daytime activity of searching over the vertical surfaces of trees for insects in their various life stages. A creeper conducts this search in a systematic way, starting at the bottom of the trunk and ascending in spirals to a point where she decides she's seen enough of that tree and flies to the base of the next one. I've often wondered whether this strategy maximizes her coverage of the tree per linear foot of travel or per calorie of energy expended, but I'm not enough of a bio-mathematician to figure that out.

The creeper's method seems to make more sense than the chickadee's, who flies about at random, checking this hole and that bark strip, doubtlessly covering the same ground on occasion. But is the creeper approach more sensible than the downy woodpecker's habit of hitching straight up and down a tree or horizontally around it? Spiral foraging gives the creeper a 360° view of the scene and all the possible menaces it holds at every turn of the trunk. She spends less time looking out for bird hawks than the woodpeckers, who are constantly on tenterhooks, expecting at every moment sudden movements in the trees around them.

A striking behavior of creepers is their quiet busyness which contrasts with the boisterousness of other small forest birds that over-winter here in the Northeast. Why are creepers so mum, what's the adaptive value of that? To bring it down to avian economics: What are the costs and benefits of making noise?

On the plus side is sociability: a single bird maintains contact with others of its kind by voice. The immediate advantages have been documented. For instance food is easier to find for a group than for an individual, especially if the food comes in bunches. Also, many pairs of eyes are better than one when predators are skulking about. On the minus side is the obvious exposure to danger that any noise brings. Human beings usually first catch notice of nearby birds by ear rather than by eye. The same is probably true of other predator species. The value-of-noise calculation seems to boil down to sociability vs danger. The solitary creeper seems to have added it all up and opted to keep quiet.

Brown creepers belong to the ecological guild of "bark-glean-ers," birds that feed upon the various life-stages of insects near the sur-faces of trees. Each bark-gleaner has a differently shaped bill, one specialized for its own habit. The kinglets have the tiniest bark-stickers, long enough to collect eggs only on the outermost surfaces. Then come the chickadees who can work their beaks under the smaller pieces of bark, but not so much as the titmice and the nuthatches. The creepers have little sickles for bills, designed to tease out eggs and larvae from under curved bark chunks. Plenty of food is packed in the bark of a for-est, enough to supply the needs of all these different beaks. How they divide it among themselves makes a fascinating study.

Like other birds whose young spend two or three weeks in the nest before they fly and another few weeks with their parents before they function completely on their own, creepers probably have some kind of pair-bonding arrangement in the breeding season, that is, a time when both male and female help out at the nest. This is also a time when they are exceptionally secretive. I've rarely seen a creeper in May and June, although they have been part of the bird life of every place I've lived for the past twenty-five years. Only once did I find a nest: a web of grass and finely shredded fiber lodged behind the out-turned strip of bark on a large shagbark hickory. I found it quite by accident and didn't know what it was until years later, when I began to learn about bird nests.

Creepers have a high, fluting song that is reminiscent of a theme from some Brahms chamber music piece. (The Carolina wren song is straight out of his *Fourth Symphony*.) I heard the creeper song for the first time twelve years ago while trudging up Slide Mountain in the Catskills. Since then I've heard it many times in late spring around Sanctuary Pond. Four or five years ago an unusually large number of creepers started singing in the Sanctuary. Since then the creeper songs have returned to the one or two I used to hear before the explosion. That irruption of creepers is one of the many inexplicable twists in the dynamics of animal populations, puzzles that go unnoticed and unexplained year in and year out.

I have never caught a brown creeper in a banding net or trap. For one thing, they don't seem drawn to the seed and suet that the chickadees and juncos can't resist. Also creepers are behaviorally not predisposed to getting netted. Blue jays, for instance, remind me of town toughs, raucous and rowdy, butting in here and there, always in one kind of trouble or another. I catch a lot of blue jays. A creeper, on the other hand, is more like the town librarian, prim and proper, keeping pretty much to her own tidy little chores, and certainly not likely to be caught hanging upside down in a neighbor's net.

December 24 - The pond ice is soft on the edges, forming pools in the middle

Calls of Distress

This morning I got my annual Christmas great blue heron call. I receive about eight or ten calls per year from Ulster County residents who have some sort of wildlife problem: nestlings falling out of a tree in May, squirrels in the garage in August, bats in the attic in October, or a migratory bird in December that won't migrate. Often the latter turns out to be a great blue heron and it happens around Christmas time.

This caller said a heron has been hanging around her wooded back yard for weeks, feeding in her pond. The pond is now beginning to freeze over, but the heron won't leave. She said the bird can flap its wings, but it doesn't leave the ground; nothing else is obviously wrong with it. In her concern she started feeding hamburger to the big wading bird, until a neighbor pointed out hamburger is not its natural food. Someone else suggested she catch it and ship it off somewhere for rehabilitation. Now she was wondering what to do. This is an old problem: how to convey my version of great blue heron needs in the few minutes that she (or I) is willing to spend on the phone. It calls for distillation.

I quickly told her not to try to catch the heron, no matter what. Legend has it that a great blue heron will defend itself by going for an attacker's eye with its powerful spear-like bill. I don't know if that's true. I've never seen them do it, but I wouldn't volunteer anyone for the experiment. I also gave the caller my five-minute philosophy on wildlife intervention: leave the animal alone unless it is faced with an immediate threat, such as dogs, and in that case, keep the dogs away. Except for such obvious cases, I believe people do more well-intentioned harm than good in jumping to the aid of beleaguered wildlife.

I make this point especially to those who call in the spring with a baby bird they've found under a back yard tree. Should they put it in a wool nest or in one made with shredded paper? Should they dig up their own worms or can they get by with canary food? Many of these people are distressed to hear they should put the bird back where they found it, out of the way of cats.

The problem is that these callers have developed an emotional bond with the animal they want to save and try to implement this concern in human ways: protectiveness, solicitousness, and ministering. Unfortunately, their gestures are usually not appropriate to the animal and are often inimical to its well being. Few people are willing to admit how poorly equipped they are, physically and psychologically, to meet the needs of the blind and featherless nestling they are tenderly holding in their hand. But it is just this tenderness that will evolve to a feeling for birds in general, for other animals and plants, to a caring for life. This too needs to be nurtured.

So, when the woman calls with *her* great blue heron, a kind of bird she never noticed before she awoke one December morning to find it wading lamely in her pond, and when she is troubled enough to ask someone for help, I make an effort to keep her feeling for this beautiful animal intact, but redirect that good will to the best interest of the bird. Everybody is cared for.

December 26 - Many springtails in the snowless south woods; Inchworm dangling from hemlock over lane puts us in mind of a story . . .

A Winter Walk Around Black Creek

This afternoon Diana and I take our "long walk": into the South Woods, around Valli Marsh, through Mario's hay fields, crossing Black Creek twice, and up our lane by the pond. This is one of our favorite strolls. We manage to cover most of the major ecosystems in the neighborhood in two hours. This hike also neatly encompasses the Sanctuary's holdings of Black Creek, a stream that keeps changing as we watch.

Most of the snow is gone from the woods now, only in pro-tected north-facing corners do we find little pockets of it, grey-white from a week's wear. The air has turned cooler after yesterday's reminis-cence of April and the woods have quieted in response. No life seems to be stirring in this corner of the Sanctuary. But as we climb the last ridge before meeting the Shattega Jeep Trail, Diana stops me and points to the dull brown duff between us, the soul of lifelessness.

"Look!"

"Springtails!" The ground is teeming with springtails!

Springtails are minute, primitive insects of the order *Collembola*. They get their popular name from a fork-like appendage under their abdomen, which they trigger periodically to spring a centimeter or so into the air, ten to twenty times their own length. They are known in our household for their defiance of winter. We usually see them on the warmer days of mid-winter, swarming by the thousands in small pools of melting snow. A closer look at a dirty pool of meltwater at that sea-son often shows the "dirt" springing vigorously about.

Despite the lack of snow in these woods we find thousands of springtails in a small patch of leaves directly underfoot. And now that we know how to look, we find many similar patches round about.

We get down on our hands and knees and move close, to sepa-rate the hops of individual springtails from the general mass of hopping. I hold my breath and catch the high-pitched thrumming of thousands of tiny tails popping off and plopping back on the dry leaf litter of the forest floor.

"Listen!" I urge D. "And we thought it was a lifeless day!"

"What's the point of all this springing around?" she wonders.

"It looks to me like a substitute for wings. Springtails don't have wings," I guess wildly.

"Maybe they're jumping up and down to mash up the leaves." Diana ventures. Since springtails are forest micro-scavengers, reducing fallen leaves to soil, this guess is not as crazy as it sounds.

We agree it would be difficult to test this new idea, so we get up and continue on our way. One thing is clear: we would not run out of springtails for the experiment.

Next, we check on the beavers who have refurbished the lodge above the Valli Road Bridge. They are doing well. The lodge is now plastered even tighter with bottom mud. The underwater cache of tree-tops seems to be growing quickly. We note the sorts and sizes of trees they have been felling this past month.

At the Ackert Bridge we stop, as we always do, to hang over the railing for a long moment. Last summer some enterprising young person built a rough cobble dam across the creek, immediately below the south side of the bridge. The winter waters have no trouble moving over and around these rocks, but the flow is distorted, here domed upward, there cleft down, in a smooth laminar flow.

We gaze abstractedly, lose ourselves in this graceful pattern, as we have many times over the last six months . . . suddenly -

"Look!" I grab D's arm.

"What?" She is alarmed at the sudden jarring.

". . . at us, in the mirror!" We are looking at a complicated reflection of the sky, the bridge, the railing, and the two of us in the domes and the canyons of the torrent below. "I never saw that until now."

Where the water swells over a cobble, the convex mirror of the surface maps the bridge into a back-bending circle, doubling the two of us and making all four images left-handed. In the canyons where the water runs between cobbles, everything is turned the other way, twisting the ends of the bridge up and making our heads touch at the top. We are looking at twice as many images as cobbles.

We wave enthusiastically to these stream people, who return our greeting in unexpected ways. We dance this way and that, hiding and seeking. They match our merriment with the same good humor. Nothing that we do can trick them into behaving quite like us, but they are clearly in our frame of mind.

Whimsically we take our leave of our doubles. But the mood settles. I walk away with a wistful feeling.

"What's the matter?" D asks.

"Funny," but not quite funny, either, "here is another world that I have failed to notice for all these years, one that was waiting to catch my eye." . . . a merry world in which bridges bend down upon themselves, going nowhere, or buckle upward, cheerily bringing bridge-walkers tête-a-tête.

December 27 - Sap begins dripping from our sugar maples

Taking Matters Smartly in Hand

On our walk yesterday, we came upon a little green inchworm (genus and species unknown) dangling on his silken thread from a hemlock branch above the lane. It seemed strange to see such a soft-bodied insect around the winter solstice, even though the last few days have been unseasonably warm. This inchworm was behaving normally, swinging from his silks, waiting for a breeze to waft him to a better food source, although we did not know what that might be in this season.

We watched him for a few moments. The cold had not much slowed him. As we followed his progress, Diana reminded me of another inchworm we watched last summer on Burroughs Drive. That caterpillar's movements appeared more erratic. Instead of laboring up the thread, leg over leg, he seemed to rise spasmodically, without any apparent effort on his part. These upward jerks were timed with his own frequent slips downward, so that he stayed approximately at the same point in space, six feet above the roadway. We puzzled over this mystery for a few minutes, trying to account for such odd behavior.

Eventually Diana glanced up and caught sight of the explanation: a large, brown spider was perched on the twig to which the silk was attached and would periodically haul up a length of it, in the manner of a fishing line. The spider clearly had her eye on the inchworm and vice versa. Why the spider didn't haul up the whole line in one swoop and eat the caterpillar on the spot was another mystery.

We continued our watch for a while. The spider had one of her forelegs on the silk as if to test for any movement by the caterpillar. Ever so slowly she would begin to draw the line in, leg over leg. The inch-worm would evidently sense this disturbance and drop suddenly, letting out more silk. At this the spider frantically pulled in as much as the inchworm let out. The spasm passed and both stopped, tentative, still about three feet apart, waiting and feeling for the next move.

We became so intrigued with this tiny life drama that we sat down on the road and watched the dance repeat itself again and again. Each arthropod seemed hypnotized by his adversary's immobility, and snapped out of the trance only when the other jumped. We wondered how long they would carry on like this, but we didn't have long to wait.

After about ten minutes the spider evidently had enough. She strode right down the thread to the dumbfounded caterpillar, bit him a good one, hefted the limp carcass back up the line, and disappeared in the foliage of the tree. End of story.

January 2 - Started banding the winter flock; Ebony spleenwort and herb Robert still thriving on a rock wall; Skating for first in evening

A Winter High

Late evening, after everyone is retired, I steal out with my skates to try the ice for the first time this season. The pond is a single sheet of mirror ice, my reward for waiting through many false starts and stops in November and December. Night holds the land, but the air is bright cold and clear. The moon has now risen over the eastern ridge; she is only twelve hours shy of being full and will light my swift ways up and down the paths of the pond tonight.

I cannot imagine an activity more exhilarating than ice-skating on a moonlit winter night. I whiz through silent spaces above the pond, fields reserved the rest of the year for dragonflies and kingfishers. Only the whispered clicking of my skates reminds me of my tenuous contact with the earth, through films of ice and water. I rush from one end of the half-mile pond to the other, gulping night and wind. Crisp air fills my body by the lungful and an electric excitement raises my spirits to the stars. Exhaustion refreshes me, I can skate till dawn.

I always bring my hockey stick and a few pucks with me when I go out skating. I make no serious attempt at the game, but love to bash the pucks aimlessly about in the mindless moonlight. For me, this is the soul of play. The gunwale of a rowboat half-sunken on the side of the pond serves as my goal. I ply back and forth in front of it, energetically whipping pucks across the dark ice in the direction of the old wood and listening for the satisfying crack that resounds between the hills above.

In all my sanctuaries (whether labeled that or not), I have had some sort of arena, often a summer and a winter one, to cover my seasonal needs for play. At my cabin in Pennsylvania, I would bicycle through ten miles of ice ruts to skate and bash my pucks against a concrete valve bunker on Lyman Lake. My all-weather field was closer at hand. The yard in front of my cabin was an abandoned potato patch where I nailed together a wooden goal and spent many an evening loping about booting an ancient soccer ball through the uprights.

Those evenings are hallowed in my memory. After dinner I would stroll to the beaver pond or down the railroad grade to see what new things were on hand since my morning walk, as I do these days on our lane. Returning after the sun had sunk below the western hill, I carried out the old soccer ball and dribbled it about the playfield, lit only by the left-over sky-glow. I bumped the tattered brown leather bag ahead of me, into the dusk. From time to time, as the mood came, I would loft the ball toward the boards of the goal, and, if it were already dark enough, only listen for the impact of my thrust. The mode of my playing was relaxed and forgetful but altogether aware; the mood was pensive attention, flowing to me and the field, ball, goal.

Skating here tonight comes closest to recreating that mood of twenty years ago. The electric night air, the flowing awareness, the thudding goal whirl together to transport me far beyond the edges of the ice. This is liberation from the everyday, which playfields have been since the beginning.

January 3 - No herring gulls overhead today

The Absence of Herring Gulls on Sunday

This morning I took a hike around the pond, that is, around the *inside* edge of the pond rather than around the outside, as I frequently do in milder seasons. Strolling about on the pond ice is our mid-winter replacement for walking up and down the lane.

The exercise of walking on these waters is uncommonly invigorating. For one thing, it means breathing bracing winter air, air that can wake up the most sluggish spirit. Sauntering down the middle of the pond also affords a 360° view, otherwise obtainable only on the mountain lookouts like Julian's Rock. Our warm-season strolls are more hemmed in with trees and hills. Anyone who has stood in the "big sky" country of the American West will appreciate the liberation of periodically having an expansive vista. Every January we walk a new path with new views upon scenes old to us from the rest of the year.

Roving around the ice this morning, I checked out what was novel in the surrounding forest since last winter's canvass: the latest in fallen trees, hawk nests, and squirrel stations. I stopped mid-ice and glanced up to survey the sky as well and saw that there weren't any herring gulls there: more practice in noticing what's not here. For every real bird in my field of view, shadows of innumerable other, possible birds fly by. The difficulty is seeing them. No field guides are published that cover this domain of the avian world.

Having spotted these non-existents this morning, I thought to myself: "Of course not, it's Sunday."

The idea had never occurred to me, that herring gulls might take Sunday off, but this makes more sense than it seems at first glance. Herring gulls, like so many of the other flora and fauna of the planet, need to accommodate their behavior to the customs of the dominant organism, *Homo sapiens*. This is the way it works:

Herring gulls are scavengers, they eat whatever comes along. In the wild this means dead fish, beached crustaceans, and other small, used-up tidbits washed up on their shoreline habitat. Where people congregate, garbage piles up and that too suits the herring gulls fine. In the good old days, when waste disposal meant heaping refuse in open dumps, gulls had a seven-day week. New environmental laws regarding sanitary landfills were a definite setback for these dump lovers. One of the new rules states that the landfill operator must cover the garbage with six inches of topsoil regularly, especially over the weekend.

These obscure state regulations are relevant to us living in the Sanctuary because our own town landfill is one mile to the northeast of us and the waste disposal site for the neighboring town lies about three miles to the southwest. Early in my tenure here I realized that the daily streams of gulls on a northeast/southwest passage were simply shuttling between the two local nodes of food opportunity. I never thought much more about it, at least not until this morning.

Is this true? That the gulls go somewhere else on Sundays because the dumps are closed? The almanac is no help: gull flights are not religiously recorded there. I am left to my impressions: I would say that herring gulls do *not* fly over the Sanctuary on Sunday. Now the question is: Am I inventing this relationship in my notoriously compliant long-term memory, or has there really been a pattern of gull-less Sundays? I can rest in the certitude that I'll never be sure.

January 4 - Tracks in the pond: 2 deer, 1 fox, a junco & deer mouse, 3 people and a toboggan

Winter Tracks - Pond

I walk out across the pond this morning an hour after the snow stops to record the early walkers. The best tracking is done several days after a fresh snow. This gives everybody a chance to make their mark, one hopes many marks. On the other hand fresh snow means fresh tracks; the imprints are clear-cut, before the action of wind and thaw disguises them.

Unfortunately last night's snow fell dry and fluffy. Animal tracks in this kind of matrix are usually indistinct because the surrounding snow blows readily into the hoof or paw print, obliterating the exact pattern of toes and nails. In some cases, this smudging makes it difficult to distinguish between possibilities, for instance between foxes and cats. Usually other characteristics of the track, like gait, pattern of footfall, stride, straddle, registration, tails, and habitat make it clear what animal passed here.

Scouting animal tracks is great fun and provides many stories during a winter stroll. In the spring and summer, I typically have my eyes trained toward the tree tops while out on walks to spot the quick movements of birds or a new pattern of branches that pleases. In the winter I'm looking at the ground, watching for some imprint left fleetingly last night or a week ago. More of these stories are recorded in the snow than we could ever hope to witness first hand. They are written in a code different from the colored surfaces and air compressions which we have become skilled at deciphering in our other life experiences. Detective work is half the fun of snow-track decoding, the other part is gaining insight into the ways of the woods.

This morning not much tracking can be done, the combination of the recent dry snowfall and the brisk winds have left little evidence behind. I start out onto the pond at our swimming ledge below the front yard. I see where a solitary junco took a few tentative hops from the edge but soon brought himself back from the desert exposure of the middle of the frozen pond. He probably spends the night in the rock dry wall above the ledge and eats by day from our front porch feeding station, as many winter sparrows do.

I trudge out to the middle of the pond but see little here. I walk toward the north end. The single-minded trail of a solitary fox makes a straight line across the pond, bending in only once and briefly to check a small dark object projecting out of the surface, a rock that someone tossed yesterday from the Peninsula. The fox's track is neat and tidy, each petite paw placed just so, in a line. The rear paws fall exactly in the prints of the fore paws. This is called "registering," a trick used by a stealthy predator to minimize the sounds she makes walking through the forest: if her front paw doesn't break a twig (which she can watch for), neither will her rear paw (which she can not). Registering is not so critical in walking across the featureless snow of the pond, but the habit is deeply ingrained.

That appears to be the whole story for snow traces this morning . . . until I spy an upheaval in the white pond surface up ahead. Earlier this morning three West Park residents played here, two of them below the age of reason, judging by their boot size. I know who one of them is, because he left his mark as clearly as the fox has left hers: the littlest one wrote his name in the snow, "Rusty George." Besides that, they made other signs diagnostic of our species: snow angels, figure 8's, and a fox and geese maze.

After fooling around the pond, the little troupe took off down our lane back to the road, trailing their half-moon toboggan behind them. I have fun tracking these snow animals, following their obvious attempts to find a suitable hill to give their toboggan a run, first on this side of the lane, then on that. I can almost hear their little shouts of anticipation and see the pouting faces when a hoped-for slide turns out to be cliff.

I find one other track on my walk this morning, an animal whose nocturnal movements I have been keeping under surveillance ever since last week's snow made them part of the daylight record. This track belongs to a deer mouse who lives in the rocks of the dam not far from the overflow. Every day a new trail starts from an opening in the rocks in the forest side of the dam and leads across the lane to the base of a post in the pond side of the dam. I wonder what business brings him so regularly between these two stations. The endpoints of his daily trek are invariable, even though the path changes from day to day. Sure enough, my mouse has made his trip this morning.

Tracks: a universal language, one of the earth's native tongues. If you are made of flesh and sometimes leave the pavement while walking about, you will make a track on the earth. After you have passed, someone else may happen by and may read your track and read you. No matter how alienated you feel from the rest of your kind or from living kind, you will have communicated, if only that you are tired, or alone, or walking south. The message disappears, the slate is cleaned by the first inch of new snow.

January 6 - Tracks along Black Creek: many deer and mice, some little sparrows, a muskrat, mink, and ?

Winter Tracks - Stream

Encouraged by my tracking success a couple of days ago, I take a longer route to the road this afternoon, following Black Creek from Valli Marsh to Copperhead Hole. The pond has been ice from shore to shore for weeks, and on a day like today (the temperature dropped well below zero last night), even the spring-fed marshes are frozen over. Most of the terrestrial life that remains active on these frigid days is drawn to the available water, in our case Black Creek. Only a rapidly flowing stream can escape this grip of crystallization.

Valli Marsh is hushed, bearing no resemblance to the Valli Marsh of a May morning - no bird chirps, no insect buzzes, hardly a breath stirs. Only by reading the printed record do I know that any life passed this way: recently a few sparrows have been feeding on the seeds of grasses growing on the marsh tussocks; three or four deer in the past few days have wandered by, testing how far from shore they can walk on the ice; and around the edge of the ice, daring little deer mice have dashed from underground tunnel to tree trunk, risking the sudden chill.

Humans can read a great deal of information from a single track. The Native Americans in this area, who did not have a written language before contact with Europeans, were quite literate in the mother tongue of the soil. I have learned a few things myself, mostly by watching animals making tracks, the same school the Indians attended. For instance: based on the size and number of hoof prints, I know that these tracks were made by one adult deer and two young of the year. If this is our doe with her two fawns, all have survived the hunting season. They were walking south, upstream. I know this from the entry and exit marks around their hoofprints. Most animals slide into a print and kick snow or dirt forward when they leave it.

I can glean more from tracks like these: whether the deer is walking, trotting, or running, and how fast; whether the deer is adult or immature, large or small; and whether it is a Virginia white-tailed deer or (where the possibility of confusion exists) one of its relatives. Clues to this kind of information can be picked up from a good book on animal sign. My favorite is Olaus Murie's *A Field Guide to Animal Tracks*, one of the Peterson Guides.

Deer belong to the order of hoofed animals with an even number of toes, the *artiodactyla*. They move about on two teardrop shaped toes that are connected by ligaments. Some people believe that the relative positions of these two toes indicate the direction in which the deer is traveling, specifically that the "arrow" points toward the front. This is a mistake, which I have never seen clarified in a field guide. The pointing of the arrow tells a story, not about the direction or speed of movement, but the acceleration. A deer standing still or walking quietly keeps the two toes approximately parallel. If the deer is jumping forward, climbing a hill, or otherwise applying force *backwards*, the front of the toes are pushed together to gain a cup-like purchase against the ground. If the deer is applying force *forwards*, by braking a descent, or slowing down on level ground, the two flexible toes are cupped the other way, again to get a good grip on the ground. I suspect the reason that most drawings of deer prints are arrows pointed forward is that most people look at prints of deer that have just jumped up and run away. That's the story of their lives.

One of the young deer at Valli Marsh is not in good condition. His hooves drag from one print to the next often leaving a continuous mark for yards at a stretch. The other two deer have left relatively crisp hoof marks, sliding into the print only at the end of the stride. I often see this dragging track at the end of the winter, especially tough winters, when many of the deer are in a weakened condition. To see such weakness in January is a bad sign. Although I would be sorry for the sight, I wouldn't be surprised to see his carcass by the stream before this winter is over, an easy victim of the feral dogs hereabouts.

The signs of deer are not restricted to their hoof prints. The marks of their passage include: hair, which they shed in the late spring or any other time of year when they get into a fight; male antlers, which are dropped in mid-winter; musk, a difficult message for a human to read; urine and feces; snorts, bleats, and the signature cadence of their hoof-falls when they run, trot, or bound; beds and wallows; browse sign and rubs, the characteristic way they nip off stems and chafe the bark from saplings with their antlers; and much more. We decipher each of these messages as best we can. The most noticeable are the droppings, the scats.

Human beings in our culture have developed a taboo against paying attention to their biological waste products, except in the most antiseptic terms. This prohibition extends for many people to the waste of other animals. That would be a crippling prejudice for an interpreter of the natural scene, because what, where, and how an animal leaves behind the digested remains of its food can reveal much that is going on in its life.

In the simplest case, a scat offers a clue to an animal's diet. A few weeks ago the few deer scats around the marsh were dry and granular. The deer were browsing on the standard fare of winter - twigs, leftover nuts, dry seeds - as opposed to the succulent grasses and herbs of summer, when their scats are moist and even-textured. Today however, the deer pebbles are smooth and creamy. I would be puzzled by this except that I know that local hunters recently dropped a truckload of apple pomace (the solid residue left after pressing for cider) in one corner of Mario's hay field, diagonally across the marsh from where I am standing.

The hunters left the pomace as a short-term humane gesture for the deer, so that more deer will be around in the long term - for them to shoot. The pomace freezes hard in mid-winter and becomes sour and rank as soon as it thaws, but the deer love it anyway. Last winter a January snow lasted into April. Day after day, as the deer came, ate, and left, defecating copiously all the way, the intricate trails leading from the pomace pile became marked not only as ruts in the snow but as a woven tracery of deer excrement. This is another kind of story that scats can tell. I missed recording the tale on film by one unusually warm day.

One more deer sign that I collected from that pomace heap was a beautiful three-point antler which a buck dropped in January while feeding or tussling. Adult males lose a pair of antlers every winter, but even regular forest walkers like myself rarely find them intact, because rodents quickly chew them up, supposedly as a calcium supplement to their diet. I wonder now if the mice avoid the pomace mess; not one gnaw mark was on the antler I found.

Continuing my walk downstream I see that a creature slipped out of the water here within the past two days and padded across the frozen flats of the stream a few dozen feet, surveyed the world, and shuffled back to the water. Hoping for a beaver I examine the messy path across the frozen snow. No, it's a muskrat, the five thin toes on the rear foot give it away. Muskrats are not too surprising in this weather, less so than beavers, who tend to keep to their lodges for days at a time during cold spells.

Farther down I pick up another track quite unlike the ones I've seen earlier this afternoon. This is an exuberant animal bounding up and down the bank, racing briefly along the bluffs, then leaping down again to the ice-locked stream. Here is someone in a hurry if only to have more fun. He is not racing to keep warm, because every hundred yards he dives in the stream to swim the next hundred feet. This maneuver identifies him as a mink. The only other animal that moves so friskily from land to water is the mink's larger cousin, the river otter, but otters are scarce to absent in the populous Mid-Hudson Valley. I have never seen one in the wild, but I hope to do so before I die.

Minks and otters are members of the weasel family, belonging to the flesh-eating order of mammals. More so than other *adult* animals (young of all sorts seem full of fun), they love to frolic. Even their tracks are energetic. Trudging along behind this mink on Black Creek tests my energy; following with my eyes his sudden plunges into the icy stream, his winding chases up the bank and mad dashes down again brings me out of breath. I can't imagine having to do it.

The mink tracks disappear again. I wonder if he took a long swim here or raced over to Sanctuary Pond (I see mink tracks in the snow there frequently). But no, up ahead I find more tracks. He splashed out of the water here and loped up a small steep rise where Black Creek constricts before plunging into the deep pool of Copperhead Hole. I work my way to the top of the rise and I am startled to see the set of prints turn into a slide. My mink evidently flopped on his belly and slid for ten feet through the saplings, took a few more bounds through the snow and nose-dived down a thirty-foot winding path to the open water below. I have seen these slides only in pictures, in fact only in pictures of otters playing in the snow. Now my question becomes: What am I looking at? Is this the work of an otter, which I have never seen before, or of a mink, which do not make slides like this, as far as I know?

I run back to the point where the slide-maker left the creek. Yes, these prints seem definitely larger than the mink tracks I was following farther upstream. All of them are badly smudged, but I can easily imagine the webbing in the hind feet, which would make it an otter. To decide between the two I need to take measurements of foot length, stride, and straddle and compare them with the figures in Murie. The winter sun now hides behind a few iron gray clouds before dropping below the south-western ridge. With one last excited look at my find for the day - my find for the year! - I hurry home full of the promise to come back early tomorrow morning to meet my otter.

January 7 - Tracks around Copperhead Hole: many deer and squirrels, a rabbit, dog, beaver, and a question mark

Winter Tracks - Pool

This morning I head straight for the misnamed Copperhead Hole with Murie and ruler in hand, to settle the matter once and for all. Overnight I have learned from the field guide that mink do indeed make snow slides, and use them in the same playful way that otters do. So the question of mink or otter will have to be settled by measurement. The tracks and slide are as I left them, no new sliding since last evening. I measure the dimensions of the tracks. There ought to be no ambiguity here, because the otter prints are almost three times larger than the mink's, and the straddle, the total width of the track from the left side of the left paw to the right side of the right paw is twice as great in the otter.

However, as I begin sampling some of the better formed prints leading up to the slide, I encounter a frustration well known to the animal track enthusiast: I measure a width of two and a quarter inches for the paw, halfway between the advertised paw measurement for the mink (one and three eighths) and the otter (three and one quarter). The thought flits through my mind that I am looking at a hybrid, a motter or an ottink. This absurd possibility gets a hearing only because the other, more probable conclusion is that I am misinterpreting these signs, I don't know what I'm looking at. It won't be the first time: I remember the first day I owned a bird guide, I walked into a neighbor's orchard and solemnly discovered a species new to science. Or so I persuaded myself, because it certainly wasn't in the book I had. Shortly thereafter a friend proved to me it was quite an ordinary cedar waxwing among the apple trees. At the time I felt stupid. Now I have a better perspective on the situation. That sleek yellow bird was *not* an ordinary cedar waxwing. It was *my* first cedar waxwing, a species new to my science.

The problem is that these mink/otter prints are not clearly defined. The tracks at the edge of the stream and across the ice are smeared with the water that was still dripping off the animal's body, and the ones higher on the bank are blurred by the dry, fluffy snow. Both kinds of weasels move along in a humping fashion, like high speed inch worms, and in doing so their hind feet drop approximately into the prints left by their fore feet, but only approximately. This makes it difficult to get a good print from a running gait, and impossible to know for sure if you are measuring the width of one print or two that are roughly superimposed. Unfortunately, I cannot settle the matter with any of the paw prints here, all of them are more or less compromised by the powdery snow and the enthusiasm of the frolicking animal.

Where experiment fails, logic fills the breach. I conclude that these must be mink tracks, because an animal can leave a print *wider* than his paw (through smudging, and so on), but not a *narrower* one. I am sorry to lose my first otter, but at least the issue is resolved. I pick up the trail of the mink again, where he jumped out of the water and splattered across the ice to the "pillow" of a large elm, the mound of roots and earth that forms when a tree keels over. At some point he climbed up on this tangled mass of vegetation and spent more time here than is usual for a member of the hyperactive weasel family. Here the tracks are clear, and are clearly those of a mink.

The mink dallied so long on this mound, I begin to wonder if it is a lodge, but I find no entrance to a subterranean chamber or other evidence of habitation. I see no scats here, but slight orange stains surround a witch's broom at the summit of the pillow. This may be a kind of scent post, to mark a territory or some other right. I sniff the stain. Strong indeed, reminiscent of skunk, but less powerful and not un pleasant. I learned last night from Ann Haven Morgan's classic *Field Book of Animals in Winter* that mink mate in January and February. Is this the scene? I stop a moment to imagine the delightful frolics that pass for mating rituals among these playful creatures.

January 8 - Flying squirrel(?) trying to get to suet on front porch

The Solstice Corporeal

About this time of winter I begin to notice that the day is a little bit longer, the sun a few degrees higher than it was two weeks ago and only then do I feel celebratory about the turning of the seasons. I know that the "real" solstice is back in December, the consensual one, the one that astronomers have plotted with the help of micrometer telescopes and super-computers. And that has a certain theoretic interest for me; I'm pleased that such measurements are possible. But they have nothing to do with my observance of this cardinal event of the natural year. That takes place on a late afternoon in the first part of January, when I become aware that this day has been ever so slightly longer than one day last week or even yesterday.

There are different kinds of winter solstice. It's a question of whose return of the sun one observes. Around December 21st, science and the community that holds with their views celebrate the solstice astronomical; the Christians and Pagans note their versions of the change on December 25 and January 1 respectively; the Maya no doubt have their holiday, as do the other cultures who keep roots in the soil and eyes on the stars. I have my own private solstice. It occurs when I unbend from lacing up my skates and say to myself, "The sun now is a little higher in the southern sky than it was the last time." It happened today.

January 9 - Great horned owls counter singing for first of season

Spring Hallo

For weeks we've been looking forward to a day like today when the snow is deep enough, a good ten inches, to go cross-country skiing. Even so we don't leave the house until late in the afternoon and decide there's not enough light to visit our favorite ski path, the Shattega Jeep Trail, which falls from a ridgetop in a fine snaking drop to Mario Valli's hay field. So we settle for skiing around the pond and up and down the unplowed lane.

As we set out, I hush Diana to listen to a distant but familiar call made strange by the presence of deep snow and bright cold.

"Canada geese," she points to the west.

I disagree, "They're up that way," across the pond, high in the southeast sky. After a minute, the birds appear far in the northeast sky, compromising between our two guesses. A flock of fifty, a mile high and headed south.

Canada geese are not unusual over the Sanctuary around the edges of deep winter, but to see a large flock on the 9th of January seems out of place to me:

"I wonder if the Hudson is frozen solid north of here. Well, if it is, they won't have far to fly to hit open water."

"How do you know?" D wonders.

"The river doesn't freeze for long below Haverstraw Bay, because of the saltwater. Also the Hudson Highlands are just north of the bay and the water moves pretty fast through there." We spot three more flocks winging south before the day is over. We ski on.

Cross-country skiing is another of the "natural history" sports, like bicycling and canoeing. At its best, cross-country is a stroll through the winter woods. It induces that relaxed state of keen awareness of one's surroundings that makes for good nature watching. Some will make a battle out of it, counter-productively, skiing faster or farther than anybody else in the club. They are kin to the bird watchers whose chief pleasure is notching their binoculars with the top count of the day or bagging the hottest rarity. I feel sorry about these peak achievers, for their own sake and for the influence they have on young people who would otherwise walk into the woods with a healthy interest in nature.

Like skating and snowshoeing, skiing taps winter for its invigorating spirit, brisk air fills my lungs, braces my mind. I move my body rhythmically and energetically through a landscape of perfect stillness, the exalted sense of aloneness in the woods. This imbalance of inner heat and outer cold, of energy within and rest without, satisfies a need for diversity in the winter woods.

The whoosh of our skis is the only sound as we skirt the pond and whiz along the snow-padded roadway of our lane. Our track meets a few others: a grey squirrel and a deer or two, but not many have crossed this path and no one has traversed it. We scoot down the last slope that leads to Ackert Road and scamper up again, like otters, to squeeze the last bit of fun out of the darkening day.

At the entrance way to our lane the sky becomes even quieter as the dusk drops a hush on a flock of tittering juncos. A winter grey suffuses through the upper branches from east to west and all is tending toward stillness. We stand silent ourselves a moment and listen. Faintly from far across the road comes a hollow hooing . . .

"Hooh hoo-hoo-hoooh . . hoooh hoooh." From another opening in those woods comes an answer . . .

"Hooh hoo-hoo-ooh . . hoooh."

The great-horned owls begin to sing to each other.

On almost any summer or fall evening we might hear a stray great horned owl give out its booming call, but only in mid-January does the sustained exchange between the male and the deeper-voiced female take up half the night. The two birds are sealing a kind of bond between themselves, a bond of nesting, of mating, of feeding and protection.

We listen quietly to these avowals, peering intently into the darkened tree tops, hoping for some glimpse of the huge night birds themselves. Great-horneds. One of the animals we would like to know better, but they make it difficult.

"Their voices seem far away," whispers Diana.

"But they could be close by." I feel sure from listening on many such evenings.

We listen in the close stillness. The hooing continues, a muffled subterranean duet, it could be the earth and moon telling stories.

We wait long minutes at the end of the lane. The great horneds do not seem to be moving closer . . . or farther away. Perhaps they are unaware of our existence or, more likely, unconcerned. I try my imitation of a great horned owl call, but it lacks credibility, even to us. I try again. Nothing. They do not believe me, and in a way I am grateful. They belong in the deep woods singing songs of renewal to each other. This is the longest moment of winter . . . and still there is spring.

January 11 - Last night 11° below zero, only the owls were warm

The Masques of Water

Walking the lane one cold morning a week ago, I noticed a fine mist rising from the snow on a knoll of the roadway ahead. This delicate film was so indistinct, such a different suggestion on a day that was otherwise brilliantly clear, that I looked at the scene and away several times before I convinced myself I was viewing matter and not some phantasm.

This vision reminded me of the playful mists that dance around the pond on cool fall mornings and vanish before the face of the sun. I believe these two phenomena are physically similar, a wet surface losing moisture which condenses when it rises into the relatively cooler air above it. We don't think of snow as evaporating continuously, it seems so solid and self contained; but much of the snow cover disappears just this way. More evidence of the sun's work . . . on the coldest day of the year.

The difference between the snow and the pond, I thought to myself, is that the snow is everywhere, stretching thousands, millions of square miles around, covering one quarter of the globe. The image was striking: a ghostly layer of vapor hovers over the earth in northern climates at every dawn, the aura of the boreal earth.

Today I am put in mind of that snow mist as I trudge out to the woodpile in the dim light before sunup. Another mist hangs over the land this morning, not hugging the earth and vaporous, but crystalline and at the height of the trees. I walk to the cherry tree in the back yard to investigate this harder, cooler haze. I find no mist at all, but many tiny leaves of ice growing along the twigs and branches, the dew-fall of a sub-zero night.

If I look closely at these ice leaves,
I can see their likeness to the cherry leaves of spring -
The veins, the ragged margins, the insect bites -
And after a moment I am wondering in a May morning,
What spring-like thing will the forest offer me today?
I straighten with a shiver -
The woods are hazy and glowing
With the promise of light,
And I cannot tell which of the mists -
From the snow or from the trees -
Is putting this cast on the scene.

This forest gauze reminds me now of the green haze of April when the first shoots emerge from their winter buds. The icy leaves today are also waiting for the sun to rise; not to push farther into the world, but to sublimate into their invisible daytime lives. Come nightfall, these moist airs will steal back to the twigs and pass for being cherry leaves once more through the cold dark.

Caught in the middle of imagining these transformations I suddenly realize that, like Thoreau, I could spend my whole life divining the inner reality of leaves, or seeds, or mists, and count myself blessed at the end.

I examine these white miniatures of the living cherry leaves which will grow here in three long months. I reflect that this moisture is related to . . . no, is the very same moisture that I saw rise off the snow a week ago. In fact these mock leaves are simply another masque of Sanctuary waters, the same water that hugs the morning snow and dances over the pond in April and September, this water that forms the core of the cherry tree and me.

January 15 - Cardinal at feeder for first this season; Algal scum in pool at end of lane

Newly Green

On the way home from the post office I noticed for the first time this season the green algal suspension in the vernal pool at the end of our lane. We see this bloom every year about now, as the cover ice buckles under the weight of accumulated snow and forms a puddle of succulent green. Discounting the pondweed and watercress which started last fall, *this* is the natural year's first green growth. This lowly algal scum, not the celebrated skunk cabbage or coltsfoot, stands at the head of "Newly Green" in the year's almanac. It's not much of a beginning, but in mid-January we count all the green blessings that come our way.

January 19 - Flicker eating staghorn sumac fruits

The Best Neighbors...

In my mind, the Sanctuary is made up of neighborhoods, each with its own character. Mapping this landscape would be difficult, particularly the corners I call "places of secret well-being." The beaver pond in Valli Marsh is one such place.

This morning I walk over to the beaver pond for a few minutes. The ice appears quite solid on all sides of the pond except at the dam where Black Creek flows swiftly north. Although the ice *seems* thick enough, exercising a little caution would be the sensible thing here. Many small springs in the marsh discharge relatively warm, underground water all winter long and can weaken the ice from below in spots that are not obvious from above. Duly noting such considerations, I stride impulsively across the middle of the pond. If I break through here, I will drop into ice-water up to my nose and enter unexpectedly the world of the beaver.

Part of this confidence comes from paying attention to the previous striders across the ice. Many deer have crossed this way. Some tracks are old and sloppy, made in short term thaws, when the deer sloshed across the surface of the ice. Other prints are clear and precise, made earlier this morning, tracks with a fine structure of snow grains scattered on each side, an effect that doesn't last a full day of sun and wind. A solitary beaver made his way across the pond, probably a week or so ago. He appears to have swum under the ice to a hole near the dam, emerged, and walked back to the lodge, slogging through the partially thawed ice. What was he thinking about? Just checking the structure? Patching up the mud pack? Clearing an air hole at the top? His tracks only circle the lodge and do not climb up on it. Other forest animals have exercised the mid-winter license to make their way over the beaver pond: raccoons, squirrels and mice. None of the pond-walkers are as heavy as I am.

But I don't fall through. I make it to the main beaver lodge, the most recent of four they've built over the past six years. The last three of these houses are bunched together in the middle of the pond. As I stand on top of the largest and newest lodge, it occurs to me for the first time that all of these lodges might be connected by passageways, like Vermont farmsteads. I wonder what kind of extended family structure this would allow. I have never seen more than one nuclear family - two adults, a few yearlings, and kits - inhabiting this pond at one time. I have heard that more than one family might set up lodges in a large pond at one time, but would they have tunnels between them?

The stick and mud lodges look to be in good shape, no doubt a vigorous beaver family is snoozing underneath me. But are they snoozing? Beavers are not true hibernators. Like many small and medium-sized mammals they become torpid in the depth of the winter, sleeping a lot, not emerging from the interior of their lodges for cold stretches at a time.

And why should they confront the cold? They have built a castle complete with moat, that even bears have trouble tearing down in the easiest of times. When the outer pack of mud is frozen solid, it would take dynamite to spring this structure apart. They also have food. Throughout the fall they have cached hundreds of limbs in a sub-surface larder near the lodge. They need only scoot out the underwater entrance for what they want: birch bark, aspen buds, poplar twigs, whatever. Beavers are provident.

A new thought intrigues me: are they listening to me tromping around their lodge? I put my ear to the air hole on top to listen for telltale beaver squeals or heavy rhythmic breathing. Nothing. What do they think when they hear this stomping and crunching a foot or so above their heads? I guess they are accustomed to racket on their roof, since the deer seem to enjoy clambering up here. And what are *they* doing here? Perhaps gazing around the marsh from a perspective they don't get the rest of the year. That's why I'm here. I wonder: Do the beavers sense me as something heavier than the dainty-hoofed deer, someone less frivolous-minded, more ominous? What would I imagine if I were a beaver?

I do not credit beavers with brilliant imaginations, but what do I know? They must guess that I am up to no good. In this they're as perceptive as I am.

In fact I'm here to look in on the beavers. They are my nearest settled neighbors. I'm here to see how they are getting on this winter . . . although they haven't asked me, which, now that I think of it, is an endearing quality in them. They've never asked me over. As a matter of fact they've given me to believe with a hundred little signs, all of them universally understood, that they'd rather I didn't come by their place at all. In return for which I can be assured they will never turn up on my doorstep, willing to while away a Sunday afternoon at my expense. Beavers are the best neighbors.

January 20 - First tufted titmouse song of winter

...My Neighborly Best

So I left the beavers to nod again for another few weeks in the rank, wet dark of their lodge. This morning I cross to the other side of the marsh and look for the marks of another marsh visitor, the trapper. The signs - apart from the usual boot prints, cigarette butts, and other loose trash- are inconspicuous stainless steel wires, with nametags attached, tied to trees on the bank or anchored along the canals cut by the beavers. At the other end of this wire, fixed to the bottom in a foot or more of water, is a steel trap, a spring-loaded jaw-like device with sharp teeth that is set to snap shut on anything that presses the trigger-plate between the jaws. A beaver that steps in one of these traps on his daily rounds drowns, because the traps are secured in such a way that the caught animal can not quite reach the surface. Beavers are remarkable in their ability to stay underwater but they can't hold their breath indefinitely. Some of them hold their breath long enough to chew off the offending foot.

I believe the trapping season has started but I don't see any traps here. Maybe the trappers are not returning to Valli Marsh this season. I muse to myself: What would I do if I found a beaver trap this morning? I don't know. In the past, I've not interfered with traps that I've found here. But I'm getting less tolerant as I get older, as life becomes dearer to me.

Disturbing a trapper's killing devices is against the law. Only once have I committed the crime of undoing a set. Years ago I found a red squirrel in a leg-hold trap not far from my cabin in the Allegheny Mountains. Both of his rear legs were crushed between the steel jaws and most of the surrounding skin and muscle were ripped or eaten away in his frantic effort to release himself. He was still fighting as I walked up.

Two possibilities were open to me as I stood over him. If I released the jaws around his legs, I was risking a bad bite. Or I could pick up a branch and brain him in one blow. Some people with genuinely humane sensibilities would have done just this. There was no third alternative. I could not walk away from this scene.

My own rule of thumb is this: What would I want in the same situation? I would want to live, no matter how badly my legs were mangled. Granted, I have more options with two fewer limbs than that squirrel did. But what does that matter?

I took a deep breath and grabbed the trap in both hands, solacing myself with the greater justice of his revenge, if he did nail me. As I pressed apart the jaws, he clung piteously to my pant leg, shivering in terror and pain. When he was free, he shot up the nearest tree, using only his two remaining limbs. He climbed as fast as any squirrel I've ever seen. For a moment I was lightened, he may make it after all. But a moment's reflection sobered me: What kind of future does a squirrel have with two ruined legs?

That dreadful scene made a powerful impression on me and I put my imagination to work devising some way of alleviating this kind of suffering. I came up with the following scheme: when I am out in the woods and find a leg-hold trap, I carefully urinate in a yard-wide circle around it. Urine is a universal boundary signal among mammals and many will not cross a closed circle of it. This works, I've tested it. The procedure is not illegal: I'm not disturbing anybody's traps, I'm only peeing in the woods. I've got my rights, too. Unfortunately this technique is not effective against underwater sets for beavers. I'm still working on that one.

I once enthusiastically explained this tactic to two smartly dressed young women in New York City, members of an Upper East Side anti-trapping campaign, who had set up an informational card table at 85th Street and Third Avenue. Their reaction to my story was undisguised revulsion. They appeared to believe I was looking for an excuse to unzip my fly and demonstrate in a tight circle around their table. That experience has tempered my gusto for sharing this gift to wildlife with just anyone, but I offer the idea to like-minded people whenever I can.

January 21 - First black-capped chickadee song this morning

The Evidence for Commonality

Yesterday morning as I walked out our back door, I heard a tufted titmouse singing his "Peter, Peter, Peter" song for the first time this season. The season I am referring to is spring. Although we are still in the middle of January, signs of the coming renewal are everywhere. The titmouse is one of many.

Another is the black-capped chickadee who joined the titmouse today with his spring song, "Teee Day Day," as I replenished the bird seed on the front porch. Unlike most birds who rarely sing outside of the breeding season, the upbeat chickadee song can be heard in every month of the year. But the particular quality of the black-cap's song on a warm mid-winter day is different from those of the fall and summer and marks it as a herald of spring. I have often wondered why chickadees sing through the year, if the function of singing is reproduction and territorial defense.

I am always heartened by bird song, all the more so in the tightest place of winter. I am particularly pleased by today's two songs because I believe these birds are responding not only to an April morning in January, but also to a change that I have felt lately, the perceptible lengthening of our days. I like to think the titmouse, the chickadee, and I respond to the subtle daily change (probably no more than a few seconds per day) on the basis of our common interest in the sun, and express that happy quickening each in his own way.

This community awakening to the approach of a new natural year was reinforced this afternoon on my way to the post office, when I met two townswomen strolling on the road in West Park. I nodded and exchanged some weather-related pleasantries. One of the women mentioned the days seemed to be getting longer now. If the chickadees and the titmice and the ladies in the hamlet think the sun is taking a longer time to pursue its daily business, then it must be so.

January 29 - Red spotted newt dead in middle of ice; Flying squirrel on feeder

Flying Squirrel for Dinner

Last night while we were eating dinner, we heard a scrambling noise beneath the windows that look out onto the front porch. It was a flying squirrel trying to get at the bag of suet. I knew what it was before I actually saw the animal. A couple of weeks ago I spotted out of the corner of my eye a sleek white body streak by the same window shortly after dark, and I thought "flying squirrel," although I didn't get a good enough look for a positive identification. Then two nights ago we heard a terrific ruckus in that corner of the room, as Pussycat tried to dive over several baskets of gloves and scarves to pounce on something that was outside the window anyway. Again I wondered if it was *Glaucomys volans*. Last night the matter was settled: when the flying squirrel finally made it to the hunk of suet, he alternately nibbled and posed for a good half hour while we finished dinner.

The truth of the matter is that I'm still not sure it was *G. volans*, the southern flying squirrel. It might well have been *G. sabrinus*, the northern flying squirrel. The ranges of these closely related species overlap in southern New York, but the distinction between them is a fine one. It suffices to me that we were sharing our dinner hour with a generic flying squirrel, a delightful treat indeed. Flying squirrels are rare, nocturnal, and shy, a combination that makes them difficult to observe for any length of time. I've caught glimpses of them in the past, briefly and by accident: scaring one out of an old elm snag I carelessly whacked, spotting another on a long glide among the moonlit trees.

A flying squirrel is small (nine inches long including a four-inch tail) and light (about two ounces), with soft, olive brown fur on his back, creamy white below. He has large, liquid brown eyes that allow him to see about the dusk without craning his neck. These traits make him well adapted for his habits and niche, soaring at night from tree to tree or tree to ground in search of nuts, insects, and the occasional bird's egg. An unusual adaptation that fits him for this lifestyle is a furry flap of skin that stretches between his forelegs and hind legs, and acts as a built-in hang glider for his volplaning sails from limb to limb.

The scrambling noise we heard on the porch last evening was one of our local flying squirrels trying to climb up the window frame. The suet hangs from the eaves trough and is centered in the front window for our birdwatching pleasure at the dinner table. For a mammal, scooting up the window frame and leaping over to the suet bag might be the most straightforward way to get there, but it would not be easy. Squirrels are known for solving spatial problems in non-straightforward ways, so I was surprised to see him try this obvious route. On the other hand, none of the gray squirrels, who nibble cracked corn on the front porch every day and who dearly love suet, have figured out how to get to this particular piece. As far as I know, they have not even tried.

In any case this flying squirrel was having a hard time going straight up the aluminum storm window casing. The window didn't have enough "bark" on it to get a good purchase. After several scuttling attempts, he did succeed in reaching the crosspiece of the frame, and inched his way along that to the middle of the window, holding on to God knows what. From there he had to make a foot and a half leap, upward and outward, but had a precarious base from which to launch such a move. He tried and ended spread-eagled against the lower pane, hanging from the crosspiece by one toenail. This seemed fairly hopeless, but, evidence of the spunk of the little squirrel, he hung there for several long moments, looking upward, apparently trying to visualize how he might yet make something of this unpromising situation. In the meantime we were getting rare good looks at his snow white belly and body flaps. Failing to figure it out, he dropped down to the sill and started scurrying uselessly back and forth under the suet.

Our spaghetti cooled as we stood at the window, betting against each other if and how he would solve the formidable problem. "I'm surprised he's acting so much like an ordinary squirrel," I complained to Diana.

"He is an ordinary squirrel."

"What I mean is he's not using his special tools for getting around. Why doesn't he climb the maple tree and glide over to the suet from there?"

"If he missed the suet bag, he'd crash into the window. Even if he landed on the bag, he still might carry it right into our front room," D pointed out.

"I suppose he doesn't know how securely fastened the suet bag is," trying to put myself in his place. "I wonder how he knew the suet was there in the first place." I pictured his daily travel route: chestnut oak to sugar maple by way of big elm, double back, watch out for the owl in the hemlocks. Our suet bag didn't seem to be on his route.

"Do you think he found the bag by sight?" Diana asked.

"Or smell," I guessed. "Maybe he watched the birds in the daytime, the way other birds find it." Who knows? Another mystery.

To my surprise the flying squirrel soon succeeded in getting to the suet by his first route. From a foot away we watched him nibble greedily on the disgusting fat. He hung exactly upside down and paused every few moments in a fine pose. I took a few photographs, but without much hope of success because of the dim light and the two panes of glass in between. We returned to our own evening meal, keeping up a one-sided exchange with our unexpected dinner companion until he hopped off the suet and scurried away through the snowy night.

February 2 - Hophornbeam seeds shedding on snow; Warm rains, 50°, the earth breathes and bathes

Giveaways

Walking along the lane this morning I notice that someone, probably a weekend hiker, has sprinkled corn kernels along the roadway from Ackert Road almost to our house. Some local resident looking to do a good turn for the birds. This corn won't last long. A whole kernel may be too much to handle for the numerous juncos and siskins around, but it should be just right for the blue jays, if the deer mice don't find it first.

Birds get a lot of human hand-outs this time of year. I haven't seen the latest numbers in birdseed sales, but the effort was substantial a few years ago and has increased, I suspect, along with other economic trends. I remember the consternation around some water coolers in the federal government when the news came down that expenditures on non-consumptive interactions with birds were greater than the monies spent by sportsmen to shoot at them. For years the government justified its breeding programs for game animals by pointing to the economic stimulation brought about by hunters buying shotguns, traveling to shooting preserves, and so forth. By the same argument they should now spend even more money helping people to watch birds. At first the fish and wildlife bureaucrats were at a loss what to do with this information, but finally instituted a few non-game bird programs.

I receive a few calls every year from people who worry about the possible negative impacts of feeding birds. For instance will heavy feeding cause birds to stay north longer than they should and expose them to cold weather dangers? I doubt it. Is it bad to cut off the feeding suddenly? Probably not, except in cases of extreme weather. Are the Madagascar sunflower seeds really worth it? My guess is no.

The more intriguing question about the people-feeding-birds interaction is: Why? Who gains most by this exchange? The bird-feeding people typically think they are acting on behalf of the birds. An outside observer might believe this business is mainly for the people. Nobody knows what the people-fed birds think. My own view is that this enterprise serves both these interests and more: it advances the human-bird relationship, which needs all the help it can get.

February 4 - Seven or eight wood ducks start off Black Creek

Earth Breathing

A few days ago we had our January thaw in early February, the temperature rose into the fifties, and warm rains washed away most of the dirty snow. This is a memorable time of year for me. All of the soil's dark smells and secrets, which have been brooding under the snow through the winter, are released at once. The Sanctuary earth has not aired itself or washed since November. Now it breathes and bathes in these warm rains and moist air. Squirting from under my pressing boot, the juices of the earth gurgle underfoot, passively engendering new life in the mash of spilled seeds from last year's grasses.

February 7 - A return to winter

The Congenital Optimist

As I stand in the middle of the hotel ruins with the desolation of winter all about, my mind is drawn back to mid-summer, when nature watchers stroll about on their own or sign up to walk with me through the Sanctuary. Few people make their way to the property in mid-winter and none of them wish to stick around long enough to do a nature hike. In an odd way I miss them now.

I miss the many questions they have about nature and the human role in managing nature. I shy away from telling people how to think about the world, but I am eager to offer them glimpses how I think. One of the most frequently asked questions has to do with the state of the environment, although people rarely put it that way:

"What do you think about this ozone thing?" they ask; or "The neighbors are all up in arms about the new garbage burning plant, but I don't know. . .;" or more bluntly "Are we doing ourselves in for good?"

I love to play jokes on nature walk participants, but always give as honest an answer as I can to these earnest questions:

"I'm optimistic about things."

My optimism may be genetic, as much a part of me as my blue eyes, but that's what I am, optimistic. I don't mean I feel good about what the human race is doing to the other natural systems on the planet; in fact, I am horrified. I believe it's going to get much worse before it gets better. But . . . "Is it hopeless? Is the whole business going down the tubes, no matter what?" My answer, without much reflection, is "No."

Why this hope, when half of our daily newspaper is now taken up with environmental disasters of every sort, local and global? Being in the business of fixing environmental mistakes, my friends and I at Hudsonia might well cheer up at the daily news: plenty of work for the next while. But we would gladly read of more solutions and fewer new problems.

Nevertheless hope I do, and trust that the race will survive the present insanity more or less intact. Nor is my optimism solely molecular. It's based also on observation of humans in bad situations. People have a world of earthy common sense. They know on some deep level that their own health is tied to the health of the systems around them, including the largest system. What they lack is breadth of vision to acknowledge this connection in every situation. We lose our imaginative power quickly if we stand to lose money in the deal. A good instance of this is the spread of NIMBYism, Not In My Back Yardism, an environmental epidemic that seems to have spread to every backyard.

The common sense that I see in people, or at least in Americans, the people I know best, is their saving grace. Once they are alerted to a real problem, Americans quickly mobilize their quite amazing energies to solve it. But they are slow in seeing the reality of obvious problems: inequality, injustice, environmental degradation. They need to see it writ large, in front of them, in bold letters. I want to help write on that board.

February 8 - Red maple buds reddening

Winter Landscape
This evening I walk to the pond and over the ice. From the far edge I watch the frozen sun pause above the Black Creek bluffs before closing one more day. The ragged undersides of the winter clouds redden slowly. February light. Naked branches around the pond scratch at the sky and ring a vibration through the woods, though the scene is perfect quiet.

The landscape is limned in white from this morning's light snowfall. On top of the Peninsula two tall white pines, the last to catch sight of the dying sun, loom over the end of the day, not ominously, but full of meaning.

I am suddenly in awe of this scene, the significance of every detail I see, hear, and feel in the landscape laid out before me. Nature is charged to bursting with a meaning that I do not know, terrifying or ecstatic according to some whim of the moment. The dead world suddenly takes life from my looking at it. The Sanctuary is realizing itself at my expense.

February 10 - Many more wood ducks on Black Creek

Ice Watersheds
The other day I got in one more hour of ice skating before the coming storm. As I rambled around the ice, I came upon several large scar-like impressions on the surface. In the center of each was one of the circular holes drilled last week by an ice fisherman. The recent thaw had

reopened the holes, making them drains for the melting on top. In seeking its way "down ice," the meltwater carved intricate channels in the surface. The flow started on the flat uplands: leaves of snow melted into twigs, twigs into branches, branches to main stems that found their common root in the central hole. The result was an oblong, tree-form watershed twenty feet in diameter, similar in appearance to watersheds twenty miles in diameter that appear on the land after thousands or millions of years of erosional runoff. I was standing on a time machine that compressed the process into a day.

With a little study I could see how the geography of the ice surface determined the structure of these watersheds, the size and shape of the channels, the angles of joining, the degree of fineness of the whole. This geography is in turn determined by a variety of causes: deer, foxes, wind-blown branchlets, and human beings carve trails in the snow. The wind itself further shapes the snow that softens and refreezes to form subtle hills and valleys. Pressures from below bend this surface every which way as it warms and cools over days and nights.

These are the same set of forces - some violent, some gentle - that shape the hard rocks of the earth. Both sets, on rock and in snow, work through the dimension of time, though on a vastly different scale. I spent the rest of the afternoon reinventing geomorphology, Sanctuary Pond scale. Reading the geologic landscape in this small edition was fascinating and fun . . . like discovering a rubber-band model of the solar system in the attic.

February 13 - Eyed elater found in wood pile

Sanctuary Snow Jobs

Two days ago we were hit with a foot of snow and yesterday four more inches fell on top of that. Last night I reluctantly called Gus Schmidt and asked him to come plow our half-mile lane. This will be the second time this season, which is twice as often as he's plowed the lane in any other year. Most winters I never call him at all.

If it were solely up to me, the lane would never be plowed. In my first three years here, I did without. I look back with fondness on those winters. I was a prisoner of the snow, forcefully removed from the twentieth century for weeks at a time, since the telephone and electric power often failed in the same big storm.

At the beginning of my first winter here (1977) I was unprepared for this circumstance of Sanctuary life. The big snowstorm of the year occurred early, the night of December 5th. On a hunch I drove my car to the end of the lane that evening. I didn't drive it back until April 10th. For the four months in between I skied the lane or the pond and packed in my groceries and other necessities, which became surprisingly few. Over the winter I came to cherish that stretch of uninterrupted snow, the symbol of an optional connection to the rest of the world, one that I could make or break at will. In those days I would be surprised to see one or two skiers or snowshoers make a Sunday afternoon effort to come this far into the woods. Now that the road is plowed in winter, anyone with wheels might show up in our front yard.

I savored this isolation: the mood at night, skiing across the frozen pond after returning late from teaching in New York City; the cold stillness, broken only by the whispering of my skis through the grainy snow; the eternal presence of quiet, moonlit and snow covered. On these midnight crossings I learned the other set of facts about the Sanctuary, complement to the names of trees and the numbers of animals that busied me by day.

When Diana came to live here in 1980, our needs changed. Eric and Jennifer had to get to school every day, and although *they* liked the idea of skiing part way there, their mother, the bus driver, didn't. The specter of a desperately ill child in the middle of the night was raised. At the same time the Burroughs Association, who owns the Sanctuary, began to worry about fire truck accessibility during the wood stove season, now that we had made the house livable. All of these concerns translated to snowplowing.

Gus arrives this morning before seven, startling us awake by the clanking roar of his plow truck fitted with four sets of heavy-duty chains. It is typical of Gus to be here before daybreak. When I moved in, he was finishing some carpentry work on the house and often woke me with his business-like hammering and sawing. I guess he inherits these traits from his father, the carpenter who built this house in the late thirties.

All of the Sanctuary's important carpentry work is done by Gus, especially at Slabsides, where a great deal is at stake. Last summer we received an official government report that said Slabsides (a National Historic Site) needed "injecting, stabilizing, and re-authenticating." They had an out-of-town expert in mind. Everyone breathed a sigh of relief when we got Gus instead to do the simple nailing and painting necessary to keep Slabsides standing another few years. We are lucky to have such a reliable fund of carpenter common sense.

Alas, what comes with the package is conscientiousness that exceeds our needs, or at least mine. Gus and I have always been at odds on the required amount of energy and care to do any given job. For instance, snowplowing: I want to get in and out of the lane; I can do that with up to six inches of snow on the roadway. Gus wants to do the job *right*, which means seeing the gravel all winter long. This difference in snow removal philosophy causes little ripples between us. I never call Gus for snowfalls less than six inches; Diana and I run over it in the truck and pack it down. When the big storm comes and a foot of snow falls, he responds to my request:

"Gee, Jim, I won't be able to get that frozen stuff below." Translation: If you had called me last month, I could do today's job *right*.

He knows I want him only to skim off the most recent foot of snow, and never refuses to do this, but not without a prickly little reminder that, one more time, I have failed to observe the professional snowplowing ethic.

Again today after I dress quickly and pile out the back door to greet him, he does not fail to mention that the last snow (four inches, a week ago) made this job *particularly* troublesome. I allow this; I am grateful that he gets up so early to help us this morning.

As Gus runs up and down our drive (one-lane in the summer, two-lanes in the winter when he plows), I busy myself with digging out Diana's car, removing a few feet of snow from around the wheels. I recall that our snow shovel is in the back of my truck, now in the repair shop. I search around the tool corner and find an adequate substitute, an old, handmade brush rake that I borrowed from Mohonk ten years ago. A shadow crosses my mind: I don't want Gus to see me using this rake to clear the snow. Another wrinkle in our relationship is his image of me (I imagine) as a mechanical incompetent, the sort of nerd who might use a rake to shovel snow. To avoid this stain, I run out to clear the snow only after he disappears down the lane for one last run. Just before he reappears, I throw the brush rake into the deep snow by the house.

Gus is done plowing except for the spot where Diana's car sits. At his finger-point I jump behind the wheel to move it across the front yard. Unfortunately too much snow still blocks the car, the wheels spin, I cannot move from the spot. I am reduced to clambering out of the dinky Honda, pulling out the buried brush rake, and hurriedly clearing a better path, while Gus waits in his man-sized plow truck behind me, smoking a cigarette, thinking thoughts. The clearing done, I toss the rake aside, jump in the car and grind it out of the snowy hole it was stuck in.

Before taking the final swipe at the snow, Gus winds his window down, a signal that we need to talk. I dearly hoped we could just wave at this late stage. I walk up to the truck. Gus pulls the cigarette out of his mouth, points with it, "Say Jim, you better move your rake or whatever, so I don't run over it." There was absolutely no emphasis on the "or whatever."

February 14 - Sycamore on dam shows snow strata

Sycamore Geology

On our stroll out to the Ackert Bridge through this virgin winter day, Diana points out the curious layering of snow on the horizontal branches of the young sycamore that sits on the edge of the dam.

"It's like a neat vertical profile of yesterday's storm," I spring my geology on her. "You can even read the story of the snowfall from the layers on the branch."

"It's beautiful."

"The storm started out with wet snow that packed tight next to the surface of the wood. And here it's dark because the storm was cleaning out the air."

Diana gently touches the parfait of snow with her finger. "This part is light and fluffy . . . full of tiny swirls."

"That's because the middle part of the storm came with cleaner, dryer air."

"How come the layers keep alternating wet and dry?" Diana gets into the spirit of stratum analysis.

I think for a minute. "Maybe the storm came through in waves of wet and dry." I am picturing the pinwheel pattern familiar to weather map watchers.

"All the same, it's beautiful."

But the comparison to the earth's record comes back to me, here are two stories from the past. The sycamore's record will melt or blow away soon, probably before this evening. But this twig-size history is not different in kind from the earth's, nor - it seems to me now - in importance. In saying this I don't mean to diminish the value of the global phenomenon or enhance the value of our sycamore history, but simply connect the two, out of time.

February 19 - Onion grass on lane, first rooted growth of spring; Two sets of great horned owls singing, South Woods & north of Ackert Road; Skunk cabbage for first, below pond overflow

Evening Absolution

This evening I check one last time the doings of the mink around Copperhead Hole. When I first discovered their activity here - their slides, the musk-marking on the upturned roots of an elm tree - I imagined this site would be favored by them for their late winter nesting. In coming down here I sense a certain uneasiness nosing into the most secret part of the life of this secret animal. I make short work of my inspection of the pool sides and the elm pillow. Nothing is different from the last time, no evidence of a new generation.

I walk upstream to look at the short, steep cascade that drops into the pool. At this time of year it should be mantled in statuary ice, bottom to top, one of those stunning exhibitions of art which winter mounts weekly. I am not disappointed, the ice is a graceful water sheathe, a frozen extension of the flow itself, literally and figuratively. As I stand at the foot of the rushing water, the cold spray freshening my face and lightening my spirit, I glance up over the top of the falls, and through the dusky cathedral aisles of the hemlocks, I glimpse the setting sun.

The whole of this moment is earthy absolution and all of my senses collude to achieve the effect: the streaming moisture across my face, the rich taste and smell of upland humus diffusing out of the torrent, the throbbing ground roar of the falls itself, and now this vision of dim grace from above through the misted yellow space between. The sun sinks, even as I take notice of the blessing. I walk home redeemed by the end of day.

February 22 - Bottom ice forming in Black Creek at Ackert Bridge; 35 Canada geese flying north

Sleeping on the Breathing Earth

Spring signs are winking at us from every corner of the property these days. As soon as the weather breaks, I expect to hear the first red-winged blackbirds tear through. This seems an odd time to make the following observation, but today is when it occurs to me.

For years I have noticed three or four small, rocky openings in the front yard which quickly lose a fresh snow and are first to melt off a major fall. I always assumed these were chipmunk entrances kept open by vents of warm air from their huddled bodies below. Although I never found evidence of their movements in and out, it felt good to have them there. This morning the truth came to me as I idly looked at them once again. These holes are openings to a vast rock talus under the front yard, part of the built-up lawn of the old hotel. I see here on the rocks around the apertures the same ice-beards, congelations of damp air, that I found earlier this winter along the dam of the pond. Tepid moist airs vent from these holes all winter long.

The feeling of living this close to the warm and breathing earth through the most breathless part of the year is deeply satisfying . . . even better than that of the chipmunks. I will sleep soundly with this new image, warm and moist as the earth-under-winter itself.

February 29 - Temperature in the 50's - mud time; Grouse tracks in snow above pond

Chickadees for Fun...

I first befriended winter chickadees a number of years ago at my cabin in the Pennsylvania woods and I have maintained the relationship ever since. I say "befriend" because I feed them when they visit, they make no bones about the quality of the fare served; and we play little games together - all the sorts of things that friends do.

It doesn't take a new bird lover long to discover that black-capped chickadees and other feeder birds, like tufted titmice and white-breasted nuthatches, will take seeds from his or her hand if they want them badly enough. I have little first hand experience with other chickadee species: the Carolina in the southeast, the boreal across the north of the continent, the mountain chickadee in the western high country. I have been told these birds are less accessible as friends than our own black-caps, but perhaps the right kind of hospitality has yet to be extended.

I now consider myself a minor authority in the technique of chumming up to chickadees and have won a few small bets from skeptical friends about the number of minutes it takes me to "tame" the little devils. "Tame" is a joke of course. Chickadees, like chipmunks, are among the fiercest of their kind and would pose a severe threat to humankind except for their size.

This is the strategy:

1) Live in a region that supports black-capped chickadees (or some other like-tempered feeder bird), i.e. any place in the mid-latitudes that has some mature native woods nearby.

2) Erect a bird feeder (any board will do) in a spot not far from shrubs or other protective brush and keep it well stocked with sunflower seeds in the winter. Summer is no good. The birds may use it occasionally, but the winter's edge of neediness is gone.

3) At the right moment, when chickadees are using the feeder heavily, go out and remove all the seeds. Put some in your hand and hold your palm outstretched exactly where the seeds were lying. Hide the rest of your body as much as possible while doing this.

It's fun to have chickadees hopping about your fingers. Diana's daughter, Jennifer, loved to play with them. Most people are probably content to leave it at that. However, if you have an experimental bent, you can get them to do much more. In the old days I had more time for this kind of fun and I spent many hours patiently coaxing the little beggars to take more risks, to bet on my trustworthiness. I never abuse that trust, but some may say that I go too far anyway.

For instance after the chickadees have become thoroughly accustomed to roaming around my hands, I hide a single seed between my fingers or press it between my thumb and palm. A chickadee, usually the boldest of the band, comes to peer into this crack and that, prying at places that look likely, and will sometimes find the seed. If not, he or she (you can`t tell the difference in the winter) will glare up at me, give me a couple of good pecks on the finger, and fly off in a huff.

Although the sexes are not distinguishable, I can tell this one from that one with a little practice. A peculiarity of plumage, a turn of the beak, or the angle of the "cap" across its head helps to identify an individual. Behavior is an even more reliable key for distinguishing them, each bird acts a little differently from his companions.

Some zoologists who covet the predictive power of the hard sciences ("physics envy," according to Freudian science historians) believe animals are machines. But this theory won't wash. Each chickadee that comes to my hand (or thinks about it and decides not to) is a sentient individual with a distinct personality. If in doubt about this, watch a few chickadees!

The more I play with my chickadees, the better I come to appreciate them as individuals. I have managed to get quite intimate with one or two of them. One I remember in particular from a few years ago, Jacques, was equal to any challenge. After he solved the simple hide-and-seek puzzle with my thumb, we moved on to more challenging games. I'd cup my two hands into a narrow funnel, letting the sunflower seed slip down to the bottom in his full view. After a little cautious circling of the crevice with the prize barely in view at the bottom, Jacques would poke his head in, grab it, and fly off. When he began to feel at ease with this, I would up the ante. The funnel would get narrower and deeper, the seed less visible. Jacques met every challenge, literally tunneling into my fist like a rodent. This is an amazing piece of audacity for a bird.

That was not the boldest of Jacques's feats. After the hand I got him going into my pockets. While he was sitting on my shoulder or head, watching, I would drop a seed into my shirt pocket or pants pocket. In he would dive, headfirst, rummaging around until he came up with the prize. Then I would test his daring around my mouth. This was a tough one for him, every animal knows what his predators eat with. First, I would put the seed on my palm, which I held extended from my chin. He flew up and took it. I brought the seed by degrees closer to my mouth until I held it between my lips. No problem for Jacques. He even managed to take the seed from my lips or from the tip of my tongue without the help of the palm as front porch, hovering in front of my face long enough to pluck off the seed. Other chickadees have gotten this far.

None, however, have matched Jacques's ultimate stunt and perhaps not another will. I placed the sunflower seed at the *back* of my tongue and opened my mouth as he flew up, anticipating the next treat. It took a few tries, but he finally screwed up enough courage to do it: he would land on my teeth, run down my tongue, grab the seed, and back out. People have expressed amazement at my daring, having an overfed, excited bird running loose in my mouth. I am much more impressed with *his* spirit, the equivalent of inserting my head in the mouth of a passing tiger, whose disposition and personal history I can only guess, hoping for the best.

March 5 - Fox, raccoon tracks on pond early morning

...and Profit...

Some of my relatives will be relieved to know that my practical faculties were not idle while I was mindlessly playing with chickadees in the Sanctuary. On the contrary, I formulated a sure-fire business plan for a tidy winter cottage industry centered around chickadee labor.

The idea first came to me in the specialty section of a supermarket when I noticed the sharp difference in price between shelled and unshelled sunflower seeds. I thought to myself, "Chickadees will do that job for free." I went home to work out the details.

The plan is based on the following behavioral trait of chickadees. When presented with a pile of sunflower seeds, a black-cap will carry off, shell, and eat one or two seeds. He will return for the surplus, as long as they last, shelling each seed and cramming the kernel into the shaggy bark of a handy tree. Black cherry is perfect for this purpose. Presumably the birds are storing this resource against a leaner day, when, given their habit of poking behind pieces of loose bark in search of food, they have a good chance of finding the seed again.

The equipment for my cottage enterprise is simple and for the most part can be assembled in your back yard: a very large gauze net, a self-feeding dispenser for the sun-flower seeds, and a hollow, perforated tube clad in simulated black cherry bark. The bottom of the tube can be fitted with a sack large enough to hold a day's worth of work. Needless to say, the area enclosed by the netting should embrace all the other daily necessities of a flock of chickadees and must *not* contain another rough-barked tree.

The size of the net raises a delicate issue. Holding captive any native North American bird is against federal law. The screened area must be large enough to be defensible against any legal definition of "captivity," and more to the point, against any such definition on the part of the chickadees. Good harvesting!

March 6 - Increasing V's of Canada geese

... and Meditation

I must clarify a point about the chickadee stunts reported above: I cannot get my chickadees to do anything I want. These birds are remarkably audacious, but only in pursuit of their own clear gain, in this case, food. Outside of this context, they are as wary and defensive as any other wild forest birds. For instance I can't approach them with a hand not holding seeds; nor would any allow me to touch him on the wing, rub his beak, or pinch his leg . . . except when "The Spell" is upon them.

The spell is an extraordinary altered mental state, which I have observed a few dozen times in my years of playing with feeder birds. I first noticed it when a chickadee came to my hand one winter day and, instead of energetically rifling through the seeds, sat quietly on the side of my finger, gazing abstractedly up at me and then off into space. When this mood persists (sometimes it doesn't), I can approach the bird with my finger, poke it, tweak its beak, pinch its wing, grasp it gently, in fact all of the things these feisty birds never allow in their normal, wild state of mind.

Ornithologists have discovered that birds experience different kinds of torpor, from an energy-conserving momentary drop of body temperature during the day to winter-long hibernation. I may be seeing something of the kind in this peculiar lassitude. What makes this behavior so unusual, however, and the reason I call it "The Spell," is that *all* of the birds within view pass into this state at the same time, not only other chickadees, but nuthatches, titmice, woodpeckers, and other feeder birds hanging around at the time. During the spell I can easily approach birds that rarely or never take seeds from my hand. Perched in shrubs around the feeder, they stop their incessant chatter and turn their eyes toward nothing in particular in the sky.

It first occurred to me that they are looking at something that I can't see, perhaps a hawk soaring beyond my range of vision. The spells seem to take place on bright, cold winter afternoons, when hawks sometimes hunt at a height. But no amount of searching with or without binoculars ever revealed a hawk or any other object as the cause of a spell.

I have often wondered what is going on during these spells and I once put a brief note requesting information in a regional ornithological journal. A few readers replied, but no one reported similar experiences or shed much light on the phenomenon. But I always take the opportunity to tell this story to fellow watchers, because I have an enduring interest in the spell, quite beyond bird study.

March 7 - First boomings of ice shifting on pond

Ice Bell

Last night, as I walked in from Ackert Road over the frozen pond, I heard for the first time this year the booming knells of deep cracking ice that toll the death of winter. This is one of the most stirring sounds of changing nature I have experienced. Standing on the ice, the message from the March pond is felt as much as heard. In bed, late nights of early spring, this rolling rumble comes as a kind of blessing, covering me with sleep.

March 8 - Turkey vulture for first, over pond; Bluebird singing overhead at end of lane

A Hole in the Dam

This morning on my daily cruise around the Sanctuary I noticed a gap in the closely cemented stone work of the pond overflow sluice, through which a sizable current (five to ten gallons a minute) of pond water was flowing. A hole in this dam is not unusual, the cobbly, earth-fill impoundment is rather porous and the flow of the stream that drains the pond is always much greater than the visible flow over the spillway. What makes this particular hole interesting is its size and its position, about eighteen inches below the overflow water level.

If this hole maintains itself through the early summer, the pond will drop a foot or more and become even more diverting. However I'm betting that the hole will not stay open; debris in the pond-water ranging from suspended clays and one-celled organisms to leaves and branches will plug it up over time. In fact the pond would probably be gone by now except for this self-sealing action of the leaky dam. I've often wondered if the Italian stone-masons took this factor into account, when they built it in the 1920's.

If, contrary to expectations, the hole does remain open through the dry mid-summer months, we can expect to see a couple of acres of new mud-flats at the shallow north and south ends of the pond, intriguing ecosystems never exposed to air over the past sixty years. I look forward to exploring these new continents.

A good naturalist develops a nose for signs of promise like this hole, meanings gleaned from a wisp of cloud moving the wrong way on a spring afternoon or an out-of-season insect on a summer's night. The question is how to acquire this sense. The answer is to pay attention.

Breathing air, taking a vital interest in this medium and its boundaries, we humans are acutely aware of the interfaces of soil/air and water/air. The other surface, soil/water, is less well known to us but is as interesting and practically important.

The physical characteristics of the water/soil boundary suggest some of its value to inhabitants on either side. For instance, it is often easier to pass through than the other two boundaries. Many an organism has escaped the worst by diving into this muck; some probably make their getaway in the other direction. I have seen snakes, frogs, and turtles leave the air for the water and the water for the ooze, all in one continuous graceful gesture. Snapping turtles are known for hiding in muck, neck tensed, waiting for someone unlucky to swim by.

The interface layer is rich in organic material. Everything that swims in or lands on the surface of the pond eventually settles to the bottom where it begins, but never quite finishes decaying. One instructive lesson in how ponds process living matter is to haul up a handful of bottom muck and carefully sort through the sample. A little leftover bit of everything is found in this palm-sized microcosm.

Big animals as well as the little ones find the pond bottom a safe haven. In the winter many amphibians and reptiles close the door on the cold by slipping into the ooze, shutting down their life systems to the limit of survival. Some of the same cold-blooded animals return to the mud in mid-summer, probably for a similar reason, to escape the other temperature extreme.

If the new gap in the sluiceway remains open this summer, all these mud flats will show themselves. The traditional hue and cry of "Hole in the dam!" translates to a whispered promise of a garden of new delights.

March 10 - Juncos singing in front yard for first; Pussy willow breaking flower buds in front yard; 3 Canada geese flying low over pond - ours?

The Return of the Geese

This week I begin the watch for the break-up of the pond ice and with it the arrival of the pair of Canada geese that have nested here for the past eight years. Normally they settle on a lake at least half free of ice. For the first few days after their return, we see four to six geese on the pond and the scene is relatively peaceful. But it goes quickly downhill.

Half flying and half skipping, the gander from last year soon starts chasing the others up and down the long reach of the pond with great squawking, flapping, and honking. Once the others are packed off (not necessarily off the pond, however), he turns his energetic attentions to the goose, whom he also chases back and forth over the water, this time not to make distance, but, paradoxically, to close the gap between them. I guess that their mating can become quite violent: I overhear scenes of clamorous honking in the dawn hours and find tufts of down and contour feathers (hers, I assume) on the pond in the morning. That's the pattern in a typical spring.

Around March 15th of last year, the six arrived on schedule to a solidly frozen pond. They spent a few days on Black Creek, some pools of which were already open. Then they came up to the pond to stand around the ice or float in the 20 square feet of water underneath the hemlocks overhanging the north end. The birds seemed at a loss what to make of this unexpected state of their home waters. One morning I saw the gander strut down the middle of the pond with two of his would-be rivals waddling out of his way as best they could. The force of degree days reduced them to this parody of their usual darting and skipping across the waters.

The question arises: How can I be sure who is the gander, who the goose, and which are proprietors by historical right and which the trespassers? Banding doesn't help in sorting out these actors, because I am not permitted to band Canada geese or other game birds (they have their own banding program), or endangered species (to minimize the impact on these fragile populations). But I don't have to tag them, I've come to recognize male and female, proprietor and trespasser in the same way I distinguish chickadees, by behavior. The nesting goose and gander have become familiar with us and will come to take bread or grain from our hands, even on the first day of their return from the South. I believe the other newcomers are young from previous years trying to carve out a piece of the pond and set up their own households. In any case they seem to be more conflicted about the risk of taking our handouts.

I separate the gander from the goose partly by size (the gander is a little larger) and by moxie, the male will take more chances with me before the young are hatched, but, oddly enough, the opposite is true when the young are around. During the three months that the young develop under parental care, he often stands aloof, head held high, ostensibly the protector, but actually not doing much in that line except to hiss occasionally when the goose, followed by the goslings, comes over to us to nibble bread from our hands. I didn't say that she *leads* them over; not much altruism is in play here. The competition for bread crumbs, between her and the young and among the latter, is fierce.

After the hair-raising mating rituals, the goose lays from five to seven oblong, baseball-sized eggs in her nest on an island off the end of the Peninsula. The nest is located in exactly the same spot every year, refurbished a little with a few new twigs and old leaves, and always a fresh lining of down, the world's best insulation, that she plucks from her own body. The precise location of the nest seems crucial to the success of egg-laying. Three years ago one of the eggs ended up a foot away from the nest; either it became dislodged or she laid it there. But that was the end of it. It remained at the side of the nest in full view during the entire brooding period; she made no attempt to slip it back underneath her.

Reproduction continues. Brooding begins on this island on April 3rd, plus or minus two days. The state of the weather seems to have no effect on this date. Last year was a good example. Late last March I saw her refurbishing the nest, on a day when the encircling ice mass left less than one foot of water around the island. She sits for thirty days, again with a one or two day leeway. Around May 1st I begin to pay regular visits from a respectable distance, to check on the progress of her young. Several days before she leaves the nest, we see one or two fuzzy yellow heads popping out from under her wing or tail. At the appointed time (she alone knows what this phrase means), she picks herself up and sails away, five to seven tiny ocher balls of fluff in line behind her. The male brings up the rear, looking arch and magisterial and at nothing in particular. Often an egg or sometimes two are left behind in the nest. They are infertile or in some way developmentally impaired; they never hatch.

What happens next is without doubt the most bizarre chapter in the saga of our geese. Within twenty-four hours of leaving the nest, the whole bunch disappears from the pond. This is the infamous "First Day Trek" I mentioned last spring. One year they never returned and I suspect the worst. In all other years the troupe returns in two or three days, often minus the same number of young ones. This baffled me for a long time, but I never had the time or patience to scout the move, which takes place early on the morning after leaving the nest. Then about five years ago we made the following great discovery quite by accident.

The day after the geese had done their vanishing act Diana was at the post office in the hamlet, which is a mile and a half from the pond and several hundred feet lower in elevation. A fellow West Parker came up and asked if she had noticed the family of geese on the railroad tracks. She hurried out in time to see the two adults on the east (river) side of the tracks, watching their hapless goslings desperately trying to join them from the west (Sanctuary) side. The little ones could not negotiate the steel rail which was half again higher than they were and offered no purchase for a webbed foot. A great deal of peeping and honking, as one can imagine. The next day they were back on the pond minus two chicks.

Considering the hazards of that three-mile, two-day trek - raccoons, foxes, dogs, cats, little girls and boys, trucks, trains - it's a wonder any of them survived. Still, this is an annual event. It's apparently in their genes. Therefore (the argument goes), this tour must have been adaptive behavior in the past, must have had some survival value. It continues to baffle me.

The geese are much safer on the pond than anywhere else I can imagine. They are familiar with every nook and cranny of it. They have a rich food resource in the curly pondweed that grows abundantly throughout the spring and early summer. Furthermore, in their own element they have an advantage over mammalian predators, except for an occasional mink, and have only one serious reptilian predator, the snapping turtle.

Snappers have a deserved reputation for being the stuff of nightmares for ducklings and other small aquatic birds, but I am confident not one gosling from here has fallen victim to the sudden lunge from below. Small goslings are lost on the trek and larger ones sometimes sicken and die, but none go to snappers. Why should this be so? The one piece of evidence I have is based largely on interpretation, but intriguing enough to pass along here. One afternoon in May a few years ago I was watching the geese feed on the pond below the stone wall that holds up our front yard. Suddenly the gander became extremely agitated, paddled a few feet behind the group and *dove* under water. There was a great roiling as the bird surfaced and dove several times. Geese frequently tip up to feed on bottom vegetation, but until then I had not (and have not since) seen one submerge completely. I could not see what he was after, but a snapping turtle makes the most sense. I'm sure that the gander, even underwater, could harass the snapper effectively enough to make the goslings not worth the trouble.

The question remains: Why does the goose family go off on its post-nidal trek? Could it be the manifestation of some primal need to get to the Hudson River as a safe haven? Alas, they can no longer make it; the genetic maps of the local fauna were not consulted when the railroad was surveyed in the latter 19th century. This is an old story.

An even more baffling question: Why do the geese come back from the railroad? If they indeed have an iron mandate from their DNA to go east, why don't they destroy themselves in the attempt? This doesn't happen. They almost always come back, decimated and a little the worse for wear, to spend the rest of the summer in relative repose around the lake. I think the problem is probably ours with ideas like "iron mandate." Evidence suggests that genetically coded instructions allow for optional and conditional actions. We need a new model of choice and determinism in the animal mind, including our own. We need new models, period.

March 12 - Pileated woodpecker drumming for first, near Ackert Road; Pond beginning to melt around edges; Red-wings singing in Valli Marsh

Accounting for Redwings

One of the most obvious signs of spring in the Sanctuary are the red-winged blackbirds, which arrive in the second week of March and take up residence in the trees surrounding Valli Marsh. Mornings and evenings they are highly visible winging in long skeins from here to there, and are just as audible the rest of the day in the marsh.

Today they've come back. I saw a half dozen of them chasing single-file over the pond, squabbling all the way. If it stays warm for a few days, dozens and eventually hundreds will make their way in an endless snake against the twilight sky from Valli Marsh to the Hudson. During the day they take up their posts on snags in the marsh and on the branches of poplar and ash that reach out over it. Their behavior here bears some resemblance to the territorial skirmishing later in the spring but differs in significant details. They still sing their famous "kon-ka-ree" song and bicker endlessly at each other or at anything else that wanders in sight. However they are not "on territory;" it seems clear to me that they are not defending their perches or any piece of marsh turf below them. Sometimes these early birds (all males) will gather in one tree and kon-ka-ree and display their flaming red epaulets, not just to each other, as they do in the mating season, but to the world in general.

So what's going on here? This is not classic territorial defense, not the sort of positional battles that will completely occupy these male red-wings in a few weeks, when the females return from the South. The most striking feature of these get-togethers in the marsh is the intense amount of communication that is taking place, one to the other and back again. What might this information be?

I have mentioned before one biologist's hunch that such a male population is counting itself: sizing up the resource against the number of new beaks that will exploit that resource; then, based on that calculation, settling on how many will breed this year. Many ecologists pooh-pooh this hypothesis for a variety of reasons, not the least of which is that the idea does not spring out of the established dogma of current ecological thinking. I love hunches like this, more or less for the same reason.

March 17 - Mourning dove singing on Peninsula; Wintergreen fruits reappear from under melting snow; Male phoebe at cottage for first; Arbutus flower buds have formed; 10 wood ducks grazing on Valli Marsh

Nesting by Trial and Error

Our phoebe came back a few days ago (once again in time to watch the ice go out) and in a week or so will be looking around for a good nest site. Usually we notice the male a few days ahead of the female, because his cheerful chirruping is one of the key landmarks by which we mark off our spring. Why *our* phoebes? We feel proprietary about some of the flora and fauna near at hand: the local flock of chickadees, the wisteria on the sugar maple at the front door, the black snakes in the old hotel foundation, the miraculously healthy American elm on the terrace, and of course the phoebes who incorporate this house into their nesting enterprise as few other wild species do.

Phoebes have been favorites of mine ever since they began nesting on my Pennsylvania cabin. When you build a house in a wilderness, where nothing like it has been before, and an untamed but vulnerable animal entrusts her young to that structure, you become solicitous no matter how weak your paternal instincts may be.

My connection to phoebes has other dimensions besides sharing houses. When I correlated the fifty years of phenological data at Mohonk, the most provocative were the relationships between the arrival of phoebes in mid-March and the weather variables of early spring, including the melting of ice on Mohonk Lake.

The phoebes spend the first weeks after arrival in feeding and in reclaiming the old territory. The male dashes from tree to telephone wire to bush top in a circle around the house several times an hour, delivering a few "cheeraw-cheerees" from each post. Except for the first one or two days of this defense in which he may have to chase away a passing rival phoebe, I have never seen his title challenged. This even though two other phoebe territories are within earshot and plenty of spare phoebes are produced every year.

In April our phoebes will begin nesting and thereby hangs a peculiar story. The first time I watched them choose nest sites, I thought it was some kind of anomaly. But the phoebes have maintained the following sequence through the years, establishing it as the rule.

The first nest-site is in the ruined foundation of the hotel that formerly stood on this site. They place the nest on a ledge of a rough brick pillar, about four feet off the ground, under a decrepit cement walkway. This site has a few good features: it is weatherproof, is sufficiently out of the way to avoid harassment by humans, and has two flyway exits. However, the location has one big drawback: it is smack in the middle of the largest concentration of black rat snakes in the Sanctuary. One might object that the phoebes can't know this when they start the nest because the snakes don't emerge from hibernation until later in April. Maybe they didn't know the first time, but why have they continued their nesting attempts at that spot for the last seven years? For much of that time I knew they were the same birds because I had banded them early on.

This first nest failed every single year. Only once was I sure that the nest was done in by the black rat snakes, who are famous egg lovers and can climb brick walls as we climb stairs. In other years I would find broken eggshells below the nest, which suggests a blue jay, pierced eggs still in the nest (house wren), or the whole nest and contents strewn over the ground, which looks like raccoon work. In any case, no egg ever hatched from that nest, and the phoebes never tried to re-nest there in the same season.

Unfortunately, the next nest site of choice was not more likely of success, a piece of drain pipe angling 45° between the eaves trough and the down-spout at the front of the house. A slanting aluminum tube does not offer much purchase for a mud and stick nest and that corner of the house is awash in waves of water during sudden squalls, a virtual certainty around here in mid-April. This nest lasted four days on the average. I'm not sure they ever got so far as to lay eggs in it, but again, once it was carried away in a flood, they never re-nested at that spot in that season.

The following nest site was variable: some years they chose the top of a vent pipe coming up from the basement in the back of the house; other years they would go for the lintel above the second floor window on the north side of the house. In any case they ended up at this window every year, no matter how long it took them, and they always brought off at least one nestful of young here.

About five years ago, in an attempt to "educate" our phoebes, I built a six-inch-square wooden nest platform immediately under the eaves in the front of the house. From my point of view it was an ideal phoebe nest site, protected from wind, rain, afternoon sun, and the prying eyes and claws of most predators. For several years the phoebes paid no attention to it, more evidence of *their* point of view. Last year they nested there once, late in the season. I am waiting to see what they'll do this year.

March 20 Red-shouldered hawk appears; The air softens and the land begins to melt

The Last Entry

Winter is taking leave of us; it drops little reminders by our front door almost daily now. We are not sorry to see it go. The bottom of this year has been snowy, cold, and long. Despite the inevitability of its going, winter will no doubt leave gracelessly over the next month, in its usual back and forth, holding on to the door-knob.

Winter has also made a commitment to return next November, but we are making no promises to be here to greet it. For several years Diana and I have been talking about living in a new environment, probably by the ocean, very likely in the Pacific Northwest. She has her own reasons, but for myself, I need to change my physical place every once in a while to maintain my spiritual health. I've lived in this Sanctuary for over ten years, longer than I've lived anywhere. The place is paling in my imagination; the material symbol for this is the real estate development on our every side.

Gathering our collective belongings and trekking across the country is not a dread but an awesome prospect for both of us. Friends ask what jobs we have lined up? Is our house all picked out? No jobs, no house. We've simply decided we want to live there, so that's where we'll go, the incidentals will have to fall in place. They *will* fall into place, that's our act of faith.

"But the weather," these same friends exclaim, "rain all winter long, you'll grow moss, turn into slugs!" We'll see, we smile. They shake their heads and say we are crazy. We agree, nodding.

Little twinges contract this picture: close friends left behind, comfortably familiar places, projects unfinished and projects not begun. Counterpoised to this is the prospect of novelty, of undiscovered thoughts, not-yet-felt feelings in a niche we now only imagine.

In another sense, this is no leave-taking at all.

"The truth is," says Diana, "you carry the Sanctuary around in you; it goes where you go and unfolds along the way, like your cabin in Pennsylvania. Someone else may hold the deed, but the Sanctuary is yours."

March 21 Spring begins, 4:39 a.m.

CPSIA information can be obtained at www.ICGtesting.com
228708LV00001B/8/P

9 781598 585957